D1180024

NO LONGER
SEATTLE PUBLIC LIBRARY

HISTORY

QA STOR.

942.09   971-391
M891S

SEATTLE PUBLIC LIBRARY

Please keep date-due card in this pocket. A borrower's
card must be presented whenever library materials are
borrowed.

REPORT   CHANGE   OF   ADDRESS   PROMPTLY

The Sun Never Sets

The British Empire has never struggled through a more turbulent decade than the nineteen thirties. Traditions were scrapped, leaders overthrown and historic crises lived through amidst growing tension and confusion. Malcolm Muggeridge, one of London's leading journalists, gives in this book a swift-moving account of the highlights in those ten shattering years—the events that took place, and the personalities concerned in them. The story is told directly and with as little indignation as possible, and no particular political standpoint is championed.

The Sun Never Sets

THE STORY OF ENGLAND
IN THE NINETEEN THIRTIES
BY MALCOLM MUGGERIDGE

Random House · New York

Copyright, 1940, by Random House, Inc.

First Edition

Manufactured in the U.S.A. by H. Wolff, New York

APR 1   1973

Contents

HISTORY
971391

Men do wrong to lament the flight of time, complaining that it passes too quickly and failing to perceive that its period is sufficiently long; but a good memory, with which nature had endowed us, causes everything that is long past to appear to us to be present.

Leonardo da Vinci

The Sun Never Sets

CHAPTER I

Yesterday and Yesterday

and Yesterday

SEATTLE PUBLIC LIBRARY

Eᴀᴄʜ moment seems more urgent than all preceding ones; each generation of men are convinced that their difficulties and achievements are unparalleled. One of the few constants in life, for the individual and for the community, is a sense of crisis. According to Johnson, Milton believed that after the Restoration the times were so out of joint that trees and grass had lost heart as he had, and grew more tardily than before. In the same way, Mr. Middleton Murry has proclaimed in all seriousness "a major crisis, not merely in the history of human life, but of life itself," [1] and the Pope "perhaps the most serious and widespread crisis since the Deluge," while Mr. Wells, in *The Fate of Homo Sapiens*, describes the Nazi movement as "the most urgent challenge the human mind will have ever had to face," and considers that it "may well bring disaster to our species."

Men aim at projecting their own inward unease onto as large a screen as possible. When they tremble, the universe must; when their great ones die, the elements must register disturbance. A tremendous thunderstorm is commonly believed to have marked the occasion when both Cromwell and Napoleon breathed their last, though in Napoleon's case it has been pointed out that no reference to this storm appears in the log of a ship which happened to be anchored off St. Helena when it was supposed to have taken place.

[1] In *Heaven—and Earth*.

3]

The passing of each sovereign and statesman is presented as the end of an epoch; and when a Lenin or a Hitler surprisingly climbs into the seats of the mighty, the foundering or birth of a civilization is announced.

In truth, there can be no crisis in any absolute sense, since life, like the King's Government, must be carried on. Life survived even the coming of the Ice Age, and will doubtless survive Mussolini. A great while ago the world began, and its end is not yet. If this earth on which we live for a little while were to-night pounded into dust, and that dust scattered, still the universe would remain to fulfil its mysterious destiny—a destiny in which we, as belonging to the universe, must participate. A crisis is inconceivable for creatures who are born and must die, who must endure their going hence even as their coming hither. A traveller going he knows not whither and coming he knows not whence, cannot be said to lose his way.

If, however, there can be no absolute crisis in the affairs of mortal men, there are periods of relative stability and instability, relatively eventful and uneventful periods; periods in which men are more conscious than at others of the precariousness of their fleshly life, and less conscious that as it was in the beginning, so it is now and ever shall be.

The decade just ended may legitimately be regarded as unusually eventful. There can seldom in ten years have been fewer days on which a chief sub-editor had difficulty in finding a lead. For chief sub-editors, if for no one else, it has been a good time.

The present is always chaos, its prophets always charlatans, its values always false. When it has become the past, and may be looked back on, only then is it possible to detect order underlying the chaos, truth underlying the charlatanry, inexorable justice underlying the false values. That man had to speak and that man to be silent, that man had to rise to power and that man fall, that victory had to be won and that defeat suffered. Looked back on, the past makes a pattern, every element of which, however trivial, is necessary to the whole; each incident, each word spoken, the tilt of each hat, the modulation of each voice, falling into its place. Then it is apparent that nothing takes place aimlessly, no one exists aimlessly; that truly the hairs of each head have been numbered, and the fall of each sparrow to the ground, foreseen.

Looking back on the ten years now ended, turning over the deposit they have left behind them—newspapers already yellow, books already musty, photographs already curious, shifting reputations, the dead whose shadows are still lively and whose voices still speak, and the forgotten dead; all the litter of a decade, swept aside to clear a space for more to accumulate—a pattern may be sought.

Change is imperceptible. It happens so gradually that an effort is required to notice it. A face seen day after day seems changeless, until a sudden realization comes that time has hollowed it and bleached it; leaves are everlasting, until lo! they have withered, and bare branches clutch at a wintry sky; an empire is great, and then is fallen. Days pass, and months, and years, signifying what?—to a ledger clerk so many ledgers filled, to a politician so much importance acquired, to a prostitute so many who have stretched themselves out beside her, to a financier such a bank balance accumulated, to a missionary so many brands plucked from the burning, to a civil servant so much progress made towards pensioned retirement, to a journalist so many newspapers produced, sold, read, and cast aside to light fires or wrap up fried fish; to all, foolish hopes which were disappointed, foolish despair which was survived.

It is difficult to realize that ten years hence Greta Garbo will seem as sadly strange as Lillian Gish does now, and Mr. Priestley's present literary pronouncements seem then as surprising as to-day his past ones do—for instance, his estimate of Vicki Baum in 1932 as "the most remarkable woman novelist now writing."

A recent revival of one of Rudolph Valentino's successes, *The Son of the Sheik*, aroused uproarious laughter; as Mr. Campbell Dixon put it: "The love scenes that thrilled millions of women in 1921 rolled audiences in the aisles in 1939. . . . The dialogue, studded with such lines as 'Lock up the jealous one, and bring in the white gazelle!' set the whole house rocking." Everything except ecstasy soon becomes funny.

Ten years is not long—a seventh of a lifetime, or a paragraph in a history book, or two Parliaments' full tenure, or a sentence for robbery with violence. Take away ten years from Lenin's life and few would have heard of him; take away ten years from Wordsworth's life and his reputation is unaffected; take away ten years from Napoleon's life and he dies in his glory; take away ten years from Keats's life and little is left; let the earth have ten years more or less to revolve round the sun, ten centuries more or less, and who would care?

If ten years is not long, ten years ago is long ago. Then, Shirley Temple had but just come crying into the world, where she was soon to delight millions, seated in darkness, solitary or clasped together, while on a white screen before them her little antics were projected. Then, the Duke of Windsor was still Prince of Wales, night starvation undiscovered, mixed-bathing in the Serpentine unpermitted, twopenny libraries unopened, trenches in Hyde Park undug and gas masks undistributed, A.R.P. unheard of, *Cavalcade* unwritten and unpraised by Mr. Agate, headphones in drawing-rooms still occasionally to be seen, young women wearing trousers and young men wearing make-up still comparatively rare, mass-observation uninvented, the country still unsaved, and Ramsay MacDonald who was to save it, still leader of the Labour Party; then Mr. Godfrey Winn was little known, the salaries of Members of Parliament had not been raised from £400 to £600 a year, the Leader of the Opposition performed his functions gratis, and the League of Nations, described by General Smuts as "the greatest adventure in history," was thought by the *Times* to have "quietly made good"; then, Waterloo Bridge and Adelphi Terrace still stood, Broadcasting House had not been built, Spain was still a monarchy, Germany still a republic, and King Carol dining with Madame Lupescu in London or Paris instead of in Bucharest; then, Mr. Lloyd George still had a party, the *Morning Post* and the *Daily Chronicle* an independent existence, and Sir Stafford Cripps had not been elected to Parliament, being known, if at all, as an earnest seconder of Bishop Soederblom's efforts to reunite the churches; then, no *Queen Mary* sailed the seas, the pound was on gold, Surrealism unexplained by Mr. Herbert Read, the Left Book Club unfounded, and the Bible to be read as literature unpublished.

Newspapers have their obituaries ready filed. We regret, or, in the case of important persons, deeply regret to announce the death of So-and-so, still breathing, ambitious, with money and passion left to expend.[1] These obituaries require periodical revision, he who once deserved a column and a half later only deserving perhaps three-quarters of a column; he whose imagined death was once an occasion for reflections in a *de mortuis nil nisi bonum* strain later becoming an irreplaceable loss to his country; this one's reputation having grown up so suddenly that no provision has been made for recording his demise.

In ten years reputations greatly fluctuate, and much obituary revision is necessary, apart from the inevitable weeding out—"Died on such a date," scrawled across used obituaries, yet these also kept a little while in the unlikely event of curiosity about the already dead and buried arising, and requiring to be satisfied.

Ten years ago, as a Cabinet Minister in office and a trade union official, Mr. J. H. Thomas would have been entitled to at least three-quarters of a column (". . . genial disposition made him popular with opponents as well as colleagues . . . hard-hitter but . . . notable talent as a negotiator . . ."), and probably a photograph. Then, after the formation of the National Government, this three-quarters of a column would have grown into a column, and perhaps a little more (". . . stood loyally by the Prime Minister . . . excellent work at the Dominions Office . . . when the bitterness of present political controversy has died down it will be seen that . . ."). Rumours of his impending resignation would have led to a certain shrinkage, length being reduced by the excision of some of the warmer

[1] Lord Alfred Douglas is one of the few who have been given an opportunity of reading the published version of their own obituaries. In 1921 the *Evening News*, acting on a false report of Lord Alfred's death, published his obituary, thereby, incidentally, providing grounds for a libel action which resulted in Lord Alfred being awarded £1,000 damages.

commendatory phrases; and for a few months after the publication of the findings of the Budget Leakage Enquiry and his subsequent resignation, he would scarcely have had an obituary at all, just a paragraph or two (". . . started life as an engine-driver . . . political career brought to a sudden end . . . undoubted flair for . . . events still fresh in the public memory . . ."). Now, little by little, his obituary will be growing again; never to recover its previous size of warmth, tending to harp back to its first draft (". . . genial disposition . . . fund of good stories . . . accomplished after-dinner speaker . . .") and to hurry over the later phases of his career.

Turning over these obituaries, used and unused, old and new, gives a vivid sense of how, as the years pass, great and small ones ebb and flow with the moon—here a peer and Lord-Lieutenant, Lord Kylsant, whose steady obituary accretion is suddenly interrupted by a term of imprisonment for fraud; here a clergyman, the Rector of Stiffkey, who would scarcely have had an obituary at all if he had not been unfrocked, starved in a barrel, and thrown to circus lions; here a pacifist and sometime chairman of the I.L.P., Mr. Clifford Allen, whose chilly obituary note blossomed into an adulatory column when he became Lord Allen of Hurtwood ("Principle was paramount with him, but on questions of procedure he was prepared to compromise"); here an ex-Prime Minister, Ramsay MacDonald, subject to more obituary revision, perhaps, than any of his contemporaries, his obituary in its published form containing vestiges of each stage of his astonishing career from a reputed dangerous revolutionary in whose eyes the Russian Revolution brought "a sort of spring-tide joy all over Europe," to one who, according to Lord Snowden, boasted,

probably justifiably: "To-morrow every duchess in London will be wanting to kiss me."

The full range of human importance is registered in
obituaries, between the minimum recorded at all:

"He was born on ——, educated at —— and ——, and
ordained priest at the age of ——. He was formerly Rector of
——, ——. He married ——, daughter of ——, of —— ——"

or, in another *genre:*

"In London, aged ——. A well-known member of the Stock
Exchange since ——, and senior partner in the stock-jobbing
firm of ——."

and the one and a half columns of a Lord Stamfordham,
the three columns of a Sir Edward Clarke, K.C., the one
column of a Lord Trent, formerly Sir Jesse Boot, and
founder of Boot's Cash Chemist, the two columns allotted
to Arnold Bennett, author, and to Sir Hugh Bell, iron-
master.

II

Lenin resolved all politics into the single question, Who
whom? [1] Like two wrestlers locked together, each struggling to pin the other down and be uppermost, or standing
apart and looking for a likely grip, or attempting some ruse,
are "Who" and "Whom." Their conflict is ceaseless, is
history. When "Who" is overthrown, becoming "Whom,"
some who were "Whom" become "Who," and there are
still "Who" and "Whom," wrestling; still the everlasting
question to be answered—Who whom?

"Who" has the advantage over "Whom" of being estab-

[1] This is a sounder classification than into "haves" and "have-nots," since
there are many "haves" with "have-not" characteristics, and vice versa.

lished in authority; "Whom" of numbers, and the energy derived from envy and a consciousness of wrongs endured. The resources of the State are at "Who's" disposal—institutions civil and religious, wealth, honours, morality, law; "Whom," uncorrupted by the exercise of power, may count on enthusiasm and disinterestedness, on the dynamic resentment of all (and that is many) who feel they have had less than their deserts. "Who" carries on from day to day, seizing opportunities to buttress up challenged authority as they present themselves, crushing or buying off opposition according to the exigencies of the moment, jolted and harassed, now seemingly almost pulled down by "Whom's" eager arms, now a little breathless, recovering and continuing to jog along, though shaken. "Who" fluctuates, but to "Whom" there is no end—changeless, eternal, necessary "Whom," "Who's" prey and "Who's" doom.

The last ten years have been a very difficult time for "Who"—confused, precarious, dangerous years. Yet "Who" survives. Judges still sit robed in red and decree punishment; policemen in blue (a greater number than before speaking like B.B.C. announcers, and the large-footed, pantomime variety, friendly with cooks, seeming scarcely to exist any more) still perambulate the streets; elderly men are still to be seen through windows in Pall Mall asleep in leather chairs with the *Times* in their lap, powdery ladies wearing furs to be seen in large cars as they pass by, or airing small dogs in Hyde Park; the *Tatler* and *Bystander* [1] continue to be available in dentists' and doctors' waiting-rooms, Eton and Harrow to be well-attended,

---

[1] These periodicals are now, along with Debrett's *Peerage*, fittingly under the same management as the *Daily Herald*, and continue to display the activities of the rich and fashionable mostly for the edification of the poor and unfashionable.

society weddings frequent, gossip-writers voluminous, expensive restaurants crowded, winter sports and the ballet popular, peerages and baronetcies, knighthoods even, much desired, tickets for theatre, and especially cinema, first-nights much sought after, débutantes many (though the American quota greatly reduced), Glyndebourne and Ascot places to be seen at, and clergymen fit, along with doctors and Justices of the Peace and bank-managers, to sign passport forms. The King in his palace and bishops in theirs, company directors at their board meetings and civil servants at their desks, governors of distant lands, Viceroy of India, lords temporal, spiritual and financial—all these and the many holding on to their skirts, survive. "Who" survives.

Sunday by Sunday Mr. Garvin fills his allotted space, not appreciably less noisy and incoherent than heretofore; *Punch* appears week by week, still with winged politicians, and jokes about hunting, and the New Rich, and servants who mispronounce, and Austen sevens, and each January 1 a Mr. C. B. Gabb surveys the year's longevity records in the *Times*. The *Morning Post* has gone and the *Daily Worker* come, Oxford and Cambridge senior common rooms gaining what retired army and navy officers have lost; the *Manchester Guardian* continues to preach enlightenment to the enlightened,[1] and the *Times*—what shall be said of the *Times*, "Who's" very voice, taking in the chaos of a troubled world and putting forth smooth persuasion; hurrying along behind tumultuous events, and, sometimes with a slight catch of breathlessness, no more than that,

1 "To the Women's Freedom League to-day Miss Elise Sprott, who has for eleven years been on the staff of the B.B.C., spoke at the Minerva Club on women and the radio . . ."

interpreting them—like the owner of a Derby runner, top-hatted, holding the bridle of his champing horse to be photographed; finding in Spain some months before the Republic was declared clear indications that loyalty to the Throne was "deeply rooted in both town and country," and "the great mass of the Spanish people undoubtedly monarchists"; in Dr. Brüning "the best since Bismarck," in General Schleicher he in whom "all Germany heard its master's voice," in Mr. Chamberlain's conversations with Herr Hitler at Munich in 1938 clear indications that "Mr. Chamberlain offered concessions from strength and not from weakness," this winning him "a respect that might not otherwise have been accorded." [1]

"Who" survives, but with less confidence than before. Doubt has crept in, and apprehension. Much that was taken for granted can now be taken for granted no longer. Even facetiousness has grown somewhat tremulous. To-day's joke has a way of becoming to-morrow's reality. With Dr. Goebbels German Minister for Propaganda and Enlightenment, it is difficult to imagine anything that might not happen. On January 1, 1930, in a review of the year just ended, the *Times* could write:

[1] Occasionally unintentional comedy is provided. For instance, on January 23, 1931, there appeared in the *Western Mail* a burlesque interview with Mr. Lloyd George by the "Junior Member for Treorchy," such burlesque interviews being a regular weekly feature in the paper. The next day the *Times*, assuming the interview to be authentic, referred to it editorially:
"In a remarkable interview which Mr. Lloyd George accorded on his birthday to the representative of a provincial paper, the 'little Wizard' is reported as saying, 'I am not prepared to commit myself *just yet* in regard to my future destiny. I may go to the Right, or I may drift to the Left. My decision will be dependent on circumstances. In the meantime, I must wait until I can discern *where the land lies*.' This no doubt correctly represents the attitude of the Liberal Party, but circumstances seem to be conspiring . . ."

"Except for sundry disturbances which were confined to localities, such as civil war in Afghanistan, conflicts between Jews and Arabs in Palestine, and continued marching and counter-marching of armed forces in China, the year 1929 was passed everywhere in tranquillity. . . ."

By Christmas 1938 the note is noticeably more subdued, and reassurance more laboriously attained:

"When, for example, the pessimist asserts that the modern world is 'full of cruelty' what precisely does he mean? If he means that there are many victims of cruelty, the phrase is tragically true. But if he means that there are many perpetrators of cruelty, or that cruelty is now condoned by the mass of mankind, his phrase is altogether false. . . ."

Thus to derive comfort from the fact that there are fewer perpetrators of cruelty than victims of it, whereas there might be one man one cruelty, suggests a serious shortage of comfortable data. Civil war in Spain could not, like civil war in Afghanistan, be easily dismissed as "confined to localities," marching and counter-marching of armed forces in Europe is more disturbing to tranquillity than in distant China, and even Arabs and Jews, by persistence in conflict, become ominous.

III

Ordinary men and women, struggling to get the means of life for themselves and those dependent on them, assume the permanence of existing institutions unless and until they cease to function. Like a clock, as long as they are going they are going, and when they have stopped they have stopped.

Yet these institutions are not static. Like living creatures, they have a will to survive, and are constantly undergoing adaptations to that end. Consider, for instance, the Church and related activities. What doctrinal adaptations, what symptomatic changes?

At the coronation of King George VI Bishops and the two Archbishops were much in evidence, and for the first time representatives of the Nonconformist bodies participated in the ceremonial. Episcopal appointments, even colonial ones, continue to arouse interest, and in little village churches, Sunday by Sunday, Rectors still pray and preach and hold up an offertory-plate to the altar, their congregations not appreciably sparser, and the offertory-plate not appreciably lighter, than ten years ago. The B.B.C. broadcasts religious services, and Toc H lamps remain alight. One spring morning in 1936 a procession of vans drove from Shoe Lane and dispersed throughout London, each bearing the poster: "Is There an After-Life? See To-morrow's *Evening Standard*"; the *Morning Post* shortly before its amalgamation with the *Daily Telegraph* published a series of articles entitled "The Empty Pew"; and the more serious dailies each Saturday devote a column to religious topics, uncomfortable texts being made comfortable, harsh sayings mitigated—as, "Take no thought for the morrow":

"So long as we are able to preserve the true balance of interests founded on a sound appreciation of life's true values we shall never allow ourselves to be the creatures of circumstance or so to fear the future as to lose faith in the loving will of God."

Clergymen continue to play their part in public affairs. The Rev. "Dick" Sheppard was much esteemed, and founded the Peace Pledge Union, which attracted a considerable membership, among others Mr. Aldous Huxley and Miss Rose Macaulay. When he died, occasioning some surprise by leaving £40,000, Miss Vera Brittain expressed the opinion [1] that if he had lived the whole course of events in the years which followed his death might have been different. His successor as Dean of Canterbury, the Rev. Hewlett Johnson, has achieved prominence as an admirer of the Soviet régime and enthusiastic supporter of the Left Book Club. When he invoked a divine blessing on this organization at an Albert Hall rally, Mr. Victor Gollancz, its founder, remarked that he for one was deeply moved, as well he might be considering the small encouragement most of his well-wishers had given to any expectation of divine, or even ecclesiastical, support. The Rector of Stiffkey occupied many columns of newspaper space both during and after the proceedings which were taken against him; Dean Inge, since his retirement from the Deanery of St. Paul's, has contributed a weekly article to the *Evening Standard*, and it was a Bishop, Dr. Blunt, who precipitated the constitutional crisis which led to the abdication of King Edward VIII.

If, however, the Church appears to function with undiminished vigour, episcopal palaces all occupied, prebendary stalls all filled, each year some 600 deacons ordained, and some 3,000,000 persons more or less regularly receiving Holy Communion, in Liverpool a new cathedral in process of being built, new suburbs acquiring places of worship, missionary endeavour, though restricted, continuing—there are signs of decrepitude.

In 1930, Dr. Barnes, the Bishop of Birmingham, aroused a certain amount of public, or at any rate newspaper, indignation, by his somewhat scornful preference for scientific

[1] In *Thrice a Stranger*.

rather than theological explanations of the universe. Statements like: "The Christian Church has never made the
unguarded statement that Jesus was God," could still shock;
at least they were worth reporting. The Anglo-Catholic
movement was still strong, its annual Congress a notable
event, and birettas still worn on Anglican heads with a
certain defiance. Now heretical utterances, however strong
and by whomever made, tend to pass unnoticed, while a
number of losses to the Church of Rome have thinned the
ranks of the Anglo-Catholic leaders, and the flock's ardour
has cooled.[1] Mr. T. S. Eliot remains, still Anglo, still
Catholic, but many others have departed, and congregations, even fashionable ones, neither resent nor are excited
by ritualistic innovations, listen to prayers for the dead as
apathetically as to a recitation of the Thirty-Nine Articles.

Doctrinally, the Church may be said to have been fighting a rearguard action. After the slaughter caused by its
encounters with science in the latter part of the nineteenth
century, scattered forces were gathered together, broken
ranks reformed, and not a very convincing offensive undertaken from the abandoned enemy lines. If the Biblical
account of the creation was invalidated by evolutionary
theories, have not they also been invalidated in their turn?
"It cannot be admitted," a leader in the *Times* contended
in 1931, "that either the clergy or any considerable body
of church people still link their religion with creationist
theories that have been obsolete for fifty years or more."
As a piece of tactics this may be admired, yet all it amounts

[1] This statement in the *Church Times*, organ of the High Church Party,
in the autumn of 1937, suggests drooping spirits—"The Church of England
is settling down to autumn work, and persons of imagination are asking
themselves the searching question, What exactly are we trying to do, and
how are we to set about doing it?"

to is throwing bad science after good dogma, involving *The Origin of Species* in the ruin of Genesis.

For fourteen years a committee of churchmen represent-ing all shades of theological opinion laboured at the task of reformulating Anglican doctrine. The result of their labours, published in 1938, is a curious document in which unanimity has been achieved by hedging which might have made even Sir John Simon blush. Angels and demons have, "at the very least, a symbolical value," though "to many of us it seems unreasonable to suppose that the only spiritual beings which exist in the universe, other than God Himself, must be human"; miracles may have happened, though "many feel it to be more congruous with the wisdom and majesty of God that the regularities, such as men of science observe in nature and call Laws of Nature, should serve His purpose without any need for exceptions on the physical plane"; the Virgin Birth remains valid, though "there are some among us who hold that a full belief in the historical Incarnation is more consistent with the supposition that Our Lord's birth took place under the normal conditions of human generation"; the Judgment Day "presents great difficulties," and the Anglican Hell, if it still retains a shadowy existence, is markedly less forbidding than Dante's.[1]

IV

The Church is under the necessity of from time to time thus formulating its adaptations to changing circumstances.

[1] Not, however, as comfortably envisaged as by a Roman Catholic writer in the middle of the last century, who, infected by the ebullient optimism of the times, pointed out that, though Hell was clearly not to be compared with Heaven, it still represented a considerable improvement on earthly existence.

In the case of other institutions, adaptations take place without needing to be formulated. If the Judgment Day "presents great difficulties," so does the House of Lords; if angels and demons have "at the very least a symbolical value," so has the Gold Standard, whose abandonment in 1931 seemed so grievous, until custom and the Exchange Equalization Fund brought reconcilement; if Hell has had to lose some of its discomfort, so has poverty, and if miracles are of dubious validity, so is unearned income.

There has been a general toning-down process, an endeavour, which tends to become desperate, to soften the asperities of social and economic inequality by pretending they scarcely exist. In 1931, protests were made in Parliament against a broadcast by a Cambridge economist, Mr. Maurice Dobb, on the ground that he was a Marxist; now the difficulty would be to find an economist employed in any university who was not one.[1] Wealth, which used to be respected, has come merely to be envied; and the well-to-do find it necessary either to be apologetic or to become socialists. Bishops explain that they are out-of-pocket on their salaries, undergraduates that their hearts are with the masses, and dons at their high-tables bridle when Stalin is

[1] A good example of how those whose views would once have been regarded as subversive, have been assimilated, and sometimes rewarded, is provided by a symposium, published in 1937, entitled *The Mind in Chains*, and edited by Mr. Day Lewis. The theme of this symposium is that "capitalism has no further use for culture," and that the lot of "intellectual workers" has become insufferable, since "the mind is really in chains to-day"—chains "forged by a dying social system" which "can and must be broken." Biographical notes show that among the contributors are two university lecturers, two schoolmasters (not at elementary schools), one Professor of Harmony and Composition at the Royal Academy of Music, one member of the Council of the Book Society, and one Hollywood scenario-writer. Capitalism may have no further use for culture, but it clearly has use for these well remunerated "intellectual workers."

criticized; while even the Rothschilds, the glamour of whose wealth and financial operations has become as established as the Scarlet Pimpernel's, are glad to have, besides financiers, a few country gentlemen and scientists in their line. Imperialism, once so strident, has found a precarious disguise in mandated territory, and India resounds with imparted parliamentary eloquence. With that strange aptness which trivial events sometimes have, when Kipling's coffin arrived at Golders Green to be cremated, the crematorium was still littered with red flags and other revolutionary insignia taken there in honour of Saklatvala, a wealthy Parsee and former Communist Member of Parliament for Battersea, whose cremation had just taken place. The strains of the *Internationale* had scarcely died away when the corpse of the inventor of the White Man's Burden was consigned to the flames which had lately consumed the mortal remains of Saklatvala.

V

To assume that each arbitrarily measured span of time has its distinctive character, a spirit of its own, is perhaps erroneous, since days and years and centuries shade imperceptibly into one another, and the most outstanding human achievements are outstanding because they survive shifting fashions, transcend their circumstances and time. Yet it remains true that as the individual has moods, so do societies, and that this mood is expressed, in one way or another, in all, or nearly all, that is going on at a particular time; in newspapers and advertisements, in clothes and in gestures, in tricks of speech, cigarette pictures, styles of hair-dress-ing, and ministerial appointments; most obviously in whatever is immediately popular.

Popularity is achieved by making manifest the contemporary mood, as Lord Northcliffe well understood when he made an immediate success of the *Daily Mail* by setting out to give the public what they wanted, rather than what they ought to want, or what would be good for them.

Since then others have copied his prescription, and, as so often happens, outdone its original application.[1] The *Daily Mail* has come to have a distinctly old-fashioned flavour.

The contemporary mood touches everything and everyone, like the light of the declining sun spreading the same glow over faces, houses, trees, motor-cars, slag-heaps and pylons. It may be seen in hikers noisily making for the countryside, their knees bare, males and females scarcely distinguishable; in road-houses, strangely named (the Monkey Puzzle, the Spider's Web), urban to the country, rural to the town; in sunshine cruises, suddenly popular; in beauty-treatment, much developed, filling whole newspaper pages, inquiries being invited and profusely received, women's page editors (not always women) ruefully surveying a mountain of letters all asking for advice about intractable complexion, pores, arm-pits, eyebrows.

---

[1] According to the *Report on the British Press* published in April, 1938, by P.E.P. (Political and Economic Planning), the circulation of the *Daily Mail* in 1930 was 1,845,000, with the *Daily Express*, 1,693,000 and the *Daily Herald* 1,082,000; in 1937 it had fallen to 1,580,000, with the *Daily Herald* and the *Daily Express* both over 2,000,000.

From Eton-crop to permanent wave covers the same distance as from Ramsay MacDonald to Neville Chamberlain, or from D. H. Lawrence to Mr. Hemingway, or from René Clair to Walt Disney, or from Mr. Beverley Nichols, cottager, to Mr. Beverley Nichols, patriot. This author is notably susceptible to the contemporary mood's fluctuations. Its slightest shift in direction or abatement of intensity is registered by him. In 1930, he was still praising the delights of rural retirement; in 1934, he turned his attention to the iniquity of war and of armament manufacturers, many who had previously scoffed at him becoming respectful; in 1936 God was his preoccupation, and in 1938, England. There for the time being he has come to rest, his cottage sold, after probably the most profitable occupancy of a rural property on record, the local village shop participating in the harvest by selling picture postcards, for instance, of Mr. Nichols's dog, inscribed: "I just want him to be his own woolly self," and of a statue in Mr. Nichols's garden, inscribed: "The sweet country rain washed his limbs, and the wind played about him."

Even sentimentality, though never diminishing, gushes and burbles differently at different times. Once Mr. James Douglas might legitimately have been regarded as sentimentalist-in-chief, but now he has been superseded. It is not that his hand has lost its cunning, or his tear-ducts run dry, but that the hearts he once touched have changed and no longer respond to his treatment. What is his dog, Bunch, now deceased, compared with the one Mr. Nichols just wants to be his own woolly self, or with Mr. Godfrey Winn's Mr. Sponge? "I wish I could keen or howl," Mr. Douglas wrote in the *Daily Express* on the occasion of Bunch's death, "like a woman or a girl or a child or a dog, but a man can't howl or keen." That was where Mr. Douglas was wrong. A man can howl or keen, a man does. "He had rickets, you know, as a puppy," Mr. Winn has written of Mr. Sponge, "and though he is much better these days, he still wobbles sideways a bit." On another occasion, Mr. Winn "said to Mr. Sponge, pointing with my gardening scissors between the chopping: 'Look at that rose, old man. An hour ago it reminded me of a woman in full bloom—wearing a pale pink dress at a party, knowing she was what is called the cynosure of every eye. Now? Her petals are falling. Softly, gently, one by one, in the noonday heat. In another hour she will be nothing but a barren, blighted stalk.' " Bunch did well to die. His day was done.

Mr. Winn, reputed to be the highest paid journalist in Fleet Street, has indeed captured the sentimentality market. In his own words, he "set his pen high," and his salary mounted with it. His writings provide his readers with their own romanticized version of life. Beside by-pass roads are many mansions, mansions of light and love. It would be a good thing, Mr. Winn thinks, "if a law compelled all employers and employees, whenever it was compatible with public safety, to change places for one working day once a year"; "charm is the plain girl's lifebuoy," he writes, and to hearten a friend who is "waiting patiently for that event which, though this is an age of sex-emancipation, still remains the most important and memorable moment in the lives of most women," quotes a remark of Carole Lombard's: "I live by a man's code, designed to fit a man's world, yet at the same time I never forget that a woman's first job is to choose the right shade of lipstick."

The same recipe as Mr. Winn uses, but with different backing, is used by Mr. H. G. Wells, whose film, *The*

Shape of Things To Come, also holds out the prospect of a
world full of charm, correctly shaded lipstick, and interchangeable employers and employees. Golden youths and
maidens in white silken shorts and open-necked shirts live
delectable, amorous lives, provided by science with innumerable conveniences and playthings, shooting through the
air at immense speed, falling without self-consciousness
into one another's hygienic arms, with no jealous squall or
inward groan to disturb their bliss—this seen from plush
seats across intervening darkness, typewriters all still, orders
all taken, washing-up done.

In Mr. Wells, too, the contemporary mood is made manifest. He has succeeded in giving the harsh materialism in
which his own life is rooted, a glow of righteousness and
joy. Prosperity, once regarded as an end in itself, he has
endowed with transcendental qualities, adding unto it
benevolence and eroticism. Bank balances dissolve into
embraces, factory chimneys blossom like flowers, and company directors discard their black coats and put on white
silk, take off their top-hats to twine bay leaves in their hair.
The black-coated worker becomes white-coated.

If Mr. Wells has been instrumental in popularizing this
romantic materialism, this sense that faulty technique,
which might be corrected, rather than any fundamental
fallacy, has prevented increased wealth from resulting in
increased happiness, religious teaching has not been behindhand. It also has become increasingly chiliastic,[1] choosing
rather to stress the Kingdom-of-Heaven-on-Earth than
expectations beyond the grave. Denunciations of slums
from the pulpit have been more common than denuncia-

[1] For a brilliant analysis of this development, see Mr. F. A. Voigt's *Unto
Caesar*.

tions of sin, and the Church Assembly has become animated, if at all, over derelict ecclesiastical properties and
the inequality of living, rather than over derelict souls and
the equality of dying.

VI

In a film, directed by Professor Julian Huxley, the evolutionary process was demonstrated, culminating in radiant
and nude youths and maidens floating heavenwards, the
decencies being ingeniously safeguarded by a light, but
opaque, mist which floated round their nether-portions;
and a Pageant of Parliament portrayed the growth of constitutional liberties and social progress. The performers
were mostly amateurs, among them society ladies, débutantes, much photographed, whose names often occur in
gossip paragraphs. From Magna Charta onwards the tale
unfolded, until the Industrial Revolution. Then the stage
was darkened, and the débutantes appeared, whimpering
and wretched, dressed in rags, to represent miserable children condemned to work underground in mines, or in
insanitary factories. After a short performance in this rôle,
they vanished, soon to reappear beaming, and, as the programme put it, "in clean white pinnies," to attend school
in charge of a kindly Froebel teacher. All the lights were
put on to suggest sunshine. Tennis-players, cyclists, hikers,
athletes, boy scouts and girl guides assembled, and to invigorating music went through suitable motions. This was
the grand finale.

The same spirit is apparent in a rather different form, in
the only successful revivalistic enterprise of recent years—
Buchmanism, about which both Mr. Nichols and Mr.
Winn, though not Mr. Wells, have written sympathetically.

This characteristically American importation has managed, by calling itself the Oxford Group,[1] to acquire snob appeal, and to get vaguely associated with Newman and Pusey. Its founder, Dr. Frank Buchman, looks like a successful business man of the Rotarian sort, and when in London stays at Brown's Hotel,[2] which was also Kipling's favourite hotel. From this quiet and select, but expensive, headquarters, he directs his organization, which has attracted a number of dons, bishops, retired army and navy officers, athletes, and even politicians, besides enthusiastic teams of young men and women mostly belonging to the middle and upper classes. An efficiently produced, illustrated periodical made its appearance in 1938, in technique identical with all forms of photographic propaganda, whether *The U.S.S.R. in Construction* or the little leaflets wrapped round constipation cures—that is, showing smiling faces, varied, male and female, but alike in that they all smile. House parties are organized, at which sins, usually of an economic, but sometimes of a sexual, character, are publicly confessed; and occasionally there are large gatherings in the Albert Hall. The platform is decorated with flags; while the audience assembles the organ plays tunes like "Land of Hope Glory," and speeches are delivered by speakers representing as wide a social range as possible. Each, whether country gentleman acknowledging that he has been in the habit of using bad language to his stable boys, or mill-

[1] An attempt to register itself as a company under this name for the purpose of receiving a bequest aroused protests in Parliament, led by Mr. A. P. Herbert, Independent Member for Oxford University. These protests were unsuccessful, and Oxford had to endure its association with Dr. Buchman's activities.

[2] According to Mr. Rom Landau's *God Is My Adventure*, when taxed with living expensively Dr. Buchman made the significant retort that God was a millionaire and so under no necessity to economize.

worker acknowledging that he has sometimes neglected to work when the foreman's eye was not on him, or housewife acknowledging that she has been responsible for unpleasantness at the breakfast table, have the same message— life was dull and unprofitable until the Groups came along, and then was happy and prosperous. These successive testimonies, so eager, so spontaneous and yet never faltering, create a growing excitement. Each member of the audience recognizes himself in one or other of the testifiers; wonders —Might not I also smile, become self-confident and prosperous, testify even? The country gentleman is genial, the mill-worker in his Sunday best, the housewife serene. Thus it might be always—everyone smiling, in Sunday best, untroubled.

The movement has been particularly successful in Scandinavia, South Africa and Switzerland, and is reputed to have found a notable adherent in Frau Himmler, wife of the head of the Gestapo, the German Secret Police. Another notable adherent was Mr. H. W. Austin, the well-known tennis player, who when he came to realize that "the trouble of the world was selfishness," energetically campaigned for Moral Rearmament,[1] which, like Blake's mental fight waged with arrows of desire, holds out the possibility of being strong and valiant without going to the expense of acquiring arms or running the risks involved in using them. Like moral courage, moral victory, moral any-

[1] A fellow-countryman of Dr. Buchman, William James, hit on a similar idea when he suggested that what was needed to ensure peace was a "moral equivalent" of war. The trouble is that war has no moral equivalent, any more than incest has; and if it had a moral equivalent, this would be as deplorable as, if not more deplorable than, war itself. Strip-tease, for instance, might perhaps be regarded as the moral equivalent of, but is scarcely an improvement on, fornication.

thing, Moral Rearmament represents an attempt to reconcile the contrary demands of flesh and spirit by including
them in one comprehensive formula. Moral Cannibalism
would probably make a strong appeal to cannibals, and
Moral Rape to the inmates of lunatic asylums.

Another movement, in essentials of a like nature, is Social
Credit, which might perhaps be described as Moral Capitalism. Its founder, Major Douglas, is an Australian; and
his proposals involve an expansion of credit to keep pace
with expanding productive capacity. To understand exactly
how this may be done requires a knowledge of economics
beyond the capacity of most, but the advantages of doing
it are easily comprehended. If wealth constantly increases,
everyone must get richer and richer, which is precisely
what everyone wants. The poor may be made less poor
without the well-to-do having to disgorge, and revolution
become unnecessary because all have more to lose than
their chains.

If the Holy Writ of this faith is somewhat forbidding, it
also has its revivalistic side. Mr. John Hargrave, described
as "The Voice of the People," delivers a monthly lecture in
London under the general title "Social Credit Is Coming";
the late A. R. Orage, Mr. Ezra Pound and other well-known
writers and poets, have devoted themselves to expounding
and propagating Major Douglas's scheme; a weekly, *New
Britain*, had a meteoric career in the same service, though
its later numbers departed a good deal from orthodoxy;
and small processions of persons in green uniforms, and
wearing sashes inscribed "Social Credit," have occasionally
made their appearance at Downing Street and other public
places. It remained for the Province of Alberta, under the
leadership of Mr. Aberhart, an eloquent preacher and

formerly head of the Prophetic Bible Institute, to attempt a practical application of Social Credit, though not with much success. In office, Mr. Aberhart pleased his flock at the Prophetic Bible Institute more than he did Major Douglas. As so often happens, relations between the prophet and the disciple soon became strained. Ideas which had inspired enthusiasm and hope, when tendered in the form of advice were unacceptable; zeal which had been gratifying, when expressed in administrative acts became misguided.

The logical end, perhaps the *reductio ad absurdum*, of romantic materialism is some form of utopia. If heaven is transferred from Eternity to Time, from beyond the skies to earth, then it must come to pass; and if it refuses to come to pass, then what has come to pass must be called heaven, and woe unto those who question its celestial pretensions.

Two rival heavens-on-earth have been put on the market whose protagonists hurl abuse at one another, and are only united in despising whoever will not admit the momentousness of their rivalry. Many attempts have been made to define the conflict between them. Mr. Wyndham Lewis, for instance, sees it as a clash between nationalism and internationalism;[1] others have demonstrated that it is between Christianity and atheism, dictatorship and democracy, capitalism and communism, tyranny and freedom, bourgeoisie and proletariat. Even the nomenclature used is uncertain, Left and Right, Fascist and anti-Fascist, meaning one thing at one moment and another at another; and, to add to the confusion, the two factions tend to range themselves behind two existent régimes, the U.S.S.R. and the

[1] See *Left Wings Over Europe* and *Count Your Dead—They Are Alive.*

Third Reich, and are therefore bound to justify the acts of the one, whatever they may be, and to abhor those of the other, whatever they may be. Since, in practice, these acts bear a marked and increasing resemblance to one another, the lot of their rival admirers and detractors is hard indeed, and was made appreciably harder by the German-Soviet Pact, surprisingly concluded in 1939. When a Rothschild is spoiled of his possessions in Vienna, socialists must complain; patriots found their hearts glowing when British ships were bombed off the coast of Spain, and fulminators against imperialism groaned when Gibraltar was threatened; the extermination by Stalin of his revolutionary associates caused those who most disapproved of the deceased's activities when alive, to complain, and won delighted approval from those whose heroes they once were.

Yet it would be misleading to conclude from this confusion that the conflict itself has no reality. It expresses a deep cleavage of opinion, a deep discord between two expressions of the same spirit of romantic materialism—a Brave New World [1] and a Brave Old World facing one another and menacingly flourishing the same weapons. More and more this conflict came to provide the underlying pattern of thought, whether in politics, literature or religion. It became an obsession from which no one was wholly immune, creeping into novels, plays, poems, literary criticism, sermons, lectures, conversation, films, music-hall turns. Spain provided an actual battleground where some

[1] In his novel of this name Mr. Aldous Huxley expressed the feeling of horror which the prospect of a scientific utopia inspired in him; and during his next phase, when he was full of admiration for D. H. Lawrence and his gospel of mindlessness, reacted to the opposite extreme. In his recent book, *Ends and Means*, he repudiates alike Brave New and Brave Old Worlds, and falls back on Buddhistic contemplation.

shed their blood, undergraduates breaking off their studies to man machine-guns; [1] and in the ideological fray all could join everywhere. It would be difficult to find a corner of the world where some little fracas has not taken place.

If Mr. Wells is the prophet of romantic materialism, Mr. Nichols and Mr. Winn its two most competent publicists, the *Daily Express* its most marketable, and contending political ideologies its most formidable, versions, D. H. Lawrence may be regarded as its poet. At the beginning of 1930, he lay dying at Vence, in the hills above Antibes, bearded and cadaverous, *Lady Chatterley's Lover* written and published, realizing according to its publisher, Mr. G. Orioli, a profit of £1,615 18s. 3d.; his last work, *Apocalypse*, unfinished, and dealing, significantly, not with purifying sensuality but with power ("As a collective being man has his fulfilment in the gratification of his power sense. . . . If his country mounts up splendidly to a zenith of splendour and power, he will be all the more fulfilled . . ."), and curiously recalling another work, *Mein Kampf*, more profitable even than *Lady Chatterley's Lover*.

He had wandered restlessly about the world looking for satisfaction and finding none, recruiting derelict ladies to found a new social order, impotently railing against Mind and its Miseries, impotently exalting Flesh and its ecstasies; his death surely a fitting prelude to the years which were to come, full of mindless ecstasy, of new social orders and dark unconsciousness.

[1] Memoirs have been written about a number of these who were killed— e.g. John Cornford, whose mental development is typical of many undergraduates of his generation. He was earnest, industrious and rebellious. His poetic impulse found a congenial subject in the murder of Kirov in 1934 in Leningrad by a young Communist. The Spanish Civil War provided an opportunity for action, for which he craved, and an immediate solution to inward conflicts. See *John Cornford*, edited by Pat Sloan.

After his death, Lawrence's influence continued to be considerable, thumbed copies of *Lady Chatterley's Lover* to circulate widely, and his associates and disciples to wrangle, most writing books about him, and their relations with him and with one another. These books constitute one of the curiosities of literature, perhaps the gem of the collection being Mrs. Dodge Luhan's *Lorenzo in Taos*.[1] Their cumulative effect was to bore even those who did not read them; and gradually scenes in which a hero or heroine is spiritually refreshed by protracted embraces, vanished from contemporary fiction, the Dark Unconscious transforming itself into the Dark Class-Conscious as easily as, in the Pageant of Parliament, rags were transformed into white pinnies.

VII

To a casual visitor, the House of Commons presented much the same spectacle ten years ago as now. The two processions members form when summoned to a division, were more nearly equal than in the two succeeding Parliaments, but otherwise might be supposed to have gone on uninterruptedly shuffling through Aye and No lobbies, somewhat melancholy, aimless, like sheep passing for no particular reason through a gap in a hedge.

Looking more closely, however, differences are apparent. When the division is over, members dispersing to resume interrupted conversations, drinks or naps, who are these who take their places on the Treasury Bench, some of them now scarcely remembered, some dead; one, Sir Oswald Mosley, for whom Mr. Garvin has predicted "dazzling promotion," greatly applauded by Left-Wingers; three soon to take, perhaps already meditating, a surprising step?

[1] See Mr. Hugh Kingsmill's *D. H. Lawrence*.

A Labour Government was in office for the second time, the wonder that it should be in office at all having quite worn off, Mr. James Brown neither more nor less interesting than any other Lord High Commissioner of the Church of Scotland,[1] and Cabinet Ministers who had been dreaded by their opponents as irresponsible revolutionaries and praised by their supporters as heroic saviours of a derelict social order, turning out in practice to be only a rather more than usually ineffectual Government. Greatly daring, they had considered whether they might not break with tradition and eschew Court dress,[2] but had decided on the advice of their leader that to do so would be unwise. Even the Commissioner of Public Works, Mr. Lansbury, yielded to the extent of consenting to wear a dinner-jacket, his mutton-chop whiskers and jovial features occasionally appearing above an expanse of white dress-shirt.

Then, looking round the Opposition, are seen those now so rooted in office that it seems inconceivable there should ever have been interludes when they were not Cabinet Ministers—Mr. Baldwin whose triumphant career was to

[1] This, the only authentically proletarian appointment, was much publicized, Mr. Brown's Lanarkshire cottage often photographed side by side with Holyrood Palace, and he and his wife shown receiving lords and ladies, the lack of embarrassment on the part of all concerned being stressed. As the post was a purely ceremonial one, no one minded, and the picturesqueness of the situation made an immediate appeal. It recalls Trotsky's account of how six factory workers and six peasants were included in the delegation to Brest-Litovsk, but took no part in the negotiations. They were allowed to attend ceremonial functions, and partake of the refreshments offered.

[2] According to the late MacNeill Weir, M.P., who was for eight years MacDonald's Private Parliamentary Secretary, MacDonald said that at his first interview with King George V on becoming Labour Premier, the question of whether members of the new Government would "conform to the etiquette of the Court and wear the appropriate dress . . . filled the mind of the King to the exclusion of all else."

terminate in well-timed retirement as a plain Earl; Sir Samuel Hoare with a Government of India Act to pilot skilfully and cunningly through Parliament, for this service rewarded by the Foreign Secretaryship, which also he had to resign, tears coming into his eyes as he explained the circumstances of his resignation; Sir Thomas Inskip, then it seemed concerned wholly with Law and the Thirty-Nine Articles, but in due course becoming Minister for Co-ordination of Defence, the announcement after weeks of speculation of his appointment to this post being greeted with an outburst of uncontrollable laughter, and his relinquishment of it after three unprofitable years, with relief; Sir Kingsley Wood, who was to be occupied successively with the Post Office, Public Health and the Air Force, and— surely not to be omitted, Mr. Neville Chamberlain, former grower of sisal and Mayor of Birmingham, described by Mr. Lloyd George as "not one of my lucky finds," and perhaps not one of ours either.

In uneasy association with these sat Mr. Churchill, his future as uncertain as his past, and behind them a flock obedient then as now, saying little, doing nothing, voting as instructed, subject to only trifling changes—a Captain Eden, forward in asking questions about the activities of the Comintern, in due course becoming Mr. Eden and sole remaining hope of the League of Nations Union; a Duchess of Atholl earnest in denouncing Soviet timber camps and Godlessness, and in opposing raising the school leaving age and Indian provincial autonomy, in due course becoming an equally earnest promoter of cultural relations with the U.S.S.R. and the object of Miss Ellen Wilkinson's enthusiastic praise; in 1938 after an unlucky by-election vanishing altogether from the parliamentary scene.

Fifty-nine Liberals, ostensibly led by Mr. Lloyd George, have since largely scattered, some falling on stony ground there to perish, some among thorns which soon choked them, and some on good ground—Sir John Simon, Mr. Hore-Belisha, Mr. Bernays—bringing forth fruit, a hundredfold, sixtyfold, thirtyfold. In 1930 they were still supposed to be united in keeping the Labour Cabinet in office, even Sir John Simon occasionally—to use Mr. Lloyd George's expression—"lending one of his countenances" to a Government measure; and all of them holding on to Free Trade, sole remainder of a once ample programme.

Thus was Parliament then, debating, putting questions, droning through the day and sometimes through the night, too, unemployment its main preoccupation as war is now, its monotonous proceedings haunted then by derelict towns and always increasing numbers of unemployed as now by bombs and the rattle of guns. These proceedings, at length or scantily reported, have not aroused much interest. There has been something ghostly about them, a twilight; they have seemed quite remote, like voices heard across water or from the depths of a wide cavern. "When the House cheers," G. F. C. Masterman wrote of the House of Commons after the War, "the sound is as the falling of autumn leaves; when it laughs it is like the plaintive rippling of a wayside stream." [1] Tumultuous events have all been registered in Parliament, but transmuted there, made to seem unsubstantial. Special meetings have been summoned, important statements made, excited shouts and cheers often heard, fine sentiments expressed; but the sound and the fury have signified little—shadow fighting, Prime Minister and Opposition leader interchangeable, all disputes ending in

[1] Quoted in G. F. C. *Masterman* by Lucy Masterman.

the same processions through the same lobbies. Mr. Hore-Belisha compared an all-night sitting of Parliament to an army sleeping with its haversack on its back, and Mr. Churchill remarked that the House was "a recognized addition to the defences of Great Britain"; but the similarity between troops campaigning and Members of Parliament debating until grey morning finds them drowsy and stale, is not easily apparent, and few there are who sleep more quietly in their beds for the knowledge that Mr. Speaker continues to take his place, and Honourable and Right Honourable Members, theirs.

Authority still resides in Lords and Commons. They must take decisions, they must govern. Nothing can be done without their approval; patronage is theirs to bestow, and the framing of policy their responsibility. It is not power which Parliament lacks, any more than Louis XVI or Nicholas II lacked power; rather the will to exercise it. Power without resolution is as vain as desire without virility, and evokes as scant respect. The proportion of voters who care to register their votes has fallen sometimes as low as thirty per cent, and since 1932 has rarely been above fifty per cent. At times it has even seemed that Parliament itself was eager to invite ridicule, as decaying things become fantastic as though to expedite decay. Perhaps sensing this, a member, Mr. Wedgwood Benn, complained that the Minister of Labour had referred to parliamentary proceedings as a "performance," and demanded the withdrawal of a remark so offensive in its implications. The last occasion on which the House of Commons (like an army sleeping with its haversack on its back) sat all night, was devoted to an acrimonious discussion of a contributory pensions scheme for Members of Parliament.

In one respect at least there has been a drastic change-over of opinion. In 1930, if the Foreign Secretary, Arthur Henderson, in an unguarded moment referred slightingly to the Treaty of Versailles, it was Mr. Lloyd George who, warmly applauded by Conservatives, indignantly demanded an explanation, and if accusations were made that Germany was secretly rearming, it was Labour members who laughed scornfully, convinced that such lying accusations were put about by armament manufacturers and war-mongers for interested motive; whereas now, if the Treaty of Versailles has any upholders, they are to be found among those who were formerly most bitter in their denunciation of it,[1] and if Clemenceau returned to earth, it would be Mr. Eden and Professor Gilbert Murray who would rejoice, not Lord Rothermere and Dean Inge.

This change-over of opinion reflects a changed Europe; how greatly changed may be realized by comparing the journeys Dr. Luther made from capital to capital in 1931 to beg for financial help, kindly but unhelpfully received in London, and in Paris plainly told that cash would only be forthcoming in return for further political concessions, with the three obsequious flights undertaken only seven years later by Mr. Chamberlain, with the French Govern-

---

[1] There are many examples of this reversal of roles, it being generally true that the more pro-German immediately after the War, the more anti-German now. For instance, Mr. Mowrer, the well-known American correspondent, describes how he went to Germany "spilling over with sympathy," after having "expended a great deal of emotion deploring the victors' treatment of the vanquished," but how very soon "his sympathetic glands had nearly gone dry," and he came to see that there was something to be said for those who wanted to drive home the Allied victory to the utmost. Similarly, Mr. Robert Dell, *Manchester Guardian* correspondent, who was expelled from France during the Versailles Conference for his pro-German sympathies, now feels that General Weygand was right in wanting to keep Germany in perpetual subjection, and he wrong.

ment's tremulous approval, to meet Hitler. When Mac-
Donald and Henderson went to Germany in 1931, the first
official visit by British statesmen since the War, they were
escorted back by four British bombing planes, these planes
arousing much curiosity as they waited near Berlin to take
off, a crowd collecting to look at them, quite unfamiliar to
German eyes at that time. So drastic a change in so short a
time has rarely been known—from anxious Dr. Luther with
shaven head dolefully carrying his *brieftasche* to Downing
Street and the Quai d'Orsay in search of credits, to anxious
Mr. Chamberlain carrying his umbrella to Berchtesgaden,
Godesburg and Munich in search of peace; from bombing
planes regarded in Berlin as curiosities worth making a
special journey to look at, to bombing planes being lavishly
produced there, and lavishly used when the occasion arose.
A Berliner would be as little likely now to go out of his
way to look at a bombing plane as to look at a sausage.
Indeed, a sausage displayed in a shop window might attract
his rapt attention, they having become rare as bombing
planes have become common.

VIII

A great shifting of power has taken place; and when
power shifts, men shift with it. Power is their everlasting
pursuit.[1] They follow it lovingly from place to place, from
person to person, from idea to idea, sometimes with resultant confusion. When power shifts rapidly, the most practised power-diviners falter. By the time they have made up
their minds to ingratiate themselves with, for instance, the
legatees of the Russian Revolution, most of these are shot

[1] cf. Hobbes—"The general inclination of all mankind is a perpetual and
restless desire after power which ceaseth only in death."

as spies and traitors;[1] by the time they have accustomed themselves to the idea that Captain Röhm must be counted among the great ones of the earth, he is put to death. Now a Tsar Nicholas is powerful and requires adulation; now a Stalin is powerful, and also requires adulation, largely the same.[2] The mighty are continually being put down from their seats and the humble and meek exalted, to become mighty in their turn and fit also to be put down.

When the Thirties began, Europe was dominated by France, with an elaborate system of alliances sustained by loans in Central and Eastern Europe, with a Maginot Line in process of being completed, deeper, stronger and more comfortable than any fortifications hitherto constructed, and with a Gold Reserve stored away which amounted to nearly a third of the total supply of gold in the world; as the Thirties proceeded, Europe was increasingly dominated by Germany, whose Führer's speeches are anxiously awaited, if they are angry spreading panic, if mild engendering a feeling of relief comparable to that of a prisoner who, expecting a term of imprisonment, is only bound over.

[1] Of the Politburo under Lenin, four have been shot, one induced to commit suicide, one exiled, and only Stalin remains; of the Central Committee of the Communist Party under Lenin, six have died natural deaths, eight have been shot, one has been assassinated, one is in prison, four have disappeared, and only Stalin remains.

[2] In *Russia Under Soviet Rule* Mr. de Basily gives a number of examples of the adulation which Stalin expects and receives. For instance, this from a speech by Avdienko, a writer, at the VIIth Congress of the Soviets. The speech was wildly applauded, and reported in *Pravda* in full in the issue of February 1, 1935:

"I write books, I am an author; I dream of creating a lasting work. I love a girl in a new way, I am perpetuated in my children. . . . All this is thanks to thee, O great teacher Stalin. Our love, our devotion, our strength, our hearts, our heroism, our life—all are thine. Take them, great Stalin, O leader of this great country. . . . When the woman I love gives me a child the first word I shall teach it shall be 'Stalin'."

After one such mild speech in the early part of 1939, the *Daily Sketch* reported that all the florists in London were sold out, though whether to provide wreaths or bouquets or household decorations was not explained.

"The great security for peace at the present moment," Lord Grey of Falloden said in 1933, "is that Germany is not armed, and not in a position to go to war." He, dying soon afterwards, did not live to see how soon and how easily this "great security for peace" was to be lost. At midnight on August 4, 1914, he had sadly reflected: "The lamps are going out all over Europe. We shall not see them lit again in our lifetime"; on the morning of September 3, 1939, six years after his death, they would have gone out once more if there had been any alight. There were none to go out then. Put out the light, when the light had been put out; lamps extinguished before, were extinguished again.

IX

Each generation has its hero, one in whom are embodied all prevailing trends and aspirations, whose very features are what his contemporaries would wish to see when they look into a mirror, whose character and achievements represent in the eyes of others what they would wish theirs to be. Heroes are mortal, like men. They die and are forgotten, lingering on, if at all, in the pages of books, in the glamour of a remembered name.

They expire with their validity, sometimes continuing to exist in the flesh, ghostly; more often expiring as heroes and as men simultaneously, like Colonel T. E. Lawrence, whose death in 1934 as a result of a motor-bicycle accident seemed inevitable, to himself and to others. His genius had left him, he wrote to a friend. The circumstances in which it could flourish no longer existed. Other wars were brewing requiring other heroes.

At the beginning of the decade, the War book and the War play were perhaps at the height of their popularity, *Journey's End* still running,[1] *All Quiet on the Western Front* still selling. The War was far enough away to be romanticized, the prospect of another war sufficiently remote for the subject to be congenial to circulating-library subscribers. Men who had been heroic explained that they were sensitive, men who were sensitive explained that they had been heroic. Mr. Robert Graves, Mr. Richard Aldington, Mr. Siegfried Sassoon, Mr. Ernest Hemingway, Mr. Edmund Blunden and others, published their War experiences, finding many readers. The fashion was for the soldier-poet, agonized at having to shed blood, listening to birds singing when the guns paused, with his Keats or Shakespeare's Sonnets in the pocket of his tunic; yet not less courageous and effective in action for that; if anything, more.

T. E. Lawrence filled this part perfectly, provided a perfect compromise between the conscientious objector to whom it was felt some amends were due, and Lord Kitchener whose glory had faded. He was the conscientious consenter; the successful man of action who wrote fine prose and the successful man of letters who won battles. As the

---

[1] It is interesting that, despite its record run, this play has never been successfully revived. An attempt was made to revive it, but instead of its former admirers, as usually happens in such cases, getting nostalgic pleasure out of being reminded of their past enthusiasm, it embarrassed them. They did not want to remember that they had once liked the play. Mr. Vernon Bartlett, for instance, confessed that seeing it again, he was at a loss to explain how it could ever have moved him.

War receded into the past, he alone emerged as its hero. Not even controversy over Earl Haig's equestrian statue, and the attacks of Mr. Lloyd George on his generalship, could make him interesting. Two rival biographies by Lady Haig and Mr. Duff Cooper were by no means best-sellers, whereas the public thirst for information about T. E. Lawrence seemed insatiable. Books about him were many, and his own books, *Revolt in the Desert*, and later *The Seven Pillars of Wisdom*, were much read and discussed.

His modesty and delight in fame pulling him in opposite directions; his passion for publicity which, like Greta Garbo's, took the extremely effective form of ostentatiously shunning it; his refusal of important posts and insistence on joining the Air Force as an aircraftsman under an assumed name, thereby attracting more attention to himself than any colonial administrator, however successful; his poverty which, as Sir Ronald Storrs has pointed out,[1] did not prevent him from indulging in expensive luxuries like speed-boats; his achievements, so remarkable, yet coming to nothing, bearing no fruit; his reputation for endurance and feats of strength combined with a slight physique, an unathletic, unhearty appearance—all this fitted him to be the hero of the years during which all desire to hang the Kaiser had gone and a desire to hang Hitler not yet manifested itself. Mr. Stephen Spender provided the Left Book Club with a statement of his political faith called *Forward from Liberalism*; in the same way, T. E. Lawrence might be described as Forward from Kipling.

The hero provides a pattern after which many aspire. His influence seeps down, evoking remote imitations, dreams. He appears in many guises; in living men, and in imagined

[1] In *Orientations*.

characters. An age may be known by its hero, its Rousseau or Byron or Walt Whitman. Even the dead are made to conform to his lineaments, furbished up to look like him. Thus Sir James Barrie, shortly before his death, undertook the difficult task in his play *The Boy David* of presenting King David as a Prince Charming, a youthful soldier whose War-memoirs would have resembled Mr. Sassoon's. The enterprise defeated him. He was too old for it; his technique out-of-date, the right moment past. The early, not the late, Thirties was the time for it; before, not after, German rearmament. It was a pre-Hitler enterprise. Mr. Auden might have succeeded, stressing David's early proletarian sympathies when "everyone that was in distress, and everyone that was in debt, and everyone that was discontented, gathered themselves unto him," perhaps detecting in Absalom's revolt a popular protest against his father's later authoritarian propensities; but not Sir James Barrie.

Not even the fame of Miss Elisabeth Bergner, who played David, equipped for the part by her race if not by her sex, sufficed to save the play from failure. She came to it fresh from her triumphant appearance in *Escape Me Never*, a dramatization of one of Miss Margaret Kennedy's several sequels to *The Constant Nymph*; a Bohemian fantasy or Café Royal idyll of the sort that has never failed to appeal since it became the fashion for young women with incomes, great or small, earned or unearned, to live their own lives in front of their own gas-fire. The combination of a Margaret Kennedy heroine and Peter Pan dialogue failed to convey the character of David. Perhaps it would have been easier but for the Bible.

X

It is commonly observed that there is an average or type produced by particular circumstances at a particular time. Everyman's appearances have ranged between Morality Plays and furniture advertisements; Strube's Little Man, battling with Income Tax demands and frightened of his wife, is one of his contemporary impersonations, another is the Man in the Street whom journalists and politicians constantly invoke. If, however, such an average man exists, he cannot be identified. When he is known he is no longer average. If the identity of the Unknown Soldier were discovered, it would be necessary to replace his bones by others, still unidentified. He is only the average soldier who died in the War as long as he is nameless and characterless.

Everyman is an abstraction, a dream figure who may evoke pity like Charlie Chaplin, laughter like Mr. Chips, or fear and adoration like Hitler,[1] but who cannot be said truly to exist. The popularity of Charlie Chaplin, which in *Modern Times* and *City Lights* survived even the talkies, has been due to his convincing impersonation of this abstraction, this average man, and consequent releasing in each individual breast of the self-pity contained there. Hitler has performed a similar feat, with Europe for his set and mankind for his audience, and with the finale still to come—the minute, lonely figure forlornly trudging along a winding road until he vanishes into the sunset, though perhaps in Hitler's case this finale may be reversed, and the sunset for-

[1] Recognition that Hitler is more an abstraction than a living man is implied in the widely believed rumour that he was dead, and that the figure which appeared at public functions was one of several doubles who were available for this purpose.

lornly vanish into him. In a story by Mr. James Hilton, Hitler would be Mr. Hits.

Intuition makes possible such impersonations of the average man. He may also be synthetically produced, like the Economic Man of nineteenth-century economists, or Rousseau's Natural Man, or the Marxists' Proletarian Man. These are symbols merely, used to balance an equation or populate a utopia. Attempts to give them a semblance of life as fictitious characters invariably fail, and when those who accept their validity look for them in the flesh, they are always disappointed; like Tolstoy, who heard a peasant curse him as he passed by, and turned to remonstrate: "But I'm Tolstoy!" only to have more furious curses called down upon him.

If, however, there is no average man, but only men, each to himself the centre of an incomprehensible universe, certain characteristic traits, a characteristic mental development, physiognomy even, may at all times be detected; but more easily in the distant past than yesterday. The distant past is like a strange land whose characteristics are at once noticeable, whereas yesterday is still familiar and therefore difficult to explore; the dead who tell no tales, may be understood, but the living who tell many, are full of mystery. Nor has the prevailing fashion for unreticent autobiography altered this. Frankness is usually more uncommunicative than reticence. By pretending to tell everything, what is not told is more securely hidden. The subtlest politicians, like Mr. Baldwin at the time of the abdication of King Edward VIII, put all their cards on the table; and outspoken autobiographies by burglars, waiters, taxi-drivers, convicts, undergraduates, society ladies, diplomats, journalists, restaurateurs, politicians, down-and-outs, monarchs, all conditions of men and women, turn out to be no more than essays in self-dramatiza-

tion. The burglar is a choice spirit out of the common run
of burglars—for instance, Mr. Mark Benny, who has described in *Angels in Undress* how when he was on a job, cultural aspirations impelled him to fill his bag with objets d'art
rather than with common-or-garden silver spoons. A small
bust of Beethoven or a Hogarth print was irresistible, even
though a fruit salver might be taken. Such a predilection,
it may be assumed, is rare among burglars. In the same way,
the waiter devotes his scanty leisure to intellectual pursuits;
the monarch is never so happy as away from court formali-
ties, and the prostitute imbibes culture from a Bloomsbury
clientèle.[1] Even Hitler, in *Mein Kampf*, makes the general
observation that as a poverty-stricken youth in Vienna he
read voraciously, though without specifying what. He, too,
though he exalts averageness, is reluctant to admit that his
tastes are average ones.

These so diverse autobiographies have in common only
the egotism which inspires them, and that is a constant,
unvarying at all times and in all circumstances. If Rousseau
had happened to be a burglar, his *Confessions* would have
been very like *Angels in Undress*, if an American journalist,
very like *The Way of a Transgressor*; if Queen Marie of
Roumania and Miss Sheila Cousins had changed places, each
would have written the other's autobiography. Burglars and

---

[1] See *Coming Sir* by Dave Marlow, *My Life* by Queen Marie of Roumania, and *To Beg I Am Ashamed* by Sheila Cousins. The last of these
was withdrawn from circulation as a result of threatened police court proceedings after an article had appeared in the *Daily Mirror* indignantly
denouncing it as an outrage on public morality, and quoting passages
regarded as particularly offensive. In view of the great latitude now permitted in describing sexual intimacies, some surprise was occasioned that
this particular book should have so offended the *Daily Mirror's* ordinarily
not over-fastidious moral sense. The reason, perhaps, was that Miss Cousins
describes her professional experiences without any relish.

prostitutes and queens have always aroused curiosity among those oppressed by a sense of the ordinariness of their lives; but when they set about satisfying their curiosity, they inevitably assume it is directed rather towards themselves than towards their unusual circumstances. The average burglar or queen, like the Unknown Soldier, is necessarily anonymous; and the insatiable thirst for contemporary autobiography is due rather to a desire to experience vicariously the excitement of an exceptional life than to acquire information about ordinary people in whom the reader may recognize his like.

This contemporary autobiography is full of amorous adventures, and often of reforming zeal; and much of it is preoccupied with politics, both domestic and foreign. Each autobiographer is concerned to portray himself, not as he is, but as he would wish to be—experienced and travelled, yet innocent and eager; fond of a kiss and fond of a guinea; given equally to piping through the valleys wild and to *wagon-lits;* tough enough to kill, and tender enough to love, and err, and espouse righteous causes. If it would be idle to look for a burglar in *Angels in Undress,* or even for Mr. Benny, it contains Mr. Benny's conception of himself and of burglary at their noblest and best.

From the abundance of contemporary autobiography dealing with high- and low-, but seldom with middle-life, a generation's aspirations may be deduced; all they would have wished to be and are not, all they might have experienced and have not. Like toreadors, Mr. Bruce Lockhart, Mr. Negley Farson, Mr. Vincent Sheean, perform in the arena; and the onlookers, lolling in their seats, sucking oranges, applauding, feel that they too have been adventurous, they too have seen men and cities.

This vogue for self-dramatization has opened up a lucrative career for down-and-outs, convicts, and other former social outcasts. A term of penal servitude has its compensations when it may later produce abundant royalties; the prostitute on her weary search for a client may take comfort from the thought that one day her reminiscences may be marketable. Pockets which once had to be picked or left intact, will freely disgorge when a pickpocket's inner life is made available at ten-and-six net; those be edified who formerly had to be preyed upon, and Miss Rebecca West throw in her blessing with, "He writes like an angel." Nor have the upper classes neglected to participate in this profitable tirade. If low-life has strange secrets to disclose, has not high-life, too? If social outcasts easily weep, and read Proust and Shelley, do not Aristocrats, too? The halls of fashion are as enthralling as doss-houses are, and Lord Castlerosse also has a tale to tell.

Rousseau, when he announced his intention to "lay open to my fellow-mortals a man just as nature wrought him; and this man is myself," started a fashion which is likely to flourish as long as creation is believed to have no more than a human purpose. If men represent creation's only endeavour, and human life its whole range, then each individual man must be remarkable, and each individual life a unique drama. Men can only be humble if they have a God, only content to be alike if they feel themselves children belonging to one family with a father in Heaven. Without a God, they must be arrogant to be able to go on living at all, unique or they are nothing. The necessity to be unique has borne heavily upon them. To make themselves unique, they have had to falsify themselves and their lives, their past and their future; like Rousseau, divulging uncommitted faults, unfelt hopes, ecstasy and misery never experienced; at last abandoning the struggle, and finding their extraordinariness in another's extraordinary ordinariness, merging their unique lives in his life, their unique selves in him, their demagogue leader, themselves.[1]

Another manifestation of the same craving for reassurance that earthly life suffices, is the veneration and idealization of Youth. It is only the young who are truly able to persuade themselves that they may live by bread alone, who are truly forgetful of death. To the ageing, unsatisfied by bread alone, unforgetful of death, Youth seems the only corroboration of their belief in earthly life's sufficiency. They look back longingly as Bunyan looked forward longingly, see the Heavenly City in retrospect instead of in prospect. Youth is their answer to death; perhaps one day by means of monkey gland, or some other wonder of science, attainable even by those who have lost it; withered flesh again glowing, spent appetites again stirring, ardour renewed; until then, to be adulated, fawned on, obsequiously led. Demagogues pride themselves on attracting Youth to their following; religious leaders groan that Youth has deserted them; politicians come forward, not always young, as champions of Youth, and men as well as women strain after youthfulness, smoothing away wrinkles, obliterating greyness, dentured, massaged, exercised, young. Youth seems glamorous and splendid. Headmasters must be young, sometimes under thirty; bishops of fifty, and, in the case of colonial diocese, even less,

[1] cf. *Mein Kampf*—"Mass demonstrations must burn into the little man's soul the proud conviction that though a little worm, he is nevertheless part of a great dragon."

have surprisingly made their appearance; politicians when they are aged plead their still youthful hearts, when they, like Mr. Eden, still in their forties, are acclaimed for that.

An example of this idealization of Youth is provided by Lord Lytton's memoir of his son Antony, Viscount Knebworth,[1] who died as a result of an aeroplane accident in 1933 at the age of twenty-nine. The memoir consists mainly of Antony's letters to his parents, and was much praised, for instance by Mr. Arthur Bryant, who wrote of it with comprehensive modesty that it would be remembered long after he and most others then alive had been forgotten. A glowing picture emerges of Antony's childhood and time at Eton—"but, by God, it's the most wonderful place in the world." Then comes the undergraduate, and a sense that "all this religious business doesn't really explain the peculiar things I feel." Choosing a career presents difficulties; the army "like the 'varsities, from a young man's point of view is *passé*," though not the Army and Navy Stores, on whose Board he is offered, and accepts, a seat. Interest in politics develops; he "adores Ramsay MacDonald," thinks that the "key to the situation is Lord Robert Cecil," and has been "soaking in disarmament lately." After an unsuccessful electoral contest in Shoreditch, he writes: "I know all about the political situation, have incidentally gone raving mad, but believe that the hour for 'Young England' is very nearly ripe." Hitchin returns him with a majority of 17,000, but Parliament brings disillusionment, a feeling that "the world appears to be shaking off the yoke of Democracy," and that the "hour is so ripe everywhere for a man, and a drive, and a policy. I hope the great National Government is the last of the *ancien régime*." After rereading *The Constant Nymph*, he reaches

[1] *Antony: a Record of Youth* by the Earl of Lytton.

the conclusion that "it is one of the best novels of this century, if not of always"; he "loves *Cavalcade*," and, though he
has doubts about Noel Coward, after seeing one of his re-
vues, he is inclined to agree with his sister when she says,
"But he is on your side." "His stuff is all right. He's good,"
he writes of him to a friend.

This ardent life, cut short before its prime, and so full of
zest ("What fun it all is . . . what with St. Moritz and
Socialism and the Surrey hills and Empire-building and the
Manor House and Bendigo and Sporting"), was felt to
embody the very spirit of Youth. Who but the very young
could adore Ramsay MacDonald, find Noel Coward good
and an ally for righteousness, and pronounce *The Constant
Nymph* a masterpiece? The elderly were happy to be
reminded that youthful hearts were still capable of such
careless rapture, and the young to know that their hour was
"very nearly ripe." Socialism and St. Moritz might seem
antipathetic, but here was one who found both fun. Not all
were viscounts, went to Eton, served on the Board of the
Army and Navy Stores; but others, at a less illustrious level,
could follow Antony's course, be brave and eager, and await
"a man and a drive and a policy." If he was an *edition de
luxe*, there were also popular editions, at seven-and-six and
two shillings and even sixpence.

How is it possible to pierce below the imagined man to
the reality? How disentangle what is really hoped from
stimulated hopes, authentic feelings from those awakened
by printed words, coloured pictures, screen shadows speaking and moving, the vast persuasion ceaselessly playing on
each human heart? Many faces spread out in an audience,
drifting along a street, littering a sea-shore, assembling to
cheer and to watch, to sing and to mourn; now happy, now

sad, now adoring, now menacing, struggling to reach a film-
star's presence, massed, sombre, without walls behind which
a platform is to be dropped, a rope tightened and a limp
corpse left dangling, then pressing forward to read the notice
announcing what has been done; besought to eat this, drink
that, become beautiful in such a way, rich in such another,
to journey to strange lands, wear such garments, be healthy
and masterful by such means, have such desires—many faces,
coagulating, then dispersing, each to some familiar corner,
swallowed up by some door, little lights lighted, shining like
stars, and then put out one after the other, only street-lamps
remaining, and silence and darkness amidst which separate
faces sleep, inscrutable.

Who shall venture to say of these sleeping faces, "Thus
they are, and thus!" counting and classifying them, habits
all observed, opinions all taken, required calories estimated,
earnings computed? What an impossible task to construct
one face which comprehends all the others, taking a feature
here, a feature there and fitting them together. What an
equally impossible task to break one chosen face down, distributing its components as a compositor uses type. If all
pursuits be noted, films which delight, football-pool coupon
filled in with a faint expectation that great wealth will result,
desires balloted and tabulated, even dreams known, secret
longings to enfold as flesh what was seen only as shadow, to
escape into strangeness and danger, no longer alone, surren-
dering to a tide of emotion—still the mystery remains. Pursuits and longings added together, do these constitute a man?
Subtracted, is nothing left? Lambeth-walking, Hitler-hiss-
ing, Deanna Durbin-loving, wireless-listening, biped, existing on this earth for a little while, and then legs no

more dancing, lips no more hissing, heart no more loving, ears no more hearing, eyes no more seeing; forever incomprehensible.

XI

Piecing together the significance of years which have passed is made easier because now Time has not only a body —events and those who shape, and are shaped by them, and a spirit whose character may be looked for in fashions of thought and of behaviour, in mental and spiritual preoccupations; it has also a voice. From nine million wireless sets in nine million homes this voice is heard nightly, giving information, news, entertaining and instructing, preaching even, with different accents yet always the same; the voices of the nine million who listen merged into one voice, their own collective voice echoing back to them.

This voice, silky, persuasive, cultivated, passionless and laughterless, emerging relentlessly from a mechanical instrument, awakened and silenced, swelling and waning, to the adjustment of a switch, ushering in each new year, bidding farewell to each old one, announcing a King's demise and a Government's fall, a new King's enthronement and a new Government's formation, presenting happenings great and small to its immense audience—may it not be regarded as, to use Coriolanus's expression, the "tongue of the common mouth?"

Sometimes accidents occur—a commentator on a Naval Review finds himself so overcome with emotion, or otherwise incapacitated, that he can do no more than murmur that there are many ships, all lit-up; forbidden words are spoken, someone inconsequently muttering, "Mrs. Simpson." Such accidents are rare, and soon obliterated. Sometimes the voice is disentangled with difficulty from other voices, not all silky, not all persuasive or genteel; clamorous, angry voices. Yet, once found and isolated, it may be listened to without fear of interruption, all discordant sounds silenced. *La voix, c'est l'homme même.*

The B.B.C. came to pass silently, invisibly; like a coral reef, cells busily multiplying, until it was a vast structure, a conglomeration of studios, offices, cool passages along which many passed to and fro; a society, with its king and lords and commoners, its laws and dossiers and revenue and easily suppressed insurrection; where there was marriage and giving in marriage, and where evil-doers and adulterers were punished, and the faithful rewarded. As many little rivulets empty themselves into a wide lake, all their motion lost in its still expanse of water, so did every bubbling trend and fashion empty themselves into the B.B.C.

Circumstances shaped it, making it an image, pure and undefiled, of the times. It was a mirror held up to nature. Beards grew on chins, tufty, rather sparse, as inevitably as reeds in marshland; sentiments crystallized with the same slow certainty that a pearl forms in an oyster. Whatever was put into it must either take on its texture or be expelled, a waste product; though different meats were inserted, the resultant sausages were indistinguishable. Nightly, the nine million listened—"News-bulletin, copyright reserved"— merely curious, or apprehensive; gently and persuasively instructed in their own and others' misfortunes, in what they should hope for and what they should dread; music to delight them, both serious and frivolous, edifying discourses, perhaps a domestic chat from Lord Elton, or a curious encounter between a Chinese poet and a Westmoreland shepherd; prayers for the prayerful, tunes for the tuneful, instruction for those who wished to be instructed. Comfortable in arm-chairs, drowsing perhaps, snug and secure, the whole world was available, its tumult compressed into a radio set's small compass. Wars and rumours of wars, all the misery and passion of a troubled world, thus came into their conscious-ness, in winter with curtains drawn and a cheerful fire blazing; in summer often out of doors, sprawling on a lawn or under a tree, or in a motor-car, indolently listening while telegraph poles flitted past.[1] Dollfuss had been murdered, despairing Jews had resorted to gas ovens, Wall Street prices were rising or falling or stationary, Lord Runciman thought war unlikely, much of Cardiff had been disposed of by its owner, Lord Bute, for some millions of pounds, and the King and Queen had received a warm welcome in Hackney —well, there it was, and now for another station; as the wave-length slowly changes, fragments of music heard, sounds and sweet airs, spluttering voices, many languages and many intonations, laughter and anger and stock prices and salesmanship and oratory all mingled together, frenzied confusion.

That a voice could be heard in innumerable homes, as though speaking there, was wonderful; and as soon as that marvel was achieved, the question arose: Whose was to be

[1] In the United States, the broadcasting of one of H. G. Wells's ro-mances, *The War of the Worlds,* led to a panic among listeners, who thought that Martian invaders had made their appearance. What they heard on the wireless was so little related to their own experience, to reality, that an invasion from Mars seemed as possible or impossible as other news items announced. If Job had heard of his misfortunes from a B.B.C. announcer, he would have been more likely to become hysterical than despairing, more inclined to drink lysol than remember that he came naked out of his mother's womb and naked must return thither. Broad-casting, by intensifying the prevailing sense of unreality, has intensified the hysteria which results therefrom. Complaints were made in 1939 that a number of suicides had resulted from listening to the B.B.C. news bulletin.

the voice, and what was it to say? In other countries the voice might be monopolized by a party, and made to utter only its slogans, or put up for sale, precious moments purchased to praise a pill, explain a soap's excellence; but in England, in Sir John Reith's words, what was aimed at was an expression of "British mentality at its best." This ideal was assiduously pursued, he the man to pursue it—a tall Scotsman, Calvinist in his origins, deeply respectful towards those set in authority over him and expecting a correspondingly deep respect from those over whom he was set, a very incarnation of British mentality at its best. Debates were arranged between persons holding different opinions, rehearsed and broadcast, so that all points of view might be known and impartially considered; an unemployed man, when what he proposed to say had been submitted and examined,[1] might give an account of himself and his circumstances, or a crofter in the Highlands describe how his days were spent. A policeman on his beat, a lighthouse keeper on his solitary vigil, a ship's captain on his bridge, all might be listened to, as well as politicians, authors, scientists, clergymen, peers and peeresses.

While Dr. Goebbels raged and Signor Virginio Gayda imagined vain things, the B.B.C. continued to purvey British mentality at its best, in foreign languages as well as in English, war itself scarcely deflecting it from its course, though necessitating the transference of its headquarters from London. The same voices speaking in the same accents were heard as in peace; the same gentle persuasion washed against

[1] The obligation to submit beforehand, and sometimes accept alterations in, all broadcast matter, was occasionally resented. Mr. Bernard Shaw refused to broadcast on such terms, and a broadcast by an unemployed man had to be cancelled because he would not agree to delete certain passages from the script he had prepared.

the nine million, patiently wearing away angular opinions;
like waves on a beach, ebbing and flowing, transforming
rocks and stones into smooth round pebbles, all alike, into a
stretch of yellow sand.

CHAPTER II

Mr. High-Mind

It is impossible for one man, however determined and cunning he may be, to impose his will on other men, for long unless they recognize themselves in him.[1] This applies just as much in an absolutist as in a democratic state. A tyrant may linger on for a little while after those over whom he rules and he have become strangers, but not for long. He must fall as surely as a prime minister without a parliamentary majority. No Ogpu or Gestapo or Ovra is strong enough to sustain the authority of a dictator who is not to a certain extent a mirror held up to his people. Even the Indian princes, most pitiable of all rulers, abdicate or are deposed or just die of inanition, when the gulf between them and their subjects becomes too wide. Louis XIV might more truthfully have said *"Le Peuple, c'est moi"* than *"L'État, c'est moi."* There is no state apart from the people. Kings, Presidents, Prime Ministers, Demagogues, Lamas, Popes, Caliphs, all who enjoy their little moment of authority, do so by virtue of momentarily embodying the hopes, fears, desires, dreads, resentments, the whole character of those over whom they have been set. The blind lead the blind because

[1] cf. Hobbes's "Every particular man is author of all the sovereign doth; and consequently he that complaineth of injury from his sovereign, complaineth of that whereof he himself is author; and therefore ought not to accuse any man but himself; no nor himself of injury, because to do injury to oneself is impossible."

[58

there are none who see. And if there were, would the sight-
less deliver themselves over to them? Rather gouge out their
eyes, too. There is no leading astray, since Leaders are made
in the likeness of the led.

Thus it was not chance or his own ambition merely which
carried Ramsay MacDonald to the Premiership. He had his
part to play, and that was the role in which he had been cast.
Grounded in resentment against his obscure birth and childhood poverty, nurtured in the Fabian Society, the I.L.P.,
and other offshoots of the late Victorian urge to improve
the conditions of the poor without seriously incommoding
the rich, brought to fruition in four and a half years of
bloody warfare followed by a fraudulent peace and hysterical reaction against the strain and agony of war, his
moment surely came. *He* had not succumbed to the fever of
war,[1] nor to the fever of peace. Conscientious objections
which once made him despised among men now added to
his prestige. "MacDonaldstein" Horatio Bottomley had
often called him during the War years, and angrily asked
on a *John Bull* poster: "When Will They Put MacDonald
In Gaol?" Horatio it was who went to gaol, while Mac-
Donald—possibilities were opening up before him beyond

[1] MacDonald's pacifism is, like everything else in his life, confused. That
he made himself greatly unpopular during the War, is certain; but what
were his actual opinions about it, and what policy, if any, he advocated, are
still the subject of controversy. It would be difficult to deduce from, for
instance, his speech in the House of Commons in August 1914, and his
letter to the Mayor of Leicester declining an invitation to address a recruiting meeting, any coherent attitude of mind. Lord Elton, in his *The
Life of James Ramsay MacDonald*, attempts to disentangle his various
pronouncements about the War, but even he admits that they were "sometimes subtle and occasionally obscure," and that they involved him "in
some queer political alliances and entanglements, which themselves sometimes coloured his views or, more often, distorted them for the public."

the dreams of the sometime editor of *John Bull* and Soldier's Friend.

At the beginning of 1930 MacDonald had been Premier for six months. His first premiership, so troubled, ending so ignominiously, was already almost forgotten. This time he felt easier, surer of himself. He had become less distracted looking than he used to be, smoother and more respectable, often in evening dress, playful with his opponents rather than angry. Gone the days when they were mangy dogs who dared to criticize, and gone the days when the *Times* was disrespectful. Already the *Times* made pleasanter reading than the *Daily Herald*.

See him awaited by his parliamentary followers, gathered in the Friends' Meeting House, an earnest company. He is late. One or two step on to the platform and speak: "The Red Flag" is sung, hymn-like. Some, as they sing it, instinctively feel in their pockets in preparation for a collection. At last he comes—their leader. "My frrriends!" They applaud in a desultory way. His overcoat flaps open revealing underneath white waistcoat and white tie. Between his fingers a cigar droops. "My frrriends!" He cannot stay a moment, he explains. He is in a great hurry. They will understand. Then he is gone, with only the fragrance of his cigar to remind them that he has been there at all. They look at one another nervously, bitterly, the next morning read in the papers that he had gone on to a reception given by Lady Londonderry.

How they distrusted and for the most part disliked him; yet clung to him. He was the only possible leader, they assured one another. He still had a large following in the constituencies. These arguments failed to convince. Uneasiness remained.

Even now it remains inexplicable why so many who distrusted MacDonald should have continued to endure his leadership[1]—unless it was that, consciously or unconsciously, they felt that what he was going to do had to be done, and that he must do it, leaving them free to dissociate themselves.

It was true, of course, that MacDonald was an electioneering asset. In the constituencies his appearance was much admired. Women especially found him impressive. He appealed to them. The only conversation between Asquith and Mr. Lloyd George after their quarrel is supposed to have taken place in the House of Commons on the occasion of MacDonald's first appearance as Premier, when Mr. Lloyd George leant across to Asquith and said: "MacDonald thinks he is the best-looking Premier in the century. Do you agree?" and Asquith answered: "No." These were interested parties. Probably a majority of the electorate would have supported MacDonald's claim. His dramatization of himself as a lonely idealist who felt it to be his duty to play a part in public life against his own inclination, was congenial. People were sick of ambitious soldiers and hard-faced business men and deceitful lawyers. They thirsted for a little culture and high-mindedness. MacDonald provided these. He managed to convey the impression that if he had his way he would be living quietly at Lossiemouth with his books. As he put it

[1] Mr. MacNeill Weir, in his account in *The Tragedy of Ramsay MacDonald* of the events which led up to the formation of the National Government, fails to clear up this point. He gives many examples of MacDonald's treachery, shallowness and vanity, but does not explain how he personally and the Labour Party generally came to have and to keep so transparent a villain for their leader. Similarly, in his pamphlet, "What Happened in 1931," Lord Passfield suggests that MacDonald's infamy was unmistakable; yet he had not thought fit to resign in protest against so infamous a leader, and in 1924 had broken with the *New Statesman*, which he had been instrumental in founding, because it had ventured to criticize MacDonald.

in his own inimitable idiom: "Take a walk in your library, guided by your imagination, enlivened by suggestions which come to you from a phrase—exploring, exploring to be alone, going wandering and roaming and dreaming alone." It was the right note.

An idea of the esteem in which he was held is given by an article entitled "Ramsay MacDonald—the Dreamer who Triumphed," by Professor Harold Laski, later one of the Left Book Club Triumvirate, which was published in the *Daily Herald* early in 1930:

Mr. MacDonald is perhaps the most complex personality in contemporary political life.

. . . He lives in a remote citadel which the outsider cannot storm. You cannot conquer MacDonald's confidence; you have to win it piece by piece.

But when it is finally won, it is difficult to lose. He has the art of keeping his friends. . . .

Widely read, widely travelled, a popular orator of the first order, a man with an obvious gift of stirring great public emotions, he had lived and dreamed and thought in terms of the first office in the State.

He made himself not merely a national but even a world figure with an ease and a grace that betoken extraordinary qualities. No one could be long in his presence without feeling that he has the magnetic art of leadership.

He compels attention. The striking features, the rich tones of his vibrant voice, the quick sensitiveness, a certain wistful hunger for your sympathy, these are characteristics that mark him out for the front rank.

He has won his place by sheer personal power; and it is essential for opponents to realize that he holds it unchallengeably. . . .

A great political reception is an ordeal from which he shrinks. What he cares for is the bookish talk of a few intimates, men like John Morley, or Mr. Birrell; even more,

perhaps, he loves the natural peace of the woods round
Chequers. . . .[1]

If MacDonald's supporters in Parliament bore with him
while, unlike Professor Laski, strongly and often vocally
disapproving of his behaviour, even a little awed by him
perhaps, like plain virgins complaining of wantonness, his
opponents found him comforting. Since the French Revolution, the rich have lived in increasing fear of the poor.
Every now and again this fear becomes intensified, as a man
who knows he has an incurable disease will go for months
feeling no more than a dull apprehension, and then, when a
particular symptom shows itself, abandon himself to blind
panic. Such a moment of blind panic was precipitated when
the first Labour Government took office. Was it reasonable
to suppose that now the representatives of the many who
worked so hard for so small a reward had come to power,
they would refrain from spoiling the few who got so much
without working at all? Yet all that happened was that a
respectable Scotsman with an irregular moustache, a rich
quavering voice and a gift for meandering oratory, became
Prime Minister. What a relief it was, like hearing sounds
downstairs which suggest a burglar and finding on investigation that it is only a policeman making sure no windows or

[1] Mr. Churchill's judgment of MacDonald at this time has worn a little,
but not much better than Professor Laski's—"Urbane, cultured, incorrupti-
ble, he is willing to drive the car of Empire down every slope, social,
military, political, so long as he can put on the brakes and be praised for
his skill in applying them."

Later, of course, Professor Laski's opinion of MacDonald altered. Instead of being one who "holds beliefs so deeply that it is difficult to
persuade him to delegate their care to others," he was a traitor, so contemptible that "there is no abandonment of principle he has not been
prepared to make."

doors have been left open by mistake.[1] If this was all the Labour Party amounted to—MacDonald—the fears it had given rise to were quite groundless. There was really nothing to worry about. By the time the second Labour Government was formed, its innocuousness had come to be so taken for granted that few even bothered to transfer money abroad —that earliest of all symptoms of unease among the wealthy.

This was the shepherd, what of the sheep? They were a mixed lot, representing a great variety of interests and discontents, many in the House of Commons for the first time after a long life spent campaigning, always before in opposition and somewhat disconcerted to find themselves in the position of having to justify what had been done and excuse what had been left undone instead of the other way round. The most solid element among them was the trade unionists, many of them ex-checkweighmen, little given to joining in debates, sure of their seats[2] and limited in their interests. Then there was the I.L.P. group, already turbulent and dissatisfied, especially as none of them had been included in

[1] An example of the soothing effect MacDonald had on those troubled by great possessions is given in Lord Elton's biography. In 1924 MacDonald went to stay at Bishopsthorpe, York, with Dr. Lang, then Archbishop of York. Dr. Lang "put a question to him 'as a good Socialist'—'Ought I to live in a house like this?'" and went on to explain that the alternative would be, not living in a slum, but "to take a suburban villa outside the town and identify myself with the bourgeoisie." MacDonald thought for a little while, and then said: "You are right. This is worth preserving. You should live here." Needless to say, he did, until another alternative than a suburban villa presented itself, and he moved to Lambeth Palace.

[2] The fidelity of Labour voters in mining constituencies is astonishing. When Mr. Mardy Jones, who sat for a mining constituency, resigned his seat in 1931 as a result of making an improper use of the free travelling facilities he was entitled to as a Member of Parliament, in the resultant by-election the Labour candidate was returned with only a slightly reduced majority, and this when the Labour vote was slumping heavily in other parts of the country.

the Cabinet. John Wheatley, the ablest of the I.L.P. group, bitterly reproached his ostensible leaders on the very first day the new Government met Parliament, warning them that though then they were the recipients of such flattery and adulation, before long they would be discredited in Parliament and in the country, deserted by their followers, their humiliation complete. He did not live to see this prophecy abundantly fulfilled.

As for the others—they included vegetarians, prohibitionists, aristocrats, drunkards, army and navy officers, ascetics, every variety of crank, or, to use Mr. G. T. Garratt's [1] apt word, mugwump. Their only common ground was a feeling of dissatisfaction with the existing state of affairs, but when it came to instituting changes, they were hopelessly divided. They all called themselves Socialists, but they never were able to make up their minds whether their part was to welcome the economic collapse which they had long and exultantly predicted or to prevent it. As Sir Oswald Mosley put it, they were like a Salvation Army band which turned out with banners flying for the Judgment Day, but when the first rumble of the approaching cataclysm was heard, turned in disarray and fled.

Their coming to power was the culmination of much patient effort, much expense of passion. How many envelopes had been licked, addressed and delivered, how many ardent words spoken, before they found themselves ranged behind His Majesty's Government. What a pouring out of spittle and ink and breath before that came to pass. A large gathering in the Albert Hall rejoiced over their electoral victories like a revivalist meeting rejoicing over sinners saved from damnation. Their failure arose not from insincer-

[1] *The Mugwumps of the Labour Party.*

ity, nor even from deceitful leadership, but from the confusion of their hopes. Marxists and Nonconformist clergymen and pacifists and checkweighmen and Clydeside demagogues could unite in opposition, but how were they to find a basis for common action when, owing to the effectiveness of their opposition, they found themselves in power?

The confusion of the back benches was inevitably reflected in the Front Bench. "We always seemed to be just about evenly divided on every issue," a member of the Cabinet remarked sadly, and described how the Prime Minister presided over their meetings, waving his arms about like a band-conductor, soothing, confusing, insisting that they were just conducting a preliminary general survey, a second-reading debate, that no one committed himself to anything. Thus they proceeded, until it was time to disperse; dispersing, a little uneasy and bewildered, but after all still in office. Mr. Clynes, then the Home Secretary, has described in his *Autobiography* how when he was a little boy he climbed a lamp-post to see Gladstone pass by in an open carriage. "Little did that small boy think," he writes, "that he too in his day would become a Cabinet Minister." This miracle had happened. Becoming Cabinet Ministers in itself constituted success. As Johnson said of women preachers, the astonishing thing was that they should have done it at all. They went to and from their offices in Whitehall, enjoyed the respectful attention of doorkeepers and permanent officials, delighted their opponents, and made the more ardent and envious among their followers embittered, by their moderation. All their lives they had been framing resolutions, referring back motions, presiding over committees and conferences. Now they were in office they went on doing the same thing. The technique of parliamentarism had come to be identified with government itself, as a Covent Garden dealer might absent-mindedly take his sick wife home a bundle of invoices to refresh her. A motion "that this House favours a substantial reduction in the unemployment figures," debated, carried, in their eyes was the equivalent of finding work for the workless. One of them, after presiding over a committee of the Indian Round-Table Conference, remarked that things had gone well, since he had managed to steer them off all controversial subjects. Henderson, looking round the Disarmament Conference, drew attention to a bewhiskered Polish delegate who, he said, was bound to give trouble because he had a look of the boilermakers' union about him.

II

The Prime Minister's first public announcement on taking office had been: "We intend to do some thinking." Later he had sternly added: "There must be no monkeying." In the event, as might have been anticipated, there was little thinking and much monkeying. It was generally understood that the thinking he and his colleagues proposed to undertake was to be directed towards solving the unemployment problem. This problem had come to dominate politics. It made and unmade governments. Each month statistics were published which, when they showed an increase, gave pleasure to the Opposition and pain to the Government, and which were as eagerly awaited by politicians as stock-exchange prices by speculators.

It was only towards the end of the last century that unemployment began to crop up in political controversy, and even then it was assumed to be as inevitable as poverty.

Keir Hardie's only proposal for the unemployed was to feed them.[1] He did not envisage the possibility of putting them to work. After the War and up to the formation of the National Government in 1931, more parliamentary time was taken up with unemployment than with any other subject. Labour members, when they were in opposition, were relentless in cross-examining the Government about their efforts to deal with the problem, and insistent that they knew what should be done and were prepared to do it. In the constituencies, on how many platforms at how many street-corners were not voices raised denouncing the cruel irony whereby, when machinery, raw materials and hands were available, and when there were so many with needs unsatisfied, machines and men were left idle, raw materials unused; claiming that a Labour Government would speedily find a means of righting this cruel and unnecessary wrong. Mr. Lloyd George based his strategy in the 1929 election on unemployment. With five hundred candidates and what remained of the party funds which fell to him when the Coalition Government disintegrated, he offered a guarantee that he would reduce unemployment to normal proportions within a year without any extra charge on the Exchequer. The electorate neglected to take advantage of this handsome offer.

A result, perhaps, of the thinking which the Prime Minister had announced was the appointment of three Ministers—Mr. J. H. Thomas, Mr. Lansbury and Sir Oswald Mosley, to deal with unemployment, the assumption being that the first would provide the geniality, the second the benevolence and the third the brains necessary for this difficult undertaking. Their partnership lasted only until May 1930, when

[1] See *Pilgrim to the Left* by S. G. Hobson.

Sir Oswald Mosley resigned, disgusted, as he vehemently explained, with the futility and prevarication of his colleagues. He followed up his resignation by issuing a Memorandum which called for a more decisive policy, and for constitutional changes which would expedite its implementation. One of the signatories of this Memorandum was Mr. John Strachey, at the time also a Labour Member of Parliament. He and Sir Oswald joined forces for a little while, and then separated, hurrying away in opposite directions, the one to try and write like Lenin, the other to try and look like Hitler.

Another result of the thinking to which MacDonald and his colleagues devoted themselves was the institution of an Economic Council "to advise His Majesty's Government on economic matters." To this Council were appointed every variety of economist, as Mr. J. M. Keynes, Lord (then Sir Josiah) Stamp, Mr. G. D. H. Cole, and the idea was that they should meet together and formulate proposals. They met together, but no proposals were forthcoming. Each individual economist, as was clear from their published articles and books, held emphatic opinions about what should be done; but these opinions, so fertile in royalties, easily marketed at so much a thousand words, clashed one with another.

Meetings were contentious and unproductive. Far into the night the assembled economists disputed, unable to agree even about the terms they used in their discussions, a new variant of the Tower of Babel. The Economic Advisory Council still has some kind of shadowy existence; but whom it advises, and how, and when, is known only to those concerned in its activities.

The Government, like others before it, fell back on hoping for a trade revival. Alas, no revival came. Month by month the unemployment returns were more depressing. By April, 1930, the highest figure for eight years was reached—1,650,000, despite Mr. Thomas's assurance at the beginning of the year that bottom had been touched. The phrase "economic blizzard" came into vogue and comforted a little. Who were Cabinet Ministers, however well-intentioned and able, to stand up to blizzards?

In addition to the blizzard, they had their supporters to contend with, a ravening pack. To some they threw commissions of inquiry—into the desirability of abolishing capital punishment, the licensing laws, parliamentary procedure; to others, promises—of a Trade Disputes Act Amendment Bill, an Eight-Hour Day Bill, a Factories Bill; to others, legislation—a Coal Mines or Unemployment Insurance Bill.

Proposed legislation made slow progress. The Government were dependent in the House of Commons on Liberal support, and any little meat the Liberals left on the bone was devoured in the House of Lords. If Lord Passfield, the Colonial Secretary, disposed of some small difficulty which had arisen in East Africa, it was only to find waiting for him an earnest advocate of making a public declaration in favour of native rights in East Africa; if he deflected this assault, there was Dr. Chaim Weizmann to contend with, and that unending wrangle as to whether *a* or *the* National Home was intended. Ah, happy days when he was Sidney Webb, peacefully turning over municipal records in quiet cellars, peacefully collecting information about the inadequate past and devising an adequate future. Ah, happy Fabian days!

It was more than an economic blizzard which swept over

the Government, a spiritual blizzard too, freezing their hearts within them. Where were the hopes which had buoyed them up when the prospect of taking office seemed so remote? Where the projects so confidently put forward, the promises so confidently made? Education!—how they had expatiated upon the benefits of education and on the right of all to enjoy them; on the gains which would accrue to society if instead of children being thrown on the labour-market at fourteen, they were kept one year, or even two or three years longer at school. Now they came forward with a modest measure, just for raising the School Age to fifteen, and trouble came upon them, not only from the Opposition and their treacherous Liberal allies, but from the religious bodies as well. Nonconformists were enraged that Church schools should receive grants-in-aid; private money was not available for equipping Church schools to fulfil the provisions of the new Act, public money was not available for replacing them by State schools; Nonconformists and Anglicans joined together in their opposition to Roman Catholic institutions benefiting financially from the proposed legislation. It was an unseemly wrangle.

In the House of Commons the Government were defeated on an amendment in the name of John Scurr, one of their own supporters.[1] When the Prime Minister was asked what

[1] MacDonald's statement before the vote on Scurr's amendment was taken, was characteristic:

"This is a question of conscience so far as the Catholics and Nonconformists are concerned, and, in the settlement of that question of conscience, it is all in the interests of goodwill and of harmony and of putting this Bill into operation when it is carried, if the Government are left a free hand, as would happen if this amendment were not pressed to a division—if the Government were left a free hand to carry on these negotiations, with the pledge definitely given that, when the substance of a real agreement has been arrived at, when the outstanding problems . . ."

he proposed to do about it, he replied that the Government accepted the amendment, implying by his manner, defiantly distraught, that a less resolute, less high-principled Premier would have behaved differently, but not he.

This performance led Mr. Churchill to recall how, when he was a child, his nurse had taken him to a fair, where, among other attractions, there was announced the spectacle of a Boneless Wonder. He had pleaded with his nurse to be allowed to see this Wonder, but she had refused. Another time, when he was a bigger boy, she had said, he should see the Wonder, but not then. The other time had never come. He had waited and waited, but in vain; and now after sixty years his patience was rewarded. His eyes rested at last (pointing to the Prime Minister) on the Boneless Wonder. When the National Government was formed and Mr. Churchill found himself excluded from it, he ruefully recalled this quip, but for which he would probably have been included in the Cabinet, and have used his eloquence and debating skill, for instance, to promote instead of impede an All-India Federal Constitution. That a politician should make so heavy a sacrifice for a joke must count to him for virtue. Does Sir John Simon joke? Does Mr. Hore-Belisha?

These empty debates, these mutilated measures, though few knew it at the time, marked the end for many a long year, perhaps for ever, of party politics as then understood. No domestic issue was going again in the lifetimes of many there present to arouse the slightest interest in Parliament or outside. Free Trade and Protection, that once burning controversy which Mr. Lloyd George tried piteously to revive, was to be settled without causing any perturbation; the Pope might be put on or taken off the rates without anyone minding, and the School Age was to be a matter of indifference to all. Deep clouds were massing, deep clouds of fear, and thus overshadowed, the Victorian dream—progress without tears, faded, was to end in tears without progress. Its closing phase was MacDonald, Socialist Prime Minister and Boneless Wonder, accepting unmeant amendments to an unmeant Education Bill. Or, almost the closing scene, the Chancellor of the Exchequer, Snowden, rising in his place to propose the taxation of land values; not their real taxation, just the principle of the thing on the Statute Book, and a preliminary survey to find out how the tax might be instituted and how much it might be expected to bring in. Making this mild proposition old words came to his lips— "The land was given by the Creator, not for the use of dukes, but for the equal use of all his children." It was his positively last appearance in the role of chastiser of the rich and powerful. But a little while and he would become their valued collaborator, if not a ducal landlord himself, a viscount, and all his powers of chastisement be reserved for his then associates.

The fruit of Snowden's efforts on behalf of the taxation of land values was the setting up of a small Government department, which even lingered on after the Labour Government's fall, though how employing its time no one knows. This department was finally abolished when Mr. Neville Chamberlain became Chancellor of the Exchequer, without having caused any perturbation to ducal or other landlords.

III

In the first Labour Government MacDonald had combined the offices of Foreign Secretary and Prime Minister ("I determined to take on my back a double burden, not that I was unmindful of the weakness of human flesh, but

I was convinced that, if our country was to pull its full weight, the authority of the Premiership would have to be cast into the same scale as that of the Foreign Secretaryship"); in the second, against his will, he relinquished the Foreign Secretaryship. His first idea had been to give it to Mr. J. H. Thomas, the one of his colleagues on whose obedience he could most implicitly rely; but Arthur Henderson, powerful in controlling the Party machine, insisted on having it for himself.

Henderson and MacDonald never got on well together. Their natures were antipathetic. Henderson, a regular chapel-goer and occasional lay-preacher, extremely respectable, with bowler hat and umbrella, was suspicious of MacDonald's marked liking for the company of his social superiors; MacDonald considered Henderson commonplace and lower middle class.[1] They represented two elements in the Labour Party whose incompatibility has been perhaps its greatest weakness—the urge on the part of prudent, industrious manual workers to improve their conditions, and the romantic discontent of would-be, and sometimes actual, aristocrats. Trade Unionism and the Co-operative Movement are characteristic products of the former; National Labour and the Left Book Club, of the latter.

[1] Though the lower middle class is the butt alike of the revolutionary and the reactionary, both of whom pride themselves on admiring aristocrats and peasants or proletarians, but nothing in between, politicians who display integrity usually belong, like Henderson and Mr. Lansbury, to this class. Their much ridiculed respectability prevents them from being easily corrupted by flattery or easily bought; their values may be commonplace, but at least they make some attempt to observe them. It is a MacDonald with his Highlander-aristocratic pretensions ("The MacDonalds were a masterful lot . . . a wild self-willed masterful lot," as he puts it in *At Home and Abroad,* a collection of essays), a Thomas conscientiously dropping his h's, a Maxton with flashing eyes and floating hair, who are most liked—that is, least feared, by their political adversaries.

Henderson was never a revolutionary; but MacDonald, like
Hitler and Mussolini and Pilsudski, only ceased to be a sort
of revolutionary when he had become accepted by his opponents as their ostensible leader.

Though MacDonald was not technically Foreign Secretary, it was in the role of appeaser of international conflicts
and champion of oppressed peoples that he most fancied
himself. In this he was true to type. The romantic idealist
invariably turns his eyes abroad. It is so much easier and
more exciting to side with the weak and defy the strong in
other countries than at home. A capital levy, say—what a
tedious troublesome business, stirring up bad-feeling, mali-
cious attacks; whereas speaking out in ringing tones for
down-trodden Asiatics, earnestly pleading that justice
should be done to a defeated enemy, brings a glow of righteousness and no brickbats which matter. The English have
shown a marked talent for combining successful imperialism
with individual fulminations against imperialist oppression.
The same generation produced a Cecil Rhodes and a Wil-
fred Scawen Blunt.[1] While Lord Byron was becoming
famous as the champion of the oppressed Greeks, his coun-
trymen were busy extending and consolidating their rule in
India; and it would not, it is safe to assume, have struck
Byron as in any way odd to finance Greek freedom with
Indian dividends, if he had been fortunate enough to possess
any.

MacDonald was in the Byron tradition in his conduct of
foreign affairs, indeed at one point had as great a reputation

---

[1] In her *Life of Blunt* Miss Edith Finch records that he felt uncomfortable
at a "barbarously gorgeous banquet" given by the Khedive because he
reflected that the cost of it would fall on the poverty-stricken fellaheen.
Yet he was never made uncomfortable by the thought that the cost of his
own luxurious mode of life must fall on someone.

on the Continent as the hero of Missolonghi. In Germany, in Central Europe, above all in Geneva, he was included with Byron, Oscar Wilde, and Galsworthy as representing England's best. Books were written about him in German, the Scandinavian languages and even French, and his features became as familiar as once Woodrow Wilson's had been. He introduced, it was felt, a badly needed element of poetry into the dreary wrangles which followed the Treaty of Versailles. When a journalist saw him early one morning looking, rapt, across the Lake of Geneva, and greeted him, he mournfully answered: "The day is for the worrrld, but the morrrning is for myself."

He was the great exponent of the nations getting together round a conference table, he presiding. Their discontents and suspicions would all melt away like morning mist in the sun of his righteousness—"I feel that looking forward into the future we must be inspired by a new faith of fraternity, with a new courage to follow large and stirring moral aims and supplement all our material achievements by things that belong to the spiritual excellencies of the peoples of the world." He flew to Geneva, descending from the skies, an angel of peace; he walked along the Quai Woodrow Wilson as though it had been the Quai Ramsay MacDonald; he addressed the members of the League Assembly in a strain of exaltation. They, too, were his frrriends, all of them, even Equador and Panama, all.

The League reached its prime with him, expired with him, too. He was its apotheosis. As in home politics he represented the culmination of progress without tears and prelude to tears without progress, so in international politics he represented the culmination of peace without tears and prelude to tears without peace. Twinkling lights of Geneva, noisy, smoky cafés of Geneva, Lake of Geneva beside which men walk unfolding newspapers in the wind—newspapers which tell of such a speech, such a resolution, such exchange rates and stock prices; conversation of Geneva, unceasing, ebbing and flowing like the sea's tide but never abating—this was a kingdom, once flourishing, now decayed and scarcely exist-ent. In its flourishing days, MacDonald was one of its great ones, his name constantly repeated in a variety of foreign accents, his rich Scottish voice often heard in private con-versation and public address.

Besides Geneva, MacDonald visited the United States and Germany. In the United States he had an enthusiastic recep-tion, his high-mindedness being greatly appreciated there. After some years of President Hoover, he was a welcome change. In Germany, too, he was cordially received. The Nazis were steadily increasing their vote, but there seemed little prospect of their getting into power;[1] and though Stresemann was dead, his policy was still being pursued. Following MacDonald's example, the French Government decided to send Briand and Monsieur Laval to Berlin, where they showed themselves on the balcony of their hotel to a small regimented crowd of minor government officials, who chanted gutturally in a monotonous, spiritless voice: "Vive la France! Vive la France!"

The U.S.S.R. represented a difficulty. Naturally, a Labour Government was inclined to favour closer relations with the

[1] Hitler's single appearance in the news in the early months of 1930 was in connection with a libel action that he brought against a Munich news-paper which had accused him of having abandoned his former monarchical principles, and which resulted in his being awarded 400 marks damages, this sum being then considered an adequate recompense for any damage his reputation for consistency had sustained. Later in the year the Nazi vote increased to 6,500,000; Lord Rothermere discovered in Hitler a cham-pion of Youth, and Europe became Hitler-conscious.

Soviet Government and the granting of trading credits; on the other hand, the memory of the Zinovieff Letter and its disastrous electoral consequences was still fresh, and the *Daily Worker*, which had just begun publication, contained regular fulminations against "the Social-Fascists and King's toadies of the Labour Government," who, "not content with keeping Indian workers rotting in Meerut Prison, are openly shooting down unarmed Negro workers in Nigeria," and repeatedly expressed its determination to expose "the reactionary schemes of the trade union bureaucracy and the Labourites and pseudo-lefts." The Foreign Secretary was bombarded with questions in the House of Commons, and the cautious statements which these questions elicited were impatiently received by many Government supporters.

Admiration for the Soviet régime had greatly increased since the introduction of the Five-Year Plan in 1929, though more among Liberals and the professional classes than among trade unionists, who from the beginning showed themselves to be less easily deluded by Soviet propaganda than university professors, writers and clergymen. Professor Julian Huxley, for instance, had no difficulty in believing that "while we were in Russia a German town-planning expert was travelling over the huge Siberian spaces in a special train with a staff of assistants, where cities are to arise, stopping for a few days, picking out the best site, laying down the broad outlines of the future city, and passing on, leaving the details to be filled in by architects and engineers, who remain," or that "Stalin himself sometimes comes down to the Moscow goods sidings to help"; [1] whereas the late Herbert Smith, President of the Miners' Federation, and Sir

[1] *A Scientist Among the Soviets.*

Walter Citrine, both of whom visited the U.S.S.R., showed an irritating disinclination to accept such absurdities on trust, and insisted on investigating actual conditions of life.

The cost of a tour in the U.S.S.R., though moderate, was beyond the means of most manual workers, so that those who availed themselves of the exceedingly competent Intourist organization were predominantly income-tax payers. Their delight in all they saw and were told, and the expression they gave to this delight, constitute unquestionably one of the wonders of the age. There were earnest advocates of the humane killing of cattle who looked up at the massive headquarters of the Ogpu with tears of gratitude in their eyes, earnest advocates of proportional representation who eagerly assented when the necessity for a Dictatorship of the Proletariat was explained to them, earnest clergymen who walked reverently through anti-God museums and reverently turned over the pages of atheistic literature, earnest pacifists who watched delightedly tanks rattle across the Red Square and bombing planes darken the sky, earnest town-planning specialists who stood outside overcrowded, ramshackle tenements and muttered: "If only we had something like this in England!" The almost unbelievable credulity of these mostly university-educated tourists astonished even Soviet officials used to handling foreign visitors, and, expressed in large numbers of books and articles in newspapers and periodicals, especially in the *Moscow Daily News*, an English newspaper published in Moscow, should provide some future Gibbon with material after his heart.

The climax came, perhaps, with the visit to the U.S.S.R. of Mr. Bernard Shaw, Lady Astor and Lord Lothian, which provided, as Mr. Eugene Lyons has put it, "a fortnight of clowning." [1] In honour of Mr. Shaw's seventy-fifth birthday, which took place while he was in Moscow, a huge meeting was held, fittingly, in the old Nobles' Club, in the room where so many political prisoners have been tried and convicted. There was at the time a serious food-shortage, and even this privileged audience included some who were on short rations. Mr. Shaw explained in his speech how, before he started off on his trip, he had been warned to provide himself with supplies of tinned food, how he had thrown these emergency supplies out of the train on his way through Poland because he knew that talk of a food shortage in the U.S.S.R. was all nonsense, and how he had never been so overstuffed in his life as since he crossed the Soviet frontier. It was the only thing the Russians were unable to forgive him—that he should have thrown away food in Poland instead of bringing it with him to Moscow.

Later, at a Foreign Office reception, according to Mr. Lyons, Lady Astor astonished everyone by suddenly prostrating herself before Litvinov, the Commissar for Foreign Affairs. She had received a telegram from a Russian Professor in the United States asking her to intercede for his family, who had been detained in the U.S.S.R. Litvinov,

---

[1] In *Assignment in Utopia:*
"Deftly Shaw skimmed the surface, careful not to break through the lacquer of appearances. If Lady Astor asked too many questions he neatly slapped her wrist. He judged food conditions by the Metropole menu, collectivization by the model farm, the Ogpu by the model colony at Bolshovo, socialism by the twittering of attendant sycophants. His performance was not amusing to Russians. It was macabre. The lengthening obscenity of ignorant or indifferent tourists disporting themselves cheerily on the aching body of Russia, seemed summed-up in this cavorting old man, in his blanket endorsement of what he would not understand. He was so taken up with demonstrating how youthful and agile he was that he had no attention to spare for the revolution in practice."

much embarrassed by Lady Astor's impulsive gesture, read
the telegram and turned irritably away, remarking that the
matter was not within his jurisdiction. Undeterred by this
rebuff, Lady Astor appealed to other important Soviet officials when the opportunity occurred, but got no more
satisfaction out of them than she had out of Litvinov.

Despite such episodes the Soviet régime continued to be
held in ever greater esteem by writers like Shaw and André
Gide [1] and Romain Rolland; clergymen like the Reverend
Hewlett Johnson, journalists like Walter Duranty and Maurice Hindus, economists like G. D. H. Cole and the Webbs,
scientists like Professor Julian Huxley. How could all these,
so learned and so righteous, be wrong? Was the *Manchester
Guardian* given to falsehood, or Fabians to hasty conclusions?
Highbrow film societies were enthralled by Russian films
like *Mother* and *The End of St. Petersburg,* and cheered to
the skies the heroes of the Revolution, as, later, they cheered
the news that these same heroes had mostly been shot as spies
and traitors. Week after week Soviet boats sailed from London for Leningrad packed with distinguished passengers, all
excited, readers of *Humanity Uprooted* and *Red Bread,*
appreciative of the crew's singing of revolutionary songs
and of the captain's interesting speech; of the Lenin's Corner,
and of the unanimous decision taken at a meeting presided
over by someone from the London School of Economics
that it would be in bad taste to offer money to the stewards,
but perhaps some books for the ship's library might be per-
missible; in each male heart a vision, never to be realized, of

[1] A number of these writers soured on the régime as time went on; for
instance, Gide, whose *Retour de l'U.S.S.R.,* published in 1938, expressed
his disillusionment after a visit to the U.S.S.R., and created some stir. Not
even Stalin, however, could shake the fidelity of Romain Rolland and
the Webbs.

a *comsomolka* with a red kerchief over jet black hair, with
dark glistening eyes and flushed cheeks, dancing a revolutionary dance; in each female heart heaven knows what
visions.

Few there must be among Left sympathizers whose circumstances enable them to satisfy the minimum requirements laid down by Virginia Woolf (a room of one's own
and four hundred a year) for an adequate life, who did not
go on this pilgrimage, eagerly looking at all they were shown
and listening to all they were told, conducting furtive
money-changing transactions at unofficial rates, sending
postcards to awed relatives, buying with valuta perhaps a
Russian embroidered blouse or shirt for fancy-dress wear.
In the U.S.S.R., they created some wonder, much indignation, too; at home, they lectured, wrote, broadcast, cultivated beards which in some cases were trimmed like Lenin's.

The Government, despite certain misgivings, resumed
full diplomatic relations with the U.S.S.R. and proceeded
to negotiate an Anglo-Soviet trade agreement. In 1924 the
naïve proposal had been put forward and seriously considered of sending to Moscow, not a professional diplomat, but
someone like Sir James O'Grady, the transport workers'
leader. This proposal, however, was icily received in Moscow. "Send us a gentleman," a Foreign Office official said
to an English journalist there, "he'll understand us." In due
course they were sent Sir Esmond Ovey, and Sir James
O'Grady went to Tasmania.

To the annoyance of the Government's pacifist supporters, Mr. A. V. Alexander, First Lord of the Admiralty,
announced the laying down of four new cruisers; work was
suspended for the second time on the Singapore Naval Base,
and the Rhineland was evacuated. In Germany a pocket

battleship, the *Deutschland*, was launched; in Roumania
Prince Carol recovered his throne, and his chief opponent,
the head of the powerful Bratianu family, died of apoplexy
brought on by rage at Carol's triumph; in Spain a Republic
was declared amidst universal rejoicing, the most happy
and bloodless revolution, it was said, which had ever taken
place, and promising a happy, bloodless future for the Spanish people; at Geneva a two-year Tariff Truce was proposed
but not accepted, and a variety of projects laid before the
Preparatory Disarmament Commission; at Sarajevo a tablet
was ceremonially unveiled commemorating Gabriel Princip,
murderer of the Archduke Ferdinand, and strangely inscribed: "On this heroic spot Gabriel Princip proclaimed
liberty on June 28, 1914."

IV

Besides Europe, the Empire required attention, and particularly India. MacDonald had visited India in 1911, and
written a book about his visit. In the course of this Indian
tour he had publicly stated that, given a British Government possessed of sufficient determination and benevolence,
the problem of satisfying the legitimate aspirations of the
Indian National Congress might be solved overnight. This
statement was naturally remembered when he became Prime
Minister, and though his first short term of office disappointed the Congress leaders, their hopes revived in 1930,
especially when the Viceroy, Lord Irwin (now Lord Halifax), after a visit to London, made a declaration to the effect
that the goal of British policy in India was the realization
there of full Dominion Status.

As in dealing with Europe so in dealing with India, Mac-
Donald's first idea was a conference. He announced a

Round-Table Conference which should include representatives of every interest concerned, from Maharajahs to
Untouchables; over which he would wave persuasive arms,
to which he would speak persuasive words, thereby lulling
divergent views into real or imagined agreement. The Congress leaders announced that they would participate in the
proceedings of such a conference only if they were satisfied
that the "very simple but vital needs of India" would be
met. As these very simple but vital needs included abolition of the salt tax, and the reduction by fifty per cent of
the land tax and military expenditure,[1] this was tantamount
to refusing to have anything to do with the Conference. At
the Lahore Congress in February 1930, a resolution was
passed in favour of *purna swaraj*, or complete independence,[2]
a green national flag being enthusiastically unfurled, even a
cracked, tuneless rendering of "The Wearin' of the Green"
attempted; and the following month Gandhi inaugurated
a new civil disobedience campaign, and started on his march
to Dandi, where he proposed to defy the Government by
illegally making salt from sea water.

Gandhi was then at the height of his fame and popularity, unable to stir abroad without many coming forward to
take the dust of his feet; famous in the United States as
"the only figure of world importance operating practically
naked," and in England for his goat's milk, non-violence
and Miss Slade. The progress of his march to Dandi was
followed with interest, abroad as well as in India. He took

[1] A number of financial claims on Great Britain were also formulated,
totalling £546,000,000. They included, among other items, the cost of the
Indian Mutiny of 1857.
[2] With characteristic subtlety Gandhi later explained that "Complete independence" was an inaccurate translation of *purna swaraj*, which really
meant "disciplined self-rule from within."

five days over it, and was followed by his personal retinue (including Miss Slade), a number of picked followers in white homespun who were liable to break into a Sanskrit hymn, and newspaper representatives, some in motor cars and one in a rickshaw. When they reached the sea he filled a pan with sea-water, which he later evaporated until some grains of dark unappetizing salt were left, these grains of salt being preserved by some there present as a souvenir.

The fact that Gandhi was not arrested for this open defiance of the law (whereby salt was a Government monopoly, and could only be manufactured under licence) gave a great impetus to the civil disobedience campaign. In the United Provinces a highly successful rent strike was organized, and a boycott of British cloth caused seriously increased unemployment in Lancashire; for the first time in many years hostile tribesmen got into Peshawar, and for some days the city was virtually in their control; in Bengal a terrorist movement, native to that dank, unhappy climate, took on alarming proportions, fixing its victims in advance, striking them down on the appointed day. In Simla, far away from this turbulence, within sight of the white Himalayas, was the Viceroy, "that lean, tall Christian" as Shaukat Ali described him—tall and solemn and inert, looking down with solemn benignity on the turbulent sub-continent over which he had been set in authority. After much persuasion at last he was moved to act. On May 5 Gandhi was arrested, and a little later the Congress Working Committee declared an illegal body. As the many delegates to the Round-Table Conference booked their passages to London, the prisons filled with 25,000 non-violent non-co-operators, mostly loquacious and later to be heard at great length on legislative bodies, but some meek and silent and anonymous.

Meanwhile in England the Report of the Simon Commission had been published, at once selling over 20,000 copies, this constituting a record for a State Paper, especially one dealing with India, a country which the English have been glad enough to feel was theirs, but in which they have obstinately refused to interest themselves. The Commission had been appointed in 1927 to investigate the possibilities of extending the measure of Indian self-government which the Montague-Chelmsford Reforms had introduced. The deliberate omission of any Indian from its personnel of seven made it unpopular in India from the beginning, and Sir John Simon and his colleagues were received in Bombay with black flags and shrill concerted shouts of "Simon go back!" Undeterred by this unpromising reception, they proceeded to conduct their investigations, and in due course presented a Report advocating provincial autonomy, but a continuation of the existing non-representative Central Government. By the time all the leading articles on this Report, including several by Mr. Garvin in which he advocated "cool heads and warm feet," had been written, and summaries of its chief recommendations published, and compliments paid to its style, comprehensiveness and insight, it had become apparent that no voice in India had been raised in its favour. Of the Indian population of 320,000,000 at least 300,000,000 were unaware that any Commission had ever been appointed to report on constitutional reform in India, or for any other purpose; would have looked with wonder on MacDonald with his irregular moustache, and have listened, astonished, to his vibrant Scottish voice prophesying their future peace, prosperity and freedom; had no idea what a Commission, Simon or other, was, or what constitutional reforms were, both pro-

vincial and central government for them signifying mainly
a policeman in a red puggaree who needed to be conciliated
with obsequious behaviour and sometimes bribes. The
others who did know what constitutional reforms were,
and all about the Simon Commission—students, lawyers,
government officials, plump Brahmins with sacred thread
and white turban—were decidedly disgruntled by its
findings.

The Round-Table delegates assembled in St. James's
Palace in the late autumn, somewhat chilly but excited, and
each in receipt of a generous allowance to meet living
expenses. They were exceedingly representative, some representing Indian womanhood, some Indian labour, some
Indian commerce; a Mr. U. Ba Pay representing Burma,
the Aga Khan representing the Aga Khan, everything
under the sun represented except the 25,000 in gaol and the
300,000,000 cultivating their small patches of overworked
soil.

King George V opened the Conference, and MacDonald
delivered the first oration. He described how he had
travelled through India, admiring its temples, resting under
its banyan trees, enthralled by its ancient wisdom and peace.
They were met together, he went on, to discuss a Constitution. Now his Indian friends must realize that there were a
great variety of Constitutions, as a Federal Constitution on
the United States model, a highly centralized Constitution
on the French model, an unwritten Constitution which had
slowly grown up with the centuries on the British model;
any number of Constitutions, some with single-chamber
legislatures, some bi-cameral, some even tri-cameral. As he
enumerated these different Constitutions he seemed, like a
commercial traveller, to be taking them out of a bag—this

the American model, this the French, this the British, this
a convenient bi-cameral attachment which was well worth
the small increase in price it involved. "I want," he concluded, "the lion (I don't know which is the lion) to lie
down with the lamb—whichever is the lamb—and when
they do demonstrate that they are lying down together the
constitution will emerge with great simplicity and quickly."

Each of the delegates was eager for an opportunity to
address the Conference. They had come a long way; their
expenses allowance was reckoned daily, and continued as
long as the Conference did; all had carefully prepared
speeches in their pockets. Speeches succeeded one another
wearisomely, one after the other. Such quantities of eloquence had seldom been heard even in St. James's Palace.
It seemed as though the speeches would go on and for ever,
and nothing else happen. The Conference was saved from
so inglorious an end by a proposal, believed to have origi-
nated with Colonel Haksar, for an All-India Federation.
This proposal was accepted in principle, and the Conference adjourned.

Two of the Indian delegates, Sir Tej Bahadur Sapru and
Mr. Jayakar, on getting back to India, acted as mediators
between the Viceroy and Gandhi, and eventually were able
to procure Gandhi's release from prison for the purpose of
discussing with the Viceroy the terms on which Congress
would agree to call off the civil disobedience campaign and
participate in bringing to pass the projected All-India Federation. Their conversations, which lasted several days, and
were attended by Gandhi in his well-known costume and
carrying suitable refreshment in an aluminium saucepan,
resulted in what became known as the Irwin-Gandhi Pact,

whose terms provided for the calling off of civil disobedience and the repeal of the decree declaring the Congress
Working Committee an illegal body. It was also understood
that Gandhi would attend the next Session of the Round-
Table Conference, and that a good number of the 25,000
in gaol were to be released.

The Viceroy was much criticized in England for thus
negotiating with an acknowledged rebel. Mr. Churchill complained of a "seditious saint striding half-naked up the steps
of the Viceregal Palace," and Lord Birkenhead referred
scathingly in the House of Lords to a policy of emptying
the gaols of India in order to procure delegates for a conference in London. It was his last public appearance, his splendid physique broken, his insolence become faltering and
uncertain; a woeful, frightening figure. A month later he
was dead. Five years before, when Lord Irwin's appointment to the Viceroyalty was decided on, he had noted down
bitterly: "How much more profitable is virtue than brilliance." The subsequent career of the man who provoked
this observation has certainly not lessened its validity.

Gandhi's arrival in London for the second session of the
Round-Table Conference created less stir than had been anticipated. Partly it was that his goat's milk and shawl and
weekly day of silence had been over-publicized, partly that
by the time he arrived the National Government had been
formed, and the maintenance of the Gold Standard was preoccupying most minds.[1] He stayed in an East End Settlement, his hostess being Miss Muriel Lester, and spent much
of his time at Friends' House, where he was to be seen most

[1] The Gold Standard was abandoned a week after Gandhi's arrival in
London.

afternoons, the centre of a little circle of admiring Quakers, who occasionally gently questioned him. Two policemen were told off to follow him about, and as he was in the habit of taking a stroll at dawn, their day began early. The three of them—the aged, wizened Indian in unseasonable loin-cloth and shawl; the two friendly but unmistakable police-men keeping some little distance behind him—were a strange sight walking through empty East End streets at cold day-break.

Another visitor in London, but differently clad and ac-commodated, was Charlie Chaplin, who had come to Europe to attend the opening night of *City Lights*. The two met, and were photographed together, Mahatma and Clown, both past their prime, and a little forlorn. Charlie's visit also had not come up to expectations. It had started well enough, with cheering crowds, and even a suggestion in several newspapers that the conferment of a knighthood on him would be a graceful and popular gesture. Then reports were circulated that he was careless about keeping appointments —for instance, one at 10 Downing Street for lunch with the Prime Minister; and the *Morning Post* unkindly recalled the fact that, though a British subject and of military age at the time of the War, he had preferred making a film about the trenches in Hollywood to experiencing them in France.

Gandhi met and talked with other distinguished persons besides Charlie Chaplin; attended a Garden Party at Buck-ingham Palace without at all modifying his costume, being examined by Queen Mary through her lorgnettes with some surprise; visited Lancashire to see for himself something of the unemployment caused by the foreign cloth boycott he had instituted in India, there meeting C. P. Scott, Editor of the *Manchester Guardian*, aged and soon to die; Gandhi and this bearded, dying Liberal for some reason not taking much pleasure in each other's company. On his way back to India he broke his journey at Villeneuve to see Romain Rolland, and when he arrived at Bombay was received for the first time in his long career with hostile demonstrations, almost cries of "Gandhi, go back!"

A third session of the Round-Table Conference took place, almost unnoticed, at the end of 1932; "fact-finding" commissions were sent to India, and returned, as Mr. Churchill put it, bearing "bulky and indigestible sheaves"; a Communal Award was published, but gave satisfaction neither to the Hindu majority, nor to the Moslem and other minorities; a Joint Select Committee was set up, heard evidence, and duly reported, its published proceedings also bulky and indigestible.

The final result of this unprecedented outpouring of words was a Government of India Act, which provided for immediate provincial autonomy, and the establishment in due course of an All-India Federation with a Federal Legislature in which a third of the representation will be reserved for the Indian States, it being anticipated that the representatives of these moribund autocracies will counteract the influence of the representatives of British-India. The Act was piloted through Parliament with great dexterity by Sir Samuel Hoare in the face of the strenuous opposition of some fifty Conservative members led by Mr. Churchill and vociferously supported by the newspapers controlled by Lord Rothermere.

In the spring of 1931, shortly before he left India to be succeeded by Lord Willingdon, Lord Irwin ceremonially inaugurated New Delhi, the new capital of India whose foundation stone had been laid by the Duke of Connaught in 1911. This town, which cost Rs144,671,768 to build, with its palatial Viceroy's House, and huge circular building to house the Legislative Assembly and Chamber of Princes, and rows of houses for government officials each graded according to the salary and status of the occupant, is surrounded by the ruins of seven previous capitals. In summer it is quite deserted, empty as Pompeii, and even in winter has a somewhat ghostly air, so new in so ancient a setting, like a freshly painted garage built on to a crumbling ruin. When he saw it in process of being built, Clemenceau remarked: *"Ça sera la plus magnifique de toutes ces ruines."* [1]

V

Egypt was another country with a nationalist movement, the Wafd, whose leaders had been encouraged to hope for concessions from a Labour Government. Nahas Pasha, who had succeeded Zaghlul as leader of the Wafd, bearing rather the same relation to him as Mr. Neville Chamberlain to his predecessor, came with a delegation to London early in 1930 to negotiate an Anglo-Egyptian Treaty. The negotiations broke down on the Egyptian delegation's refusal to abandon Egypt's theoretical right to participate in the administration of the Sudan; and Nahas returned to Cairo, there soon to resign, leaving King Fuad, that astute monarch, in control of the situation, as, indeed, he remained, with a few short intervals, until his death in 1936, ruling through Court favourites, amassing great wealth, and growing fatter and fatter, for ever memorable to all who met him for the curious, unexpected barking noise he constantly made owing to a bullet hole in his throat which resulted from an attempt on his life by his brother-in-law.

[1] Quoted in *Indian Ink* by Philip Steegman.

The High Commissioner in Egypt, Lord Lloyd, disapproved of the proposed Anglo-Egyptian Treaty, and resigned. His resignation looked like creating a political crisis, until Henderson was able to convince the House of Commons that his predecessor at the Foreign Office, Sir Austen Chamberlain, found himself as much in disagreement with the High Commissioner as he did. Such a display of integrity was ruinous for Lord Lloyd's career. Virtue, if it is to bear out Lord Birkenhead's claim and prove more profitable than brilliance, needs to be pliant.

The spirit of the age was against admitting disagreement in any circumstances. If Lord Lloyd, as innumerable Government officials did in India to their great advantage, had pretended to himself and to others that he believed in the possibility of appeasing conflicts by assuming they did not exist, his promising career would have proceeded without interruption, leading, perhaps, to the Viceroyalty instead of to the British Council for Cultured Relations with Foreign Countries.

Egypt also produced its quota of words, written and spoken, these dying down to a faint trickle when graver preoccupations arose, and only momentarily swelling in volume on the occasion of the marriage of King Farouk, Fuad's successor, to Princess Farida; then again abating. Nahas Pasha made another short appearance as Premier; negotiated another Anglo-Egyptian Treaty, this time successfully, and was little more heard of. Students still from time to time paraded the streets in Cairo and Alexandria, filling the air with shrill shouts; Egypt was admitted to membership of the League of Nations, and the right of resident foreigners to be tried by special courts, abolished;

cafés continued to be full, Pashas and Beys to be rich, many hoping for employment as government officials not to find any, and the Nile to overflow its banks, fertilizing a strip of land on either side, green and narrow in the wide yellow desert.

India was the Prime Minister's speciality, Egypt the Foreign Secretary's; the Colonial Secretary, Lord Passfield, found himself in great difficulties over Palestine. The proposal to repatriate the Jews to their ancient home, so easily acceded to in the stress of war, so pleasing in prospect to Protestants brought up on Old Testament history and to accept the majestic claim of the children of Israel to be God's Chosen People, was proving bitter in execution. Both Arabs and Jews were able plausibly to blame the British Government for a broken promise; and the feeling of resentment thus engendered grew steadily more intense, the Jews claiming that the Arabs could be conveniently accommodated in Transjordania, the Arabs protesting against the steady influx of subsidized Jewish immigrants.

It is difficult to imagine anyone less equipped by nature than Lord Passfield to deal with so turbulent a situation. No one could fail to be impressed by the immense amount of information he had managed to pack into the small compass of his mind, by his diligence, well-meaningness and desire to be scrupulously impartial; but his small, rotund figure, his confused eyes and thick voice, impressive at a Fabian lecture, were pitiably inadequate to mediate between inflamed Jew and Arab. Confronting him with their bitter antagonism was like confronting an elderly specialist on sex repressions with a sergeant-major in maniacal pursuit of a small girl.

As the Congress and Wafdist leaders had expected sympathetic treatment from a Labour Government, so did the Jews. Lord Passfield, however, leant towards the Arab side, thereby bringing down much trouble upon his own, and, until it virtually repudiated his policy, the Government's, head. Sonorous Hebrew curses were called down upon him, and it was even said of him, as of Herr Hitler and Dr. Goebbels, that so cruel a chastiser of the Jewish race must be himself a renegade Jew. His wife, the redoubtable Mrs. Sidney Webb, who, by refusing to become Lady Passfield, found an original means of extracting notoriety from her husband's peerage and of annoying the *Times,* was included with him in these imprecations; and in various parts of Palestine the two of them were burnt in effigy, their figures, often seen at Summer Schools and other enlightened gatherings, his short and plump, hers tall and lean, consumed with flames amid the shouts of angry Zionists. From this predicament they escaped when the National Government was formed, and Lord Passfield resigned his office, thenceforth devoting themselves to a sympathetic and detailed study of the Soviet régime,[1] and being no more burnt in effigy.

VI

Thus the Government bumped along, dependent on the uncertain support of fifty-nine Liberals, harassed by discontented supporters, helpless before increasing unemployment and deepening depression, assembling conferences and opening negotiations, enraging many who had hoped for too much, scandalizing many by refusing to be adventurous

[1] The result of their labour was published in 1935 in the form of two large volumes entitled *Soviet Communism: A New Civilization?* In the Russian translation of this work the interrogation mark in the title was omitted.

(as, by refusing to discontinue the Meerut Trial [1]), yet, like the Abbé Siéyès during the Paris Reign of Terror, remaining in existence, and that, given all the circumstances, being a not inconsiderable achievement.

Nor were either of the Opposition parties in a particularly happy plight. The fifty-nine Liberals, technically under the irresponsible leadership of Mr. Lloyd George, found themselves in most divisions divided in three, one-third voting with the Government, one-third against, and one-third abstaining, and were rapidly approaching the point when they had nothing to lose but their seats and what remained of their leader's money—the famous Coalition War Chest, cash value of many peerages, baronetcies and knighthoods bestowed in the days of the Coalition Government, but now sadly depleted. The more ambitious among the fifty-nine were even meditating abandoning altogether, so cruelly remote did office seem.

The other Opposition Party, the Conservatives, 260 strong, were also far from contented. Their leader, Mr. Baldwin, had lost them an election by placarding the country with the slogan "Safety First" surmounted by his, he had mistakenly hoped, reassuring features. They hankered after tariffs, which Mr. Baldwin had forsworn; they were uneasy about the Government's India policy, which Mr. Baldwin had with some reservations endorsed; Mr. Churchill had felt constrained to withdraw from the Conservative Party Shadow Cabinet, and another ex-Minister, Mr. Amery, was openly rebellious. It is even possible that Mr. Baldwin might

1 Three Englishmen and twenty-six Indians had been charged with sedition. The case was allowed to drag on for four years, severe sentences being imposed, though on appeal greatly reduced.

have been ousted from the Party leadership [1] but for one of those fortunate accidents from which he has so often bene-fited. Just when his position was most insecure he was lucky enough to be the object of a combined onslaught by Lord Beaverbrook and Lord Rothermere.

It is impossible for these two peers to attack without benefiting, or to praise without harming. The public will read their newspapers, but has so engrained a distrust of their judgment and motives that it will not be influenced by them, except contrariwise. Thus, they find themselves in the curious position of wielding immense influence which they cannot use to enhance their own sense of importance. Lord Northcliffe found, to his deep sorrow and chagrin, that he could not even influence readers of his newspapers to the extent of persuading them to alter their headgear. The only wearers of the *Daily Mail* hat were his own employees, who, according to Mr. Tom Clark,[2] used to carry their normal bowlers and trilbys in a bag to put on as soon as there was no danger of meeting their employer. One of the first clear symptoms of the mental derangement to which Lord North-cliffe finally succumbed was his appearance at Dover agon-izedly watching passengers go aboard cross-Channel steam-ers in the hope of seeing at least one or two wearing the hat he had so ardently tried to popularize.

There are, indeed, few more tantalizing situations in life than a Press Lord's. He has money, he has his circle of paid flatterers; he can have as much publicity as he likes since the headlines are his own to get into, and can make others fa-mous or infamous as he pleases. Yet whenever he attempts

[1] His succession to Lord Willingdon as Governor-General of Canada was seriously considered.
[2] *My Northcliffe Diary.*

to exercise his potential authority, he finds himself frustrated.

This inability to translate circulation into enduring political influence has been particularly galling to Lord Beaverbrook, for whom politics have a great fascination, and whose Presbyterian ancestry has endowed him with demagogic gifts [1] and a passion to exercise them. Despite his intimacy with Bonar Law and his part in putting him in office, he was not offered the Colonial Secretaryship after which he aspired when Bonar Law became Premier. Bonar Law's death and Mr. Baldwin's succession to the Premiership, put the Colonial Office, or any other, more than ever outside his reach. If he had only known it, when he acted as a pall-bearer at Bonar Law's funeral he was also acting as pall-bearer at the funeral of his own political career.

The calamitous electoral consequences to the Conservative Party of Mr. Baldwin's Safety First policy, and the Labour Government's indecision and loss of prestige, seemed to provide an excellent opportunity for another attempt on Lord Beaverbrook's part to make himself felt politically. With three newspapers—the *Daily Express*, the *Evening Standard*, and the *Sunday Express*—at his disposal for publicity purposes, he launched his Empire Crusade, whose object was: "To develop the industries and resources of all parts of the British Empire to the fullest possible extent, and for that purpose to make the Empire a single economic unit, removing so far as possible all obstacles to Freedom of Trade between constituent parts."

The response to this Crusade on the part of the public

[1] A *Manchester Guardian* reporter, later to become well-known as book critic on the *Evening Standard*, in giving his impressions of Lord Beaverbrook's oratory, felicitously described him as "a pedlar of dreams."

SEATTLE PUBLIC LIBRARY

was, according to Lord Beaverbrook's newspapers, astounding. "In the whole history of British politics," the Editor of the *Daily Express* wrote, "there has never been anything more heartening than the response of the public to the appeal of the conveners of the Empire Crusade." Enthusiastic accounts appeared daily of offers of help which had been received from "rich and poor, employed and unemployed, men and women of all ranks." The response from clergymen was reported to have been "astonishing," and a poignant account was given of an unemployed man who "provided the most moving incident in a thrilling day" by laying a pound note down on the desk at Crusade Headquarters and saying it was his contribution "for the sake of his fellow unemployed." "It is almost," Lord Beaverbrook said to a meeting in the Paddington Baths, "as if we were sent from heaven."

In a by-election at South Paddington an Empire Crusade candidate, Vice-Admiral Taylor, was run against the official Conservative candidate, and after a noisy campaign, triumphantly returned. In Whitechapel, the nominee of Lord Beaverbrook and Lord Rothermere, Brigadier-General Critchley, a pioneer promoter of dog-racing, was unsuccessful; and in the St. George's Division of Westminster, Mr. Duff Cooper was faced with the incursion of Sir Ernest Petter.

"A Vote for Duff Cooper is a Vote for Gandhi," the *Daily Mail* informed its readers; and the constituency was decorated with streamers announcing: "Gandhi is Watching St. George's." St. George's, however, obstinately refused to watch the *Daily Mail*, and Mr. Duff Cooper was returned. This preoccupation with India on the part of Sir Ernest Petter's more active backer, cooled whatever enthusiasm

Lord Beaverbrook had for the contest. With all his imperial ardour, the Crusader-in-Chief has never much interested himself in India, or given a more than tepid endorsement to Lord Rothermere's strong views on the subject. Nor did he follow suit when, for a short time, Lord Rothermere came out as a strong supporter of Sir Oswald Mosley and his British Union of Fascists. The two Press Lords, in fact, collaborated only with difficulty. At one point during the South Paddington contest, they each had a candidate in the field, Lord Rothermere having also founded a party for the occasion—the United Empire Party.

Despite this rivalry between United Empire and the Empire Crusade, the relations between their two founders and benefactors continued to be friendly. Lord Rothermere publicly regarded Lord Beaverbrook as a somewhat irresponsible but gifted idealist, a dreamer of dreams, one who "unfolded before our eyes a vision of enduring prosperity," while Lord Beaverbrook, publicly, regarded Lord Rothermere as a statesman of solid worth and integrity, not easy to move, but once moved resolute in his course. Occasionally, they paid each other compliments in their newspapers. For instance, the *Daily Mail* announced that there was only one man worthy of succeeding Mr. Baldwin as leader of the Conservative Party, and that man was Beaverbrook; and, when a train on which Lord Rothermere was travelling ran into the buffers, the *Daily Express* reassured its readers as to the safety of this distinguished passenger, and in a leaderette drew attention to the irreparable loss the country had been spared.

Such exchanges of graceful compliments served to keep the peace between them; and they found a common cause, if not in the Empire, at least in a common detestation of

Mr. Baldwin. All their newspapers, representing an aggre-
gate circulation of at least six million, were turned on to
attack him, with the result that his leadership of the Conservative Party was enthusiastically endorsed at two Party
meetings, and each abusive reference [1] he made to Lord
Rothermere and Lord Beaverbrook was warmly applauded.

After so signal a victory, there was little more the Press
Lords could do. Lord Rothermere's retort to Mr. Baldwin's
charge that he represented an "insolent plutocracy," was
to point out that such an expression came ill from one whose
"father left him an immense fortune which, so far as may
be learned from his own speeches, has now almost disappeared"; and Mr. Baldwin contemptuously dismissed Lord
Rothermere's claim to a voice in shaping the Conservative
Party's policy on the ground that "in so far as he is anything, he is a professing Liberal." There the matter ended.
Lord Rothermere in accusing Mr. Baldwin of having lost
a fortune, Mr. Baldwin in accusing Lord Rothermere of
being a professed Liberal, had exhausted their armoury of
abuse. Each had said the worst thing he knew about the
other. Mr. Baldwin's leadership of the Conservative Party
was established; and United Empire and the Empire Crusade, like Mr. Baldwin's fortune, have almost disappeared,
a faint trace of the latter remaining in the figure of a crusader

[1] "The papers conducted by Lord Rothermere and Lord Beaverbrook,"
Mr. Baldwin said, "are not newspapers in the ordinary acceptance of the
term. They are engines of propaganda for the constantly changing policies, desires, personal wishes, personal likes and dislikes of two men. What
are their methods? Their methods are direct falsehood, misrepresentation,
half-truths, the alteration of the speaker's meaning by putting sentences
apart from the context, suppression and editorial criticism of speeches
which are not reported in the paper. What the proprietorship of these
papers is aiming at is power, but power without responsibility—the pre-
rogative of the harlot through the ages."

in armour which still appears on the front page of the *Daily Express*, and in occasional references, wrung from unwilling gossip-writers, to the fact that "if I were a rising young politician I should join the Empire Crusade Club. At last night's crowded and enthusiastic meeting, Mr. Brendan Bracken . . ."

Lord Rothermere, perhaps, found this enforced retreat from politics less painful than Lord Beaverbrook did. He had always the satisfaction of remembering, and occasionally reminding readers of the *Daily Mail*, that he had once been offered and had refused the throne of Hungary. If London was indifferent, there was always Budapest, where a plaque has already been set up in his honour. Lord Beaverbrook had no such solace. Not even Canada, his native land and a beneficiary under his Empire Free Trade project, had thought fit to immortalize him in a public monument; nor had he been given an opportunity to refuse any throne, except the Board of Trade. Though he continued to persuade himself that he had a hand in public affairs, in this much assisted by Low, whose cartoons subtly flattered while seeming to ridicule him by including him among leading politicians, he pined for a more solid political role than in the drawings of a cartoonist whom he employed, and in the columns of newspapers which he owned. When important events took place at home or abroad he worked himself into a state of great excitement, shouted through telephones at his editors and leader-writers, until it suddenly dawned on him that all this excitement, all this shouting, signified nothing; that he was not in a position to affect what was happening in any way.[1] Then his spirits drooped; self-pity and

[1] cf. the Astronomer in *Rasselas* whose madness took the form of believing that he "possessed the regulation of weather, and the distribution of

sometimes petulance overcame him, and his little court had
to find means of restoring his spirits.

If Lord Beaverbrook, alone or in combination with Lord
Rothermere, made a poor showing against Mr. Baldwin,
that master of political strategy, he was more successful
when the conflict was with his fellow Press magnates. In
the struggle for circulation which a popular newspaper
must constantly wage, attempts had been made to get readers by offers of gifts, free insurance, and other benefits. To
put an end to this ruinous competition, an agreement was
reached between the national dailies to renounce all free
gift schemes, but proved no more adequate as a safeguard
of peace in Fleet Street than agreements between the nations
to renounce aggression have as a safeguard of peace in
Europe. An unexpected offer by the *Daily Herald* to provide registered readers with a set of Dickens's novels, in
sixteen volumes and worth four guineas, for eleven shillings, led to the reopening of hostilities on a more lavish
scale than before.

When it was complained that the *Daily Herald* offer
amounted to a contravention of the agreement to renounce
free gift schemes, Mr. Elias (shortly after the abdication of
Edward VIII raised to the peerage as Baron Southwood)
contended that the claim that the set of Dickens's works was
worth four guineas was "just a figure of speech," and that a
profit could be made on the sixteen volumes at eleven shillings. Thereupon, the *Daily Mail, Daily Express* and *News-
Chronicle* offered their readers sets of Dickens's works for

---

the seasons. . . . The sun has listened to my dictates, and passed from
tropic to tropic by my direction; the clouds, at my call, have poured
their waters, and the Nile has overflowed at my command; I have re-
strained the rage of the dog-star, and mitigated the fervours of the crab."

ten shillings and disposed of 120,000, 124,000 and 65,000 sets respectively at an average loss of £1,200 per 10,000 sets. Now the pace quickened. Canvassers were dispatched to remote parts of the country with pens, pencils, cameras, tea-sets, knives and forks, boots, coats and pants [1] to distribute in return for an undertaking to become a registered reader of the newspaper they represented. The *Daily Express* alone distributed no fewer than 10,000 pairs of silk stockings; then, reverting to culture, offered twelve classical volumes for 10/-. *John Bull* retaliated with twelve classical volumes for 8/9, whereupon the *Daily Express* dropped its figure to 7/6, at that price distributing 115,000 sets at a loss of £12,000.

The next move was with the *Daily Herald*, which offered its readers an encyclopaedia also worth four guineas, for 11/-, thereby spurring on the *Daily Express* to come forward with its own encyclopaedia at an even lower rate. It has been estimated that this war cost the newspapers participating in it between £50,000 and £60,000 a week, the whole campaign, according to Sir Emsley Carr, costing more than £3,000,000; that £1,325,000 was spent on increasing the circulation of the *Daily Herald* from 400,000 to 1,750,000, or approximately £1 per reader, and £123,000 on increasing the circulation of the *Daily Express* by 300,-000 or approximately 8/3 per reader.[2] When at last hostil-

1 It was said that a whole Welsh family could be clothed from head to foot for the price of eight weeks' reading of the *Daily Express*.

2 In an exceptionally witty article by an Unregistered Reader, which was published in the *Evening Standard*, and from which most of the above facts are taken, it is pointed out that this exorbitant price for new readers would not have mattered so much if they had been freehold; but they were leasehold, and on a very short lease. To get his set of Dickens's works or pair of silk stockings, a new reader had only got to sign on for a few weeks; then, when these few weeks had passed, he was again in the market, and fell to the highest bidder.

ities came to an end, all the participants being financially exhausted, the *Daily Express* had won, and was able to claim a circulation of over 2,000,000, the largest daily paper circulation in the world.

Fleet Street still had not quite finished with Dickens, though some millions of his novels had reluctantly been distributed by the national dailies at a considerable loss to themselves. It was known that Dickens had left behind him a *Life of Christ*, which he had written for his children, and which was not to be published until they were all dead. The death of Sir Henry Dickens released this *Life of Christ* for publication, and the *Daily Mail* acquired it at a cost of £40,000, or more than £1 per word.

Posters appeared in the tube stations and other prominent places of Dickens's head looking out from a crown of thorns; but before publication had begun the *Daily Express* produced an effective counterblast in the shape of an article by Mr. Thomas Wright for the first time disclosing the details of Dickens's seduction late in life of an actress, Ellen Ternan, as related by her to Canon Benham when "she was tortured by remorse" at the thought of this irregular intimacy. Whether as a result of Mr. Wright's disclosures, or of the public's satiety with Dickens's works, or because the subject had only a limited appeal, the *Life of Christ*, both in its serial publication in the *Daily Mail* and in its later publication in book form, failed to arouse much interest; and it would be safe to assume that if there are any other unpublished Dickens manuscripts, whatever else may happen to them they will not be acquired by the *Daily Mail*, the *Daily Express*, the *News-Chronicle* or the *Daily Herald*.

CHAPTER III

Washing down bacon-and-egg with hot tea, an eye on the clock; rocking along five a side between Croydon East and London Bridge, or, packed together, between Holborn and Chancery Lane, people absorb the contents of newspapers. Headlines surprise them, large print gets into the blood stream, and little print lingers round the heart. The kingdoms of the earth are spread out before them, and all human activity.

Some country or town or mountain peak, formerly a name, perhaps not even that, is suddenly made familiar—a remote Greenland ice-cap, where Mr. Augustine Courtauld spent seven months alone and in darkness in a little snow hut, when removed thence stating that he found this solitary mode of life not uncongenial. Abyssinia, where the lately crowned Emperor conferred on his grateful subjects a bi-cameral legislature, and abolished slavery in his kingdom, announcing his virtuous decision to the Anti-Slavery Society in a letter which began: "The Conquering Lion of the Tribe of Judah, Haile Selassie the First, the Elect of God, King of the Kings of Ethiopia, may this reach the President of the Anti-Slavery Society"; Düsseldorf, where a murderer was active, at his trial coolly explaining that he had made a point of mingling with the crowd which collected round his victims when they were discovered, this greatly interesting the many psychiatrists who assembled to observe him, and who suggested that his brain might, like Lenin's, profitably be dissected after his execution; Manchuria, where a Japanese invasion began, resistance being offered by Chinese War Lords, among them Feng, a Christian one, whose soldiers sang hymns as they marched along, thereby pleasing missionaries: Chicago, where the Mayor, Big Bill Thompson, proclaimed his intention of "landing King George V one on the snout" if he attempted any interference with Chicago's affairs.

A name becomes momentarily prominent, a face picked out from among innumerable other faces, as when a searchlight plays on a crowd, catching one face, white, staring, and then passing on to another—Miss Amy Johnson, who flew solo from England to Australia in twenty days, tumultuously welcomed on her return, a song made about her and a triumphal procession organized along the Strand and Fleet Street, she standing up in a car and all cheering as she passed, the *Daily Mail* presenting her with £10,000, and in its columns greatly extolling her as a manifestation of the unconquerable spirit of Youth; Lord Kylsant charged with "drawing up and circulating a prospectus, the contents of which he knew to be false in an important particular," and sentenced to a year's imprisonment in the second division, after six months released, broken in health, and soon to die; Texas Guinan refused permission to land at Marseilles when she arrived there with a "party of lovely kids," even then some of the lovely kids unaccountably missing when she started on her return journey; the Bishop of Birmingham in dispute with some of his High Church clergy who refused to abandon practices which he contemptuously dismissed as magic; Miss Millie Orpen, a typist who, acting as a common informer under the Sunday Observances Act of 1781, was awarded £5,000, this sum being later remitted and by her forgone; Professor Piccard who ascended ten miles into the stratosphere, and Zaro Agha who claimed to be 150 years old, and a Mrs. Stocks who moved a resolution at a meeting of the National Society for Equal Citizenship protesting against the fashion of longer skirts, finding in this fashion a dangerous reversal to male ascendancy.

Place-names become momentarily familiar, different moods are awakened—desire, fear, hatred, grief, cupidity; like the conductor of an orchestra with his baton stirring up sound and stilling it, calling forth a little sentimental tune or a roar of passionate music. All that happens is digested, each morsel broken down by the requisite juices; what is nourishing absorbed into the blood stream, and waste products discharged. Each event has its corresponding emotion as each note on an organ keyboard has its corresponding sound; and the play of these emotions, between gulps of food and drink and puffs of tobacco smoke, constitutes public opinion.

The R101 glided away, the admiration of all, to fly to Karachi, the Air Minister, Lord Thomson, aboard, he having expedited the flight, perhaps dangerously, in his eagerness to make a dramatic appearance in India, where he hoped soon to be installed as Viceroy. Admiration turned to grief when it was learned on an October Sunday morning that near Paris the airship had crashed in flames, all the passengers and crew except three, dead. There were protracted obsequies, a long procession of flag-covered coffins transported from France to Westminster Abbey; an immense output of verbose grief from pens which specialized in such themes, sob brothers and sisters, as well as more ponderous practitioners. MacDonald appeared, haggard and drawn, at a Labour Party Conference at Llandudno, the last he was to attend, and expressed his sense of personal and public loss. Perhaps the disaster was emotionally over-capitalized; look after the tears and the pennies will look after themselves. A fund which was started to provide for the families of its victims was poorly subscribed, and a plan to set up a fitting monument to commemorate them, met with a meagre response.

A sweepstake, organized in Dublin for the benefit of Irish hospitals, proved popular, its prize-fund reaching £1,181,815. The tickets were shaken up in a large drum, and extracted by young women dressed as guardsmen; and all English newspapers prominently announced the list of winners, some with much personal detail. Outside the café of Emilio Scala, who won the first prize, a little crowd collected, looking up reverently at its shuttered windows; and the suggestion was made that a similar sweepstake organized in England would relieve the hospitals of increasing financial strain. Opposing this suggestion, Sir Reginald Poole wrote: "I do not suppose that the poor fail altogether to realize that it is largely the money of the well-to-do which really enables the hospitals to exist, or that the poor are ungrateful. This lottery scheme would certainly put an end to any such sentiment of gratitude, for after all there would be no question of gratitude as the well-to-do would have no reason to subscribe." Whether Sir Reginald Poole's or some other argument proved convincing, the suggestion was dropped.

The film version of *All Quiet on the Western Front* was banned in Berlin and Vienna after causing disturbances there; and a production of *Coriolanus* at the Comédie Française had to be suspended owing to the delight and execra-

tion aroused in different sections of the audience by Coriolanus's contemptuous references to elections and the elected.
A proposal on the part of Germany and Austria to join
themselves together in a Customs' Union was submitted to
the League Assembly, which passed it on to the International Court at the Hague. There, a decision that such a
Union was illegal was belatedly reached, the voting being
generally supposed to have been based on political rather
than judicial considerations.[1]

The results of a census taken in April, 1930, were published, showing that the population of England and Wales
was slightly under 40,000,000, that the birth-rate had enormously fallen,[2] and that London was steadily growing, soon
to have 9,000,000 inhabitants, the largest number of human
beings so far collected together in one place; at the same
time a builder announcing that in his experience it was
garages, not nurseries, which were in demand.

Off Ushant, Italian divers persistently jumped into the
sea, some losing their lives, to recover gold from a liner,
S.S. Egypt, which had foundered there in 1922, causing a
few to wonder whether this hardihood was worth while to
provide more ingots to lie in bank vaults in London, Paris
and New York. The divers concerned appeared to have no
such doubts, and persisted, in time recovering the gold and
disposing of it. Trotsky's house at Prinkipo was burnt down,
many of his papers being lost; but this misfortune failed to
induce the Home Secretary, Mr. Clynes, to reconsider his
refusal to allow Trotsky to come to England. Pictures began

[1] The countries to which the judges who voted against the legality of
the Union belonged were: France, Poland, Spain, Italy, Roumania, Col-
ombia, Salvador and Cuba, and for: Japan, U.S.A., England, Germany,
Holland, Belgium and China.
[2] To 16.3 per thousand, the lowest recorded, and half the 1871 figure.

to be telegraphed, and a tick was found by a purchaser in a pound of butter, sent by him to the Natural History Museum, and there pronounced of a kind "entirely unknown in Europe, and clearly of Asiatic origin," questions being asked in Parliament about the matter and indignant letters appearing in the Press.

Dr. Brüning and Herr Curtius were entertained at Chequers without any noticeable result; and a large meeting was held in the Albert Hall preparatory to the opening of the Disarmament Conference, and addressed by MacDonald, Mr. Baldwin and Mr. Lloyd George. "We are going to Geneva," MacDonald said, "determined by persuasion, by arguments, by appeals to what has been written, appeals to measures already taken, appeals to history, appeals to common sense, to get the nations of the world to join in and reduce this enormous, disgraceful burden of armaments, which we are now bearing from one end of the world to the other," [1] and was much applauded.

Flood-lighting in honour of the International Illumination Congress attracted many into the streets to stare up without visible emotion at a radiant Tower of London, St. Paul's Cathedral and Buckingham Palace. A Cambridge undergraduate who had tied himself up and gagged himself so securely that he was found dead, created much interest; the unveiling of a memorial to Lord Curzon in Carlton House Terrace, less. Those opulent houses looking down on to St. James's Park might have been regarded as in themselves adequately commemorating him, the one in which he lived and, according to Mr. Harold Nicolson, diverted

[1] MacDonald's last act as Premier was to initial a White Paper stating the case for British rearmament. This White Paper appeared with his initials, J.R.M., at the end, it was said by an error; if so, perhaps a Freudian one.

himself by listening to the servants talking on the house
telephone, in due course becoming the premises of the
Savage Club, whose Bohemian revelry was somewhat
abashed under high, embossed ceilings.

Mr. Jacob Epstein's statue Genesis, a heavy featured
woman in an advanced stage of pregnancy, after being on
show in London and reproduced in most newspapers, was
taken to the chief provincial towns, and there seen at a
shilling a time, long queues forming, and some, though they
had waited and paid, when they came into the presence,
averting their gaze. French deputies were provided with a
device whereby they might vote by pressing one of three
buttons without leaving their places, this, however, not having any noticeable effect on the stability of the Governments
they formed. A Dutchman created more amusement than
moral indignation by persuading a prominent firm of London printers to provide him with an issue of Portuguese currency, as well as trunks in which to take it away; and Rouse,
an amorous commercial traveller with a high-pitched voice
who lived in Barnet, was convicted of having set fire to his
small saloon car when a tramp to whom he had given a lift
was in it, in the hope that this tramp's charred remains
would be mistaken for his, and the proceeds of a life insurance policy he had taken out be available to enable him
to begin again as someone else. The tramp's identity was
never discovered, a large number of derelict persons of no
fixed abode and with no family connections being rounded
up, any one of whom might have been incinerated without
his disappearance causing any concern, or even arousing
curiosity. Newspapers competed for an exclusive statement
from Rouse's widow of her opinion regarding her husband's
guilt or innocence, one, the *News of the World*, reproduc-

ing what purported to be a facsimile letter from her to the
effect that Rouse had told her he was guilty.

Sir Oswald Mosley carried his revolt further by founding
the New Party, whose policy mainly aimed at reforming
constitutional procedure, and a weekly, *Action*, first edited
by Mr. Harold Nicolson, later Member of Parliament for
Leicester in the National Labour interest; the Pope broadcast for the first time, the Holy Father's voice being heard
in all parts of the world; Mr. Eugene O'Neill excelled himself by producing a play, *Strange Interlude*, whose performance lasted five hours without one laugh; and the *New
Statesman*, a Socialist weekly, originally Fabian, amal-
gamated, first with the Liberal *Nation*, then with the *Week-
End Review*, whose editor, Mr. Gerald Barry, had formerly
been editor of the *Saturday Review*, but had fallen out with
its then proprietor, Lord Beaverbrook, on a question of
policy, and started the *Week-End Review* by way of protest. This confused situation in due course sorted itself
out. Under the editorship of Mr. Kingsley Martin, the
New Statesman and affiliated periodicals became the chief
organ of Left-Wing intellectuals; [1] Mr. Gerald Barry became editor of the *News-Chronicle*, sole relic of Liberal
daily journalism; and the *Saturday Review* fell into the
hands of Lady Houston, appearing until her death in 1937
with a Union Jack and a Red Flag and the legend "Under
Which Flag?" on the front cover, a cure for colds devised

[1] Not always, however, satisfying their somewhat exacting demands, "But
for Guidance in the task of . . . casting off the skin of nineteenth-century
coal-and-gas ideology and substituting an up-to-date hydro-electric-bio-
logical mental wardrobe," a correspondent wrote plaintively at the beginning of 1938—"for this we mostly look in vain. Yet if the *New Statesman and Nation* will not supply this urgent need, where else are we to
look for help?"

by Lady Houston herself on the back cover, and in between much patriotic matter.

Cross-word puzzles became daily instead of weekly features in most newspapers; air mails to all parts of the world were instituted, and the activities and internecine feuds of American gangsters were followed with interest, Al Capone, Jack Diamond and others becoming better known than most politicians, new words and expressions like "racket" "bumped off," "taken for a ride," coming into common usage, and gangster plays, novels and films proving increasingly popular; for instance, *On The Spot*, a play believed to be based on the great Al Capone himself, which had a long run and provided Mr. Charles Laughton with the first of many successful and lucrative gangster parts. This literature, whose theme was violence and crime, whose style reproduced the rattle of machine-guns, or at any rate of typewriters, and in which there was only action and appetite, owed its popularity to the relief it afforded from the boredom and desolation of mechanized life. It represented the poetry or mysticism of mass-production, the craving for violence and bloodshed, set up by days spent in exhausting but monotonous activity; unnecessary when, as in the U.S.S.R. and Germany, the same craving is catered for by State organized and publicized terrorism. Its leading purveyor was Edgar Wallace, a genial, rather pathetic figure,[1] frenziedly pouring out words into a dictaphone, frenziedly making and getting rid of money, appearing at Blackpool in a yellow Rolls Royce as a Liberal candidate in the 1931 General Election, and dying exhausted and in debt a year later, having written in all 150 novels, eighteen plays,

[1] See *Edgar Wallace* by Margaret Lane.

and innumerable short stories and newspaper articles; of words, many millions.

II

It was the twilight of post-War enlightenment, almost the end of Mr. High-Mind. Perhaps the verse in the National Anthem about frustrating knavish tricks was "un-Christian, indecent, disgraceful," and ought to be dropped; perhaps even the Elgin Marbles ought to be returned to Greece whence they had been taken. Politicians with military rank mostly preferred to be plain Mr.; Eurasians were Anglo-Indians, boarding-houses guest-houses, garages service-stations, and Mr. John Masefield, not Kipling, was made Poet Laureate when Robert Bridges died. René Clair's films, *Sous les Toits de Paris*, *Le Million*, sentimentally satirical, drew large and appreciative audiences, and the membership of the League of Nations Union went on increasing.

The question of design in industry was investigated, birth-control clinics were opened, and psychoanalysts multiplied. A compassionate Minister for Justice in the Spanish Republican Government, Victoria Kent, decided that prisoners serving long sentences should be allowed to spend allotted days each month with their wives, or, if bachelors or widowers, permitted to absent themselves from prison occasionally on parole; and Mr. Duff Cooper got into trouble with the *Daily Mail* by delivering in Berlin a lecture entitled, "An Apology for the British Empire." What were we coming to, Lord Rothermere asked his readers, when our young men apologized in foreign countries for having an Empire, and refused to be mollified when the precedent of Sir Philip Sidney's *Apologie for Poesie* was pleaded. For the first time a state subsidy for opera was granted, and a performance of Wilde's *Salomé* allowed, though not much appreciated.

One after the other, the best-known figures in the War were dying, each given his long obituary and memorial service, perhaps also made the subject of a memoir, and then forgotten; year by year the two-minutes' silence on Armistice Day was becoming more formal, and the unveiling of new War memorials rarer. Fewer and fewer, as buses passed the Cenotaph, raised their hats; gradually, the Great War [1] became the War, then, more ominously the last war. The 1917 Club, a dingy establishment in Gerrard Street founded to commemorate the Russian Revolution, and much frequented at one time by MacDonald, went into liquidation. It also belonged to the War and its aftermath, and as the War was swallowed up in the past, so was it swallowed up and could no more exist, its members growing old, their hopes becoming unsubstantial, and love, free or confined, beyond their capacity.

A controversy on the compatibility of Christianity and Socialism led to Lord Rosebery's momentary emergence from retirement to remark that the two were clearly in direct opposition, Christ's teaching being, "What is mine is thine," and the teaching of Socialism, "What is thine is mine." Others took a less simplified view, some, like the Rev. Conrad Noel and the Dean of Canterbury, boldly claiming that Christ was a revolutionary Socialist; while Mr. Middleton Murry, proposing to take Anglical Orders, hopefully envisaged a synthesis of Marxism and Christianity under the auspices of the Church of England.[2] St. Paul

[1] Even the Boer War was known in its day as "Great." Conan Doyle called his book on it *The Great Boer War*.
[2] In *The Defence of Democracy*.

and St. Marx, he argued, were labourers in the same vine-
yard; both looked forward to a millennium, the one after
death and the other after the Proletariat's final triumph,
and it required only a trifling adjustment to reconcile their
two visions. Such attempts to vest Socialism with the moral
authority of Christianity were matched by attempts to vest
Capitalism with the moral authority of Socialism. Was not
taxation a convenient form of the confiscation Socialists
demanded? The wealthy pleaded, and tendered to apologize
for their possessions, unless they were very large. "The
Christian Church . . . has never taken the rigid view that
the poor are saved and the rich lost as such," the writer of
the weekly religious article in the *Times* mildly contended.
The comfortable conviction that wealth was the reward of
virtue, was sustained with difficulty, or not at all. Wealth
was a lottery-prize awarded to the quick-witted and the
fortunate. Its possessors were endowed with glamour, but
not sanctity. Photographs of the aged John D. Rockefeller
until his death appeared in newspapers each year on his
birthday, along with an account of the elaborate and expensive precautions taken to keep him alive: toothless,
withered, a gilded skull, he symbolized the power of money,
something to be feared, envied, fawned upon, rather than
venerated. Similarly, the matrimonial and other adventures
of Miss Barbara Hutton, the Woolworth heiress, were
eagerly followed, her photograph often reproduced, and
her way of life often described; but the curiosity which pursued her was relentless and loveless. She was a prodigy.
Wealth's glow, once seemingly benign and virtuous, had
become phosphorescent; the appetite for money unrestrained, a raging lust. In his Encyclical *Caritate Christi
Compulsi*, Pope Pius XI diagnosed the cause of the world's

confusion as "that lust of earthly goods which the Pagan poet branded with the name of 'the accursed hunger for gold,' and which St. Paul does not hesitate to call the root of all evil," and in the United States Senator Hiram Johnson, summing up the results of an inquiry into American loans, spoke of "this sordid tale, at once grotesque and tragic . . . due to the money madness of our people, the greed and even worse of our international bankers." An attempted synthesis of Christianity and Socialism, and a readiness on the part of the wealthy to apologize for their wealth, might obscure this "accursed hunger for gold," but could not restrain it, or prevent its ravages.

An occasion for righteous indignation in which all Governments could participate since the interests of none were involved, was provided by the publication of a report by a Commission appointed by the League of Nations to inquire into conditions in Liberia. This Report, according to the *Times,* "exposed a maladministration so cruel and so corrupt, and an exploitation of native workers by their Negro masters so shameless, that the civilized world will not be satisfied until effective measures have been taken to substitute a system of justice for a régime of brute force and to establish decent conditions of labour." Other newspapers wrote in the same strain. It was one of the few occasions on which the Press and the League Assembly were unanimous, though whether their unanimity appreciably affected conditions in Liberia, is doubtful.

III

Something vastly more important than conditions in Liberia required, and soon held, the civilized world's attention. The Economic Blizzard had continued blowing with unabated intensity, unemployment figures mounting until three million was approached, the Unemployment Insurance Fund falling into arrears, and increased borrowing powers having to be obtained from Parliament to keep it solvent. Abroad, Austria and Germany were rapidly approaching a condition of bankruptcy, and Australian finances were so strained that a default seemed ominously probable. To meet reparations payments, Germany had had to raise long-term loans; then, to meet the interest charges on these loans, to raise more short-term ones at a higher rate of interest, and so on.[1] Money had been cheerfully forthcoming, the interest tempting. Now the terrifying prospect arose of the whole edifice crashing, long-term, short-term, and shorter-term loans, all forever lost. A new expression became current—"Frozen Credits"; money congealed and immovable, like a duck-pond after a frost. The whole monetary system was showing unmistakable signs of distress, and might at any moment collapse. Money was sick, and its many friends hurried to its bedside to revive it.

Successive German Governments wrestled with their difficulties, and the National-Socialist vote increased, some, particularly in France, by no means displeased, assuming that a bankrupt Germany would be able to launch no more pocket battleships, nor again become formidable; the *Times*, more in sorrow than in anger, remarking that "a Germany in which it seemed likely that either Communists or National-Socialists might gain the upper hand over the moderate and constitutional parties would find it hard to persuade foreign investors to maintain, to say nothing of extending,

[1] German indebtedness abroad on June 30, 1931, amounted to about 27 milliard marks, 15 milliard long-term loans, and 12 milliard short-term loans.

the credits which are necessary for her financial stability."
Foreign investors extracted what comfort they might from
this assurance that it was for them to maintain or not maintain credits, to extend or not extend them, as they pleased,
but still trembled for their money. It was a money crisis
which had arisen; here money becoming frozen, there moving restlessly from place to place, like a dog trying to settle
to rest but finding each chosen place unsatisfactory and
looking round for another.

Such crises have little meaning to the ordinary person,
with no credits to freeze or keep liquefied, no tendency to
flee from the pound or the franc; rather the reverse. Money,
to him, is coins and pieces of paper laboriously acquired,
a little hoard laboriously accumulated to provide for emer-
gencies, and to keep him from being a burden on others
when he is old and can earn no more, perhaps also to ensure
a respectable funeral; a polished coffin to lie in, a hearse
to carry him to the burial ground, and a tombstone announcing that he once was alive. On or off the Gold
Standard is much the same to him; balanced or unbalanced
budgets he scarcely notices, only perhaps remembering the
surprising appearance of million-mark notes on the streets
of London for sale at a penny each.

To the few who were directly affected, the crisis was
extremely serious. Money to them is something much more
than a means of life and respectable burial; coins soon worn
smooth in being passed from hand to hand, pieces of paper
soon stale and creased. It is power. They rely on it to save
them from having to shed their blood in defence of what
blood was shed to gain; [1] to sustain their authority, and en-

---

[1] In 1939, Mr. Neville Chamberlain assured an audience that "German
statesmen, if weighing the pros and cons of a conflict with England,

sure obedience without the necessity of being formidable
and comfort without the necessity of violent seizure.
Frozen credits to them are a doom, and the Gold Standard
is a prop which comforts them.

The monetary system had emerged from the War badly
damaged then had been laboriously repaired—Mr. Lloyd
George got rid of, the Gold Standard re-established, the
claims for reparations made in the ebullience of victory
reduced to manageable proportions by, first the Dawes,
and then the Young Plan, the American Debt funded. It
seemed as though the world was settling down to its old
comfortable ways again, money being money, a foreign
investment a foreign investment, with nothing more formidable to contend with than the reincarnation of the
Liberal Party as the Labour Party, of Morley and Campbell-
Bannerman as Henderson and MacDonald. Appearances
were deceptive. What was thought to have been repaired
seemed now to be more decrepit than ever; and if Mac-
Donald more than lived up to the role which had been
assigned to him, a growing awareness of the absurdity of
over-production existing side by side with want was giving
rise to more ominous cries than for Peace, Retrenchment
and Reform.

What were the Government to do? They had insisted
on the advantage of no longer treating Germany as a

---

would reflect upon our immense financial strength which might well
prove decisive," this being interpreted by an "eminent economist" for the
benefit of readers of the *Daily Sketch* as signifying: "Our financial resources are far greater than those of Germany, and a rich country MUST
always prove victorious in a protracted struggle with a poor one." In the
same way, the rich merchants of Mecca were confident that they had
nothing to fear from Mohammed because he had no money, and a bankrupt France after the Revolution was confidently expected to prove an
easy conquest.

defeated enemy, but now money, not benevolence, was wanted; they had inveighed against Capitalism, and now found themselves its legatees, like prohibitionists unexpectedly made responsible for the management of a derelict brewery. Either they had to salvage what they had condemned as cruel and unworkable, or to await a catastrophe which they did not understand and for which they had no stomach. Neither course appealed to them. They just did nothing at all, only hoped.

Long acrimonious debates took place in Parliament on the merits and demerits of the Alternative Vote and university representation, and each session left behind its trail of Commissions of Enquiry. Many there were of these—on capital punishment, on licensing laws, on whatever might be expected to arouse controversy other than on party lines. They accumulated like dirty plates and dishes in a lazy household; in due course producing their reports, mostly bulky, which were conscientiously noticed when published, and then referred to rarely. Sunday Observances received consideration, and mixed bathing in the Serpentine; and not very convincing attempts were made to repeal the Blasphemy Laws and to legalize the voluntary sterilization of mental defectives. A Member of Parliament, Mr. John Beckett, later to become editor of an organ of the British Union of Fascists, by way of protest seized the mace and walked away with it; another Member refused to obey the Speaker's ruling and was ejected by the Sergeant-at-Arms, five fellow Members clinging to him.

There were resignations—Sir Charles Trevelyan, Lord Arnold, Mr. W. J. Brown, who gave as his reason for resigning from the Labour Party that "continued membership of it had become incompatible with any kind of intellectual integrity"; deaths, among others Mr. Vernon Hartshorn's; ominous by-elections all showing a heavy fall in the Labour Party vote. Snowden, his own followers silent, his opponents applauding, delivered a solemn warning in the House of Commons: "I say with all the seriousness I can command, that the national position is so grave that drastic and disagreeable measures will have to be taken if budgetary equilibrium is to be maintained." A Friends of Economy Movement was launched under the direction of Lord Grey, among its supporters Mr. Neville Chamberlain, who proclaimed that the "first duty must be to reduce national expenditure," little anticipating then that in a few years' time he would be delighting a Birmingham audience with an announcement that it was proposed to spend £1,000,000,000 on armaments in the course of the years 1938-40. The Movement's main forum was the correspondence columns of the *Times*. There day by day appeared letters complaining that money was being squandered and wealth taxed out of existence; among them one from Sir Reginald Bacon which argued that financial deterioration began in 1894, when Sir William Harcourt introduced increased death duties, which "up to date have been responsible for destroying at least £2,000,000,000 of the capital of the country by taking that sum from the investing and employer section of the community." Leaving budgets unbalanced was called "sinning against the light"; and attention was drawn to the fine example of Australia, where in spite of Mr. Lang, the turbulent Prime Minister of New South Wales, the virtuous counsels of Sir Otto Niemeyer had been followed, dividends on Government stock all paid, and disaster averted.

Momentary exaltation was caused by President Hoover's

proposal for a year's moratorium on war-debts, but the
relief thus afforded proved short-lived. The French Government haggled over the terms of the moratorium, still convinced that a bankrupt Germany would be weak and
defenceless; and a conference in London was unable to
reach any conclusion, and dispersed without any more tan-
gible result than a Standstill Agreement.

Standing still was the one impossibility. Important European banks closed their doors, and rumours were current
that money was being withdrawn from London in alarming
quantities; frightened away, it was contended, by the growing insolvency of the Unemployment Insurance Fund. After
Snowden's solemnly delivered warning about the grave condition of the national finances, some action had been called
for, and, inevitably, yet another Commission of Enquiry
had been set up, with, for chairman, a civil servant, Sir
George May. The publication on July 31, 1931, of the Report of this Commission, anticipating a Budget deficit of
£120,000,000 the following spring, and recommending
economies totalling £96,578,000, including a twenty per
cent cut in unemployment pay, accelerated the withdrawal
of money from London. The Bank of England borrowed
from France and the United States to meet this drain on its
resources; soon exhausted what had been borrowed, and
asked for more. More was not forthcoming. The Government were faced with an empty till.

It was on a warm August evening that the Cabinet met
at 10 Downing Street, after their deliberations adjourning
to the garden, there meditatively sitting while darkness came
on, a little bewildered group, one woman among them, Miss
Margaret Bondfield. Perhaps the situation which had arisen
was sufficiently complicated, yet to them at that moment

it seemed simple enough—money was required and they were expected to find it. They had advanced, not very formidably, against the Kingdom of Mammon, and now found themselves its forlorn garrison. Bankers had been the particular object of their scorn, and now they waited to hear whether bankers would help them; heard they would not. What economies they agreed to, or refused to agree to; whether or not they were deliberately deceived, is not now of much importance. They sat on forlornly in their garden, and then dispersed to assemble no more, with them expiring the last flicker of nineteenth-century Liberalism; little more henceforth to be heard of Proportional Representation, taxation of land values, free trade, even; progress without tears over and done with for ever.

The following day the formation of a National Government was announced with MacDonald as Premier. "Thank God For Him" Mr. Garvin headed his next article, and this refrain was taken up, echoing and re-echoing. Mr. Clifford Allen traced a likeness between MacDonald and Lenin, soon afterwards becoming Lord Allen of Hurtwood; a lady wrote, with no apparent relevance, that "there was no greater sacrifice than love"; and Mr. Noel Coward was ready with *Cavalcade*. Nothing could have been more suitable; it played to large and enthusiastic audiences, the *Daily Mail* serialized it, royalties came rolling in. The recent past was recalled, its most dramatic episodes—the Boer War, Mafeking, the sinking of the *Titanic*, the War, Armistice Day; once popular songs, still remembered, were sung, and past fashions portrayed. The days that are no more!—tears, manly and womanly, flowed in the stalls, and the pit and gallery wept like anything to see such quantities of sentiment. At the end, a glass of champagne was lifted, white dress-shirt gleaming, bare arms and back fleshly, hearts broken but bank-balances intact; and a toast was drunk to England's recovered greatness, it almost seemed to MacDonald. He had saved the country. Money was saved, England was saved—or so it seemed at that time. The audience rose spontaneously to their feet, the National Anthem was played and sung with deep emotion. God save our gracious Pound, Long live our noble Pound, God save the Pound.

Both MacDonald and Mr. Coward had reached the climax of their careers. By routes how different, they had arrived at the same point, the one purveying sentimental idealism, the other sentimental cynicism, sweetly bitter and bitter sweet, my working-class friends and my idling-class friends, Mr. High-Mind and Mr. Low-Mind stood hand in hand, to England's greater glory. This was their supreme moment, higher than this they were not to go.

Great was it at that time to be alive, so most newspapers insisted, and their readers perhaps felt. England had shaken off lethargy and prevarication, and Englishmen shown, as of old, their hearts of oak by balancing their budget and reducing unemployment benefit. The Armada and other triumphant episodes were mentioned as comparable with the National Government's valiant defeat and utter routing of unsound finance; and it was remarked, of the opening of the new Shakespeare Memorial Theatre, that the ceremony came aptly at a moment when "England had awakened anew to a consciousness of her own worth and a confidence in her own future"—this fortress built by nature for herself against budget deficits, and currency depreciation.

Satisfaction was almost universal, MacDonald had acted, Mr. Coward had spoken, and the Archbishop of Canterbury

offered thanks. A great victory had been won, and was enthusiastically celebrated. Later, when more serious dangers
than even budgetary disequilibrium threatened; when more
than the reluctance of foreign bankers to provide loans
had to be overcome, more than the Gold Standard to be
defended, enthusiasm was not so easily forthcoming. The
country again required to be saved; but this time blood, not
economy in public expenditure, was necessary; national determination, not a National Government. A sick man who
gets relief from a drug is the more reluctant to face the
operating table; if he can make himself whole with a pill,
why endure the surgeon's knife? If MacDonald had saved
the country by joining forces with Mr. Baldwin and Sir
Herbert Samuel and balancing the budget, if that was a
glorious victory fit to be celebrated, England's awakening,
why procure another victory, dearly bought with life and
limb and sorrowful partings?

IV

Both MacDonald and Mr. Baldwin were insistent that
the National Government was a temporary expedient.
"Conservatives have consented to take part in the National
Government for a limited period," Mr. Baldwin said, "but
there is no question of a permanent coalition." The Liberals
alone kept quiet, like uninvited guests at a reception effac-
ing themselves and taking up their station near the buffet.
With the exception of the *Daily Herald* and the *Manchester
Guardian*, the Government had the enthusiastic approval
of the whole Press, though the *Morning Post* relieved its
feelings by, for a few weeks, referring to MacDonald as
"titular" Premier.

MacDonald himself showed certain symptoms of uneasiness. The very completeness of his victory abashed him a little. His new admirers were so enthusiastic, and his old ones, with a very few exceptions, so uniformly hostile. It was all very well for the *Times* to write that he had "gained the reward of those who dare greatly and win through"; but what precisely was his reward to be when he came to claim it?

To reassure himself, he visited Seaham Harbour, a scattered and desolate mining constituency which had returned him at the last general election with a majority of nearly 30,000.[1] "Do not," he had written to Mr. William Coxon, secretary of the divisional Labour Party, "believe what is being published in the papers, Labour or other." It was wise advice, then as always; but now it was incumbent on him to tell them what they were to believe. The audience which listened to him seemed more bewildered than excited. When he pleaded with them—"My working-class friends——" the response was slight. He searched about his mind for something that would touch them; at last found what he wanted. If he had not formed a National Govern-

[1] MacDonald inherited this constituency from Sidney Webb, who had represented it in Parliament before he became Lord Passfield. When he handed it over to MacDonald, he mentioned that most of the collieries there were owned by Lord Londonderry, whose agents were far from popular among Labour voters. Any personal relations between MacDonald and the Londonderry family would, therefore, be a disadvantage as far as his candidature was concerned. This, MacDonald said, was awkward, as he was already "on Christian name terms" with them. In the National Government, Lord Londonderry succeeded Mr. Lansbury at the Office of Works, later becoming Air Minister. Lady Londonderry has described in her volume of memoirs, *Retrospect*, how on one occasion MacDonald rang her up at Londonderry House and asked if he might look in for coffee on his way to the Palace. "When he arrived," she writes, "he was arrayed as an Elder Brother of Trinity House in full dress. This was the first occasion he had worn it, and he had come especially to show it off."

ment, money would have depreciated in value; a shilling worth perhaps a penny, perhaps even less, no more purchasing a pound of butter but only, say, a quarter of margarine. His working-class friends saw the point of that: from such a calamity he had delivered them. Henceforth, to drive home the argument, he carried about a pocketful of inflated German marks, which he constantly produced and flourished at audiences, and even argumentative acquaintances.

When the new Government met the House of Commons, Henderson was leader of the Opposition, and behind him were ranged Labour Members, a dozen or so only having attached themselves to MacDonald, to be known hereafter as National Labour, but not to signify much politically. Debates tended to resolve themselves into a series of bitter exchanges between MacDonald, Snowden and Mr. Thomas, and their former ministerial colleagues, in the course of which the rule that Cabinet proceedings should never be divulged was frequently contravened.

It is one of the peculiarities of parliamentary procedure that, though it is intended to ensure that issues shall be clarified and all information of public importance be made available, its effect is usually to spread confusion and increase obscurity. Each individual speaker is concerned to assert his own consistency and virtue, with the result that their utterances tend to cancel out, leaving no remainder. Everyone concerned in the events which led to the formation of the National Government had his say, in some cases several times over. Vehement accusations and counter accusations were made. Henderson going so far as to ask to be put on oath. Yet all these speeches, angry interpellations, assertions and denials, do not reveal whether a condition of

further borrowing from France and the United States was
some reduction in unemployment benefit with a view to
making the Unemployment Insurance Fund solvent. This
was the point round which controversy raged most furiously. The nearest it came to being elucidated was when
MacDonald, in answer to a supplementary question, stated
that "the handling of the unemployment cuts was necessitated by special conditions of borrowing, and they must
remain." This statement, however, was subsequently repudiated.

There is nothing which gives the well-to-do greater satisfaction than to be asked to economize for the good of their
country. The money saved gratifies their avarice; the fact
that in saving they are performing a public service, adds a
glow of self-righteousness. Even when the expenditure concerned is not their own but the State's, they are still doubly
pleased, feeling at once more virtuous and more secure. The
new Government's appeals for national self-sacrifice did
not, therefore, pass unheeded. A lead was given by the
King, who asked that his Civil List of £470,000 should be
reduced by £50,000. Other members of the Royal Family
followed suit, the Prince of Wales presenting the Exchequer
with £10,000 from the income of £65,000 he received
from the Duchy of Cornwall. Employers contracted their
expenditure, and provided their employees with an opportunity to accept a voluntary reduction in their salaries,
usually enforcing the reduction when this opportunity
was neglected. Even, the Prime Minister proudly announced, certain of the unemployed had dispatched small
postal-orders to him as a contribution towards reducing the
Budget deficit, and as an expression of their approval of his
leadership. In token of his admiration for these mostly vi-

carious sacrifices, an American, Mr. Edward Harkness, provided £2,000,000 to be spent "for the benefit of Great Britain." The fund, known as the Pilgrim Trust, was administered by a committee consisting of, among others, Mr. Baldwin, Mr. John Buchan and Sir Josiah Stamp. One of its early benefactions was the alteration and equipment of the Muniment Room in Westminster Abbey, and the endowment of an Archivist.

Snowden's supplementary Budget instituted economies totaling £70,000,000. All official salaries were cut by ten per cent, and a saving of £25,000,000 was effected on unemployment pay. Teachers in State schools complained that the cut in their salaries contravened the Burnham Award, and judges that their remuneration was not subject to a parliamentary vote; but the unemployed, according to MacDonald, were delighted. The discontent of teachers could safely be ignored, and attention to judges' grievances postponed. A mutiny in the Atlantic Fleet, then exercising from Invergordon, was a more serious matter, and required immediate attention.

The trouble was due to resentment at the inequality of the reductions in pay which had been ordered.[1] For the first time since the Mutiny at the Nore in 1797, ships' companies in the British Navy refused to obey orders and put to sea. A protest meeting was held ashore, an officer who put in an appearance being propelled towards the door and through it into the street outside, without any technical infringement of the King's Regulations; and when the men returned to their ships they adopted Gandhi's tactics of non-

---

[1] A vice-admiral's pay of £5 10s. 0d. a day was to be reduced by 10/-; a lieutenant's of £1 7s. 0d. a day by 1/-, and an able-bodied seaman's of 5/- a day by 1/-.

violent non-co-operation. Bursts of cheering broke out from time to time, passing as though by arrangement from ship to ship, and occasionally the "Red Flag" was sung, its rendering greatly facilitated by the fortunate coincidence that a well-known hymn has been set to the same tune. The First Lord of the Admiralty, Sir Austen Chamberlain, hurried to Invergordon to conduct a personal investigation there; and it was announced that, as far as the Navy was concerned, pay cuts were suspended. Later, they were reintroduced in a greatly modified form without any objections being raised.

Abroad, the Invergordon Mutiny was regarded as the beginning of the break-up of the British Empire.[1] Britannia, it was felt, was clearly not in a position to go on ruling the waves, and therefore London was no longer a safe place to deposit money. The flight from the pound which had been slowed down by the formation of the National Government, gained renewed impetus; hearts reassured by the cut in unemployment pay and other economies, were made anxious again by insubordination in the Navy. Once more Mr. Montagu Norman had to announce an empty till, and the refusal of French and American bankers to replenish it. Less than a month after MacDonald had formed the National Government, there was a recurrence of the same situation which had led him to break with his old associates and find new ones among former opponents. This time he could not save the country. He had saved it already. His previous performance was not capable of repetition. On August 25

[1] Especially in the U.S.S.R. The course of the Russian Revolution has now been sanctified there as the pattern of all true revolutions; and as a mutiny in the Black Sea Fleet heralded Lenin's assumption of power, so it was assumed that a mutiny in the Atlantic Fleet must herald the outbreak of a proletarian revolution in England.

he had delivered a solemn warning that "if there were any collapse in the pound we should be defaulting on our obligations to the rest of the world and our credit would be gone"; on September 21 he announced the abandonment of the Gold Standard, the sterling-dollar rate falling at once to $3.23.[1] As Prime Minister in a predominantly Conservative Cabinet, he was content to see it abandoned. Frightened foreign investors went on receiving the gold they demanded as long as a Government intent on destroying the Capitalist System was in office; when it was replaced by one intent on defending the Capitalist System, they received paper of uncertain value.

The passing of the gold pound was deeply mourned. Bury the Great Pound 'mid a nation's lamentation. Mr. Beverley Nichols, who happened to be abroad when the calamity occurred, wrote a poignant account of how he presented a pound note, only to be given a dirty look, compounded of malignancy and suspicion, instead of the obsequiousness his British money had always hitherto commanded. In the South of France, in Switzerland, Italy and the Tyrol, pensions emptied; small oil-stoves for making afternoon tea were sadly packed away, and a melancholy trek homewards began, a flight to the pound, of those who, now that the Gold Standard had been abandoned, must return to income tax and Bayswater. Foreign travel, formerly much

---

[1] Commander Stephen King-Hall, in *Our Own Times*, pointing to the Invergordon Mutiny as the direct cause of this, in his view, necessary change in fiscal policy, mentions that he has often reflected upon "the strange combination of circumstances which caused the Royal Navy to be used by a far-seeing Providence as the unconscious means of . . . releasing the nation from the onerous terms of the contract of 1925 when the pound was restored to gold at pre-war parity." "In 1805," he writes, "the Navy saved the nation at Trafalgar; it may be that at Invergordon it achieved a like feat."

recommended as broadening the mind and breaking down the barriers between nation and nation, was blamed as unpatriotic; the Duke of Connaught announced his intention of wintering in England, and Sunshine Cruises which did not involve the use of foreign currency, became popular.[1] Skiing resorts that winter were empty and desolate; and Swiss hoteliers who had catered extensively for English tastes, groaned and thought wistfully of Holland, their little libraries of Tauchnitz editions unused, the English they had laboured to acquire, unexercised, and the authentic plumpudding they were accustomed to dish up on Christmas Day, not required.

Instead of, as had been predicted, England becoming scorned and rejected among nations still righteously on gold, these, too, some soon, some later, some regretfully, some gladly, followed England's example and abandoned the Gold Standard. When even the United States, despite an immense gold reserve, took this step in 1933, it was clear that the Gold Standard no more existed, and would probably never be resurrected. Gold continued to be precious, more precious than ever. As its price soared, it was dug out of the earth with even greater eagerness than before; deposits hitherto not thought worth working, now worked; gold-mine shares doubling, trebling, in value, and greatly enriching those who bought and sold them judiciously;

---

[1] Although most newspapers ardently supported the campaign against foreign travel, they continued to publish advertisements of foreign steamship companies, and Mr. George Lunn, in a letter to the *Observer*, "ventured to predict that the whole country would heave a vast sigh of relief to hear that the Duke of Connaught had gone again to Cannes, because we English value more highly the good health of our great nobility than that they should suffer the extremes of an English winter, which is most certainly taking a very grave risk which even these strenuous circumstances do not justify when such important lives are at stake."

shops which specialized in buying old gold doing a large
business, new ones coming into existence, sometimes queues
forming of persons with golden objects to dispose of. In
India, ornaments reserved for ceremonial occasions, sole
treasure of penurious households, were sold and exported
to the value of £40,000,000 annually, to be melted down
and stored away, no more gleaming on arms and ankles and
fingers, become geometrical, immobile, in underground
vaults; and in the U.S.S.R. special *torgsin* shops were established which offered food unobtainable elsewhere in exchange for gold, the hungry bringing a strange litter of
ancient coins, brooches, trinkets, tooth-stoppings even, and
after these had been tested and weighed, receiving propor-
tionate quantities of delicacies like butter and sausage for
which their bellies had long craved.

From many places, expected and unexpected, came gold,
most to find its way at last to the United States, there remaining. Little trickles flowed into rivulets, and these into a
main stream, which emptied into bank vaults and was lost
to view.

People soon got used to the idea of being off gold. It
really seemed to make very little difference; and soon it
was being said that what had looked like a calamity was in
reality a blessing, many claiming that for years past they
had been advocating controlled inflation regulated by an
Exchange Equilization Fund. Instead of, as the *Morning
Post* had contended, abandonment of the Gold Standard
amounting to an amputation which left England hobbling
along as best it might on an artificial limb, the operation
was thought of as the removal of an unnecessary appendix;
and before long the Government was taking credit to itself

for having allowed to happen what it had been formed to prevent.

Even so, the abandonment of the Gold Standard had important consequences. It led to the institution of currency restrictions in a number of countries and an intensification of those already in force in others; to a drastic curtailment, and for a time the complete cessation, of foreign lending in London, and an all-round raising of already high tariff barriers. As far as England was concerned, the fact that so flagrant a departure from orthodox finance went unpunished, was even rewarded, prepared the way for other departures from orthodoxy in the future. It was like the first visit of a respectable householder in distress to the pawnshop. As he creeps along with his surreptitious bundle in the dusk, he expects passers-by to recoil, disgusted, from him; when they do not, he takes heart, and the next time goes more brazenly, until he is as indifferent to being seen on his way to the pawnshop as on his way to church. MacDonald aroused fear and trepidation, as well as winning votes, with his gloomy prognostications about the consequences of detaching the pound from gold; but Mr. Neville Chamberlain was not much heeded when eighteen months later he envisaged the woe which would follow a default on the American Debt—"Default would have resounded all over the world, and might have been taken as a justification for other defaults by European Powers, and might have had a most profound effect upon the whole conception of the meaning of obligations of all kinds." Nor was anyone surprised that when, after one more half-yearly payment, and an inconsiderable token payment, England defaulted, the event, far from resounding all over the world, was scarcely noticed. "They hired the money,

didn't they?" Cal Coolidge asked in his simplicity; but only
Finland responded, paying up like a man. The rest of
America's debtors pleaded poverty, and refused to repay
any more of the money they had hired, a few following
England's example and making token payments, these rep-
senting the faint agitation of almost extinct conscientious
scruples, the single egg left in a robbed nest.

A Bishop, by way of illustrating his contention that
Europe was "a much more savage place than it has been for
perhaps 1,000 years," recalled how "during the Crimean
War, Russia, the most backward nation in Europe, continued to pay the interest on its foreign loans to the very
nations it was fighting against." In the light of so sublimely
civilized an act, default on the American Debt, even the
expedient of a token payment, made a poor showing.
Henceforth, not only might enemies expect to go unpaid,
but allies as well. The vast sums which at the end of the
War were owing and owed,[1] proved, like the League
Covenant, to have only a paper existence. When all hope
of realizing them had been abandoned, they continued to
make a fugitive appearance in the budgets of France and

[1] England was owed £3,400,000,000, and owed the United States £850,-
000,000. By the terms of the settlement negotiated by Mr. Baldwin in
1923, England was to make annual payments to the United States of
£33,000,000 from 1923 to 1932, and of £38,000,000 from 1933 to 1984. Under
this arrangement, £326,000,000 was paid, and then payments ceased.
Reparations figures were even more astronomical. In *The Truth About
Reparations and War Debts*, Mr. Lloyd George quotes the report of a
committee, set up in 1918, and consisting, among others, of the then
Canadian Finance Minister, a Governor of the Bank of England, and a
distinguished economist. The report estimated the capital liability of the
Enemy Powers at £24,000,000,000, and "saw no reason to suppose they
could not provide £1,200,000,000 per annum as interest on this amount."
It went on to remark that "the fear of economic ill-effects from the re-
payment of the cost of the War is not well-founded."

the United States, and then disappeared altogether, never to be heard of again.

Finance's great empire was crumbling, its laws disregarded, its territory contracting, its weapons unavailing to put down insurrection; in London, still strong enough to keep Cabinet Ministers meekly waiting in a garden, but faced with open defiance in remoter places where the circumstances for engineering stock-exchange panics and flights to and from currencies no more existed. Loans were still pumped out from France, money-transfusions to revivify sickly alliances; England still could reckon on invisible imports, cash returns on imperial and foreign investments, to rectify an ostensibly adverse trade balance; but the money-transfusions were losing their effectiveness, and the cash returns becoming difficult to collect. Cobbett despised "the idea of paying bits of paper by bits of paper"; [1] the elaboration and inflation of credit, beginning in his time and subsequently reaching proportions then undreamt of, filled him with apprehension; and the prophesied wrath to come when what was thought of as wealth-certificates, figures entered in ledgers, turned out to be illusory, nothing.

Inevitably, the financier was discredited along with his occupation, especially in the United States, where ruined

---

[1] "When the foreign loans first began to go on, Peter McCulloch and all the Scotch were cock o'whoop. They said that there were prodigious advantages in lending money to South America, that the interest would come home to enrich us; that the amount of the loans would go out chiefly in English manufactures; that the commercial gains would be enormous; and that this country would thus be made rich, and powerful, and happy, by employing in this way its 'surplus capital,' and thereby contributing at the same time to the uprooting of despotism and superstition, and the establishing of freedom and liberality in their stead. Unhappy and purblind, I could not for the life of me see the matter in this light. My perverted optics could perceive no *surplus capital* in bundles of bank-notes."

financiers and speculators fell like autumn leaves from up-
stairs windows, and a searching investigation was conducted
into the activities of famous private banking houses like
J. P. Morgan and Company and Kuhn Loeb and Company, a number of facts not calculated to increase the public
esteem in which their principals were held, being made
public.

Jokes at the expense of financiers were as common in
the *New Yorker* [1] as jokes at the expense of curates in
Punch; books which exposed the practices and practitioners
of high finance, circulated widely; and the attempts of Mr.
Samuel Insull to find some spot in Europe whence he could
not be extradited to face charges of embezzlement in the
United States, were followed with interest, but without
much sympathy.

Mr. Insull found a temporary refuge in Greece, but not
even the Greeks showed any readiness to avail themselves
of his handsome offer to "try by some financial combination to reciprocate the hospitality of this small but great
country."

In England, the slump in financial combinations was in-

---

[1] Though the *New Yorker* had an extensive circulation in England, an
attempt to produce an English periodical on similar lines (*Night and
Day*) proved a failure, succumbing to libel actions and that insular morality in the English which makes them enjoy obscenity in French, but turn
out in indignant Watch Committees when it is purveyed in their native
language. If Mr. Peter Arno had been born an Englishman, he would
either have had to change his name to Armitage and draw funny char-
women or symbolic Britannias, or emigrate to the United States. As an
American whose mordant drawings appeared in an American periodical,
he was much appreciated. Even Swift needed to be Irish, and Mr. Bernard
Shaw has enjoyed a similar advantage over native-born satirists.

tensified by the suicide on March 14, 1932, of Ivar Kreuger, the Swedish match magnate. Few had heard of Kreuger when he died, and the disorganization of stock markets caused by the announcement that he had shot himself through the heart in his Paris flat, came as a surprise to the general public. At first the Press treated him as a noble casualty on the battlefield of international finance. He had struggled bravely, but adverse circumstances had proved too much for him. "The impinging of forces that even the League of Nations had been unable to withstand" had brought him down, the *Economist* wrote, and Mr. J. M. Keynes that he had been crushed "between the icebergs of a frozen world that no individual man can thaw and restore to the warmth of normal life." [1] It was noted as a touching circumstance that his suicide had been considerately timed to take place after the closing of the Paris bourse so as to give French speculators a short respite before having to wrestle with the difficulties he knew his death would make for them; like Carto's solicitude for friends at sea on the stormy night he took his life. The fortunate coincidence that an American millionaire and philanthropist, Mr. George Eastman, whose finances were in perfect order, should have killed himself on the day after Kreuger did, provided an opportunity to run the two suicides in together, the note Mr. Eastman left behind him ("My work is done. Why wait?") being made to do service for both.

As little by little details of Kreuger's transactions, and of the insolvency he had left behind him, became known, his admirers became more reticent. The final blow was the discovery that his liabilities exceeded £50,000,000, and that

[1] Quoted in *The Work, Wealth and Happiness of Mankind* by H. G. Wells.

he had forged forty-two Italian Treasury Bonds for £500,-
000 each to replenish his dwindling assets. Even, it was felt,
being crushed between the icebergs of a frozen world
scarcely justified such irregularities. The *Daily Express* and
other popular newspapers, began where the *Economist* and
Mr. Keynes had ended, entertaining their readers with accounts of the luxurious flats Kreuger had in all the capitals
of Europe, and the mistresses he kept to enliven his leisure
hours. From being an austere master-financier whose careful plans were upset by circumstances beyond his control,
he was transformed into a swindler and debauchee whose
balance sheets were as fraudulent as his way of life was
reprehensible.

Reading of the magnitude of his transactions, how he
lent enormous sums of money to governments and floated
so many companies that the mere investigation of his affairs
was a lengthy and arduous undertaking, it seemed wonderful that so elaborate a structure should have been built on
so trifling a foundation as matches. The only reality behind
the millions of pounds he manipulated, were these little
sticks of wood dipped in sulphur used to light a fire in the
morning or a pipe after breakfast. By means of them, he
made himself so powerful that his death disorganized stock
markets in all parts of the world; affected prices, trade,
employment, and had serious consequences for many who
had never heard his name until a headline told them of his
suicide. If this might be done on matches, what might not
be done on more substantial commodities? it was wondered;
and did the provision of harmless necessary matches really
require operations so vast and so complicated and so dangerous?

Kreuger was a portent, reinforced later by Stavisky, the

counterfoils of whose check book gave many French politicians sleepless nights, and whose activities made it necessary for the Chamber of Deputies to be surrounded by
troops when it met; even then, angry shouts from without
disturbing its deliberations, and members preferring to
remain where they were that night rather than venture into
the tumultuous streets. A Jabez Balfour, when his frauds
were discovered, was just a sinner, one who had erred and
strayed like lost sheep; but Kreuger and Stavisky were regarded rather as symptoms of a prevailing corruption than
as notably corrupt themselves. Financiers were under a
cloud, and finance became a somewhat shameful, though
still lucrative, occupation.

From demagogic and other throats came the cry: "Poverty in the midst of plenty!" This cry, it is true, would always, to a greater or smaller extent, have been valid; from
the beginning of time many who gathered in the crops have
gone hungry, many who collected fuel lacked fires, and
many who sat long hours sewing and tailoring been themselves inadequately clothed. Yet now this state of affairs,
once commonly accepted as part of the lot of poor humans
struggling along from birth to death, came to seem unreasonable and unnecessary. Economists, amateur and professional,
demonstrated its absurdity; orators at street corners stri-
dently made the same point, and newspapers, ponderously
or jauntily according to their character, asked why increased
production should not result in increased consumption, instead of causing a slump, with all its attendant misery.
Over-production might provide stock-brokers and bankers
and captains of industry with a satisfying explanation of
economic disorder, but scarcely impressed those who found
difficulty in satisfying their simplest necessities, even in

obtaining work—simplest necessity of all. Under-consumption was to them a more congenial and meaningful slogan than over-production.

Until concern for production and consumption became irrelevant in the light of a deeper concern—a concern for life itself rather than for the means of life, for the very continuance of any existence at all, whether over-producing or under-consuming, the machinery whereby commodities were produced and exchanged was subjected to a minute scrutiny and much criticism. A variety of suggestions, mild and drastic, were made for improving its working, or for replacing it altogether; many had their say on the subject, some at great length. There were advocates of currency reform, others who thought salvation lay in overhauling the banks; public works were not forgotten, and President Roosevelt's New Deal had its admirers. The International Labour Office contributed data, and sometimes actual proposals; and the Brazilian Government deserved gratitude from demagogues, if not from coffee-drinkers, by ostentatiously destroying large quantities of coffee,[1] thereby making available a ready and much used illustration of a favourite theme. These burnt bags of coffee were consumed again and again, the flames from them, indignation; the smoke, confusion, and the ashes which remained, despair.

The Greeks only became interested in their administrative institutions when they threatened to break down, and the interest thus expended failed to prevent their decay. Utopias flourish in chaos, doctors in a pestilence, and economists and chartered accountants in a slump. As unemployment increased, so did the London School of Eco-

---

[1] In December, 1931, the destruction of one million bags a month was ordered.

nomics; a by-product of depressed industrial areas were
University Extension Lecture courses in economics, conscientiously attended, with essays handed in and discussion
groups formed. In Welsh valleys, in Lancashire and by the
Tyne, desolation spread; but in Tunbridge Wells and
Bournemouth visiting Oxford and Cambridge economists
with Marxist leanings were eagerly questioned, spoke knowingly of trade-cycles, pump-priming and even of dialectical
materialism. Here, bedded in the earth, it was frequently
pointed out, were raw materials, and here machines capable
of transforming them into useful or pleasurable commodities; here were hands eager to extract these raw materials
and work these machines, and here desire for what they
would produce. Might not materials, machines, hands and
desire be brought together, and the health, wealth and happiness of mankind greatly increased thereby? It seemed
not. They would not come together, despite the ingenuity
and labour devoted to that end; only came together when
the resultant, instead of health, wealth and happiness, was
death, destruction and misery. Derelict factories and ship-
yards continued idle until war spurred them into renewed
activity; in peace they were paralyzed, but the threat, and
then the reality, of war brought back their life—like an
indolent giant who cannot summon up the energy to move
his huge limbs except to kill.

V

Once the National Government had performed the surprising feat of coming into existence, its initiative was exhausted. The lamp had been rubbed, the jinn had appeared,
but no instructions were forthcoming as to how its formidable powers should be exercised. The Conservative members

of the Cabinet believed in tariffs, the Liberal members of the
Cabinet in free trade, the Labour members of the Cabinet in
continuing to be members of the Cabinet, and the Prime
Minister in continuing to be Prime Minister. Formulating a
policy acceptable to all and likely to impress the electorate,
therefore, presented great difficulties. Economizing on public expenditure was all very well, but did not, in itself, constitute a political programme. England, Mr. Coward and
others insisted, had recovered her greatness; but some manifestation of this recovery other than a balanced budget, was
called for. There was the Government, there the Prime
Minister who had dared greatly and won through, and there
the country for whose sake he and his colleagues had sunk
their differences and taken upon themselves the burden of
office. It was an inspiring spectacle, like the moment in a
play when, to the audience's applause, hero and heroine fall
into each other's arms, but not one which could be indefinitely protracted. Either a curtain or further action was
required.

The Cabinet deliberated. Should they go to the country,
or continue in office with the comfortable parliamentary
majority they enjoyed? If they went to the country, what
proposals were they to put before the electorate? If they
remained in office, how were they to employ their own and
Parliament's time? Their deliberations were long and
mysterious, and aroused some irritation even among their
supporters. It almost seemed as though they were going to
prove as ineffectual as their predecessors.

If Cabinet Ministers had foreseen the sweeping electoral
success which was in store for them, and the simplicity of
the device which would ensure it, their hearts would have
been easier. But they did not know. Doubts still gnawed

at them. Might not the unemployed, despite postal orders dispatched in gratitude to the Prime Minister, be expected to vote solidly against a Government which had reduced unemployment pay? Teachers were complaining, judges felt they had been wronged, seamen had mutinied and civil servants grumbled. Authoritative statements which had been made about the consequences which would follow the abandonment of the Gold Standard, would provide hecklers with useful ammunition; and how was it possible for Sir Herbert Samuel and Mr. Neville Chamberlain to persuade themselves and others that they were in agreement on fiscal policy? The Cabinet were unanimous on nothing except that they had saved the country and must go on saving it. Such a position had serious electoral disadvantages, and made a general election seem a hazardous undertaking.

In this perplexity a step was taken which, in the light of subsequent events, became merely laughable. The Prime Minister drove down to Churt to interview Mr. Lloyd George, who was recovering from an illness. MacDonald's purpose was to find out the terms on which Mr. Lloyd George would participate in the National Government. He went without much expectation of success, and came away probably on the whole relieved that so incalculable an ally was not available. Their interview is unlikely to have proceeded very smoothly. MacDonald had already experienced what being dependent on Mr. Lloyd George's support was like, and cannot have much relished the prospect of more and closer collaboration; his ponderous and incoherent earnestness, always distasteful to Mr. Lloyd George's impish nature, was more than ever so now that he had come to be admired by the *Times* and to be the associate of Mr. Baldwin and Sir John Simon, not to mention Sir Herbert

Samuel. They spent half an hour or so together, and then
parted, MacDonald to speed back to his anxious colleagues,
Mr. Lloyd George to meditate in his darkening sickroom on
the strange vagaries of political life, whereby a man whom
he had once tried to send to Russia with a view to his pro-
pitiating revolutionaries there, but been prevented by the
refusal of the Seamen's Union to countenance the trans-
portation of so subversive and unpatriotic a passenger,
should twenty-three years later invite him to join a predominantly Conservative and entirely respectable Government.

It was the last occasion on which Mr. Lloyd George came
within measurable distance of office. His following was
soon to dwindle to a family group, his influence to become
negligible. Henceforth, his was to be an individual performance, often sparkling, always irresponsible, but of no serious
account in the House of Commons or outside. As an amateur
farmer he achieved some fame, giving his name to a popular
brand of raspberries. His journalism, particularly in the
United States, continued to be profitable; and his War
Memoirs in nine volumes and serialized in various newspapers before publication, provided him with an opportunity to exercise his gift for invective and to jeopardize many
established reputations. His ribald locks and cloak were
familiar to all; at eisteddfods he was always welcome, often
appearing in druidical robes, and he still found occasion to
disconcert the pompous and trouble the complacent. When
his voice became faint, his gestures continued to be animated; one war provided him with his opportunity, another
found him mumbling not very coherently and making ex-
pressive movements with his hands.

With the possibility of strengthening, or at any rate enlarging, their ranks by the inclusion of Mr. Lloyd George disposed of, the Cabinet's dilemma remained unresolved. As Lord Beaverbrook put it, they were like a motor-car in which Mr. Neville Chamberlain had his foot on the accelerator, Sir Herbert Samuel had his hand on the emergency brake, and Mr. Baldwin sat in the back seat wondering what it all meant. No place was provided in this image for the Prime Minister. He, perhaps, was the exhaust.

What the Cabinet needed was an electoral slogan—a slogan which should involve no commitments, presuppose no agreement among themselves, and yet inspire confidence in them and their capacity to agree together and manage the country's affairs energetically and skilfully. Out of their long deliberations such a slogan emerged. Who invented it, whence and how it came into existence, has never been told. Probably no single brain was responsible, no sudden suggestion made and delightedly endorsed. As when a steamer is sailing the babble of voices, the rattle of cranes, the groaning of hawsers, all dissolve into one long siren blast announcing departure, so did confused discussion, speculation and advice, all dissolve into one cry—a Doctor's Mandate.

It was a sagacious slogan. No one asks a doctor to specify in advance what treatment he intends to prescribe. His benevolence and skill are assumed. The obscure hieroglyphics he scrawls on a piece of paper are taken on trust, handed to a chemist, and the medicine given in exchange swallowed without question. In the capacity of doctors asking only to be allowed to heal a sick country, Government candidates approached the electorate. Whether they would prescribe ice-packs or a hot-water bottle, a low or a nourishing diet, was dependent on the circumstances of the

case. Perhaps tariffs might be required, perhaps not. Mr.
Neville Chamberlain had an open mind on the subject, so
had Sir Herbert Samuel. They all had open minds.

A general election is at all times an astonishing spectacle.
All, even the unemployed and inmates of public institutions, become ladies and gentlemen for the occasion. Old,
forgotten people are fetched out into the light of day, and
respectfully escorted to polling booths. Lordly motor-cars,
be-ribboned, make their appearance in bleak streets, and are
loaded with those whom, ordinarily, they hoot insolently
out of their way. Canvassers circulate—resonant ladies in
tweed costumes, young men with parliamentary or B.B.C.
aspirations—knocking at unfamiliar doors, and ingratiating
as salesmen when their knocks are answered. At street corners voices are raised above the traffic's noise; in school-
rooms, blackboards still bearing traces of the day's lessons,
voters assemble, seat themselves at desks, and hear a candidate's solicitations. For a little while, the humble and meek
are exalted, and filled, if not with good things, sometimes
with free refreshment. Authority bends in obeisance to its
source, like a proud king momentarily humbling himself
before an ancestral shrine; then soon straightens again and
continues as before. When their victory has been announced, lawyers wearing rosettes are carried shoulder-high
like heroes to the accompaniment of not very uproarious
cheers, and then are rarely seen until their constituents'
votes must again be solicited.

The Doctor's Mandate general election proceeded like
others before it. In most cases the addition of "National"
to a candidate's previous designation, made little difference
to the electoral campaign, though at Seaham Harbour the
Prime Minister found that on this occasion it was at his

meetings, not at his opponents', that the Union Jack was displayed and the National Anthem sung; for him that private cars were available, a long procession, two hundred or more. Whether or not he observed and considered the significance of such a change, he made no comment upon it, but threw himself energetically into the campaign,[1] addressing many meetings still from time to time producing his inflated German marks; on one occasion, as a variation, producing a toy shovel, and explaining that whereas previously he had come to them with a pickaxe to pull down, now he came to them with a shovel to construct.

Labour candidates, even in constituencies hitherto regarded as safe, found the going hard. The virtue they took to themselves for having opposed cuts in unemployment pay, was offset by the Labour Government's disappointing record and the confused circumstances of its resignation. They might insist that they were the victims of a bankers' ramp, and the only true champions of the working classes; but the leaders under whom they had previously campaigned had deserted them, and the promises they had previously made had been, at best, inadequately kept. To add to their discomfiture, they were freely and plausibly presented as faint-hearts who had abandoned their posts and forgotten their principles in the hour of danger. Though courage and integrity are little in evidence among politicians, any suggestion that they are not well endowed with these qualities, damages their reputation; as bookmakers are damaged by

---

[1] He was submitted to persistent heckling, which on one occasion led him to remark that it was preposterous to accuse him of having betrayed his party for the sake of office when he had been offered, and had refused, a position of the highest distinction. Newspapers were asked not to comment on, or give any prominence to, this statement, which was generally taken to refer to the Viceroyalty.

accusations that they lack sportsmanship, and prostitutes by
accusations that they lack womanly tenderness.

The various political leaders were admitted to the microphone, their voices thus reaching most homes. Perhaps the
most successful of them at this new and important form of
electioneering was Snowden, whose desiccated malice made
a great impression.[1] When he said that the official Labour
Party programme, *Labour and the Nation*, was "Bolshevism
run mad," listeners were impressed. They felt, as Mr. Baldwin put it, that he ought to know, since he had been largely
responsible for preparing the document. It was as though
Washington had condemned the American Declaration of
Independence as republicanism run mad. MacDonald's eloquence was too scattered to broadcast well. A microphone
was pitifully inadequate to contain the tumultuous stream
of words which poured from his lips. He explained how
he and his colleagues would explore every avenue, leave
no stone unturned, cut their coats according to their cloth,
and scrupulously refrain from attempting to put a quart into
a pint pot. No practicable suggestion for promoting the
country's well-being would be neglected, but, he assured
the electorate, "when we detect quackeries we shall expose
quackeries."

The electorate were inclined to accept his assurance;
quackery should be cast out in the name of the prince of
quacks. To reinforce their inclination, a twinge of fear
was required; and what so adequate to create this as a suggestion that their savings, their little hoards of money, were
endangered? The Labour Government, they were told,

[1] His broadcasts are believed to have been a decisive influence in the
election, though when he tried to repeat the performance in 1935, this
time in the Independent Liberal interest, he had little success. The votes
he won for the National Government, he could not detach from it.

when it resigned was on the point of laying rapacious hands on the Post Office Savings Bank deposits. Only the Prime Minister's heroic action in forming a National Government had saved these deposits; let another Labour Government take office and they would assuredly be taken. The credit for this brilliant improvisation belongs to Mr. (later Viscount) Runciman, who, perhaps on the strength of it, was sent to mediate in Czechoslovakia. With that occasional candour which has impeded his political advancement, Mr. Churchill admitted later in the House of Commons that to accuse the Labour Government of intending to raid the Post Office Savings Bank deposits, was absurd, like accusing a cook of intending to raid the savoury to improve the soup's flavour; but by this time the return to Parliament of 500 supporters of the National Government, Mr. Churchill among them, had been secured.

On the morning the election results were published, in hotel breakfast-rooms and other places where strangers congregate, habitual reserve was broken down and happy handshakes were exchanged. A great sigh of relief went up from income-tax payers and recipients of unearned increment. It was like a dream come true—the Labour Party almost obliterated, Mr. Lansbury the solitary ministerial survivor, a one-man shadow-Cabinet, and 400 Conservative Members of Parliament with a Doctor's Mandate and no restrictive pledges whatsoever. The very magnitude of the victory aroused qualms among some who had contributed to it. Professor Gilbert Murray, in a letter to the *Manchester Guardian*, explained that though he had voted for the National Government, he proposed to vote Labour at the next election. This virtuous decision indicated his irritation at having unnecessarily violated his principles. Like all good

Liberals, he only believed in supporting Conservatives when there was a possibility that they might otherwise be defeated. There may have been some others who, like Professor Gilbert Murray, looked forward to neutralizing their support of the National Government when they were next given an opportunity of voting, but most were full of unqualified delight at its great victory. A spiritual renaissance had taken place; a new era of what one writer called "courageous and clean budgets," had begun. The *Morning Post* explained the change by the preference of the English electorate for being represented in Parliament by gentlemen, though without adducing any evidence in support of this contention; and the *Daily Herald* mournfully admitted that a defeat had been suffered too devastating even to be called a moral victory. On his way to Geneva to preside over the opening session of the Disarmament Conference, Henderson walked up and down the deck of his Channel steamer, occasionally pausing and taking off his bowler hat as though to ask a question; then recollecting himself, putting on his hat again, and continuing his perambulations.

CHAPTER IV

IT is inevitable that after a bloody and exhausting war the main preoccupation, at any rate of the victors, should be with peace. Like a sated debauchee creeping away from the scene of his excesses, they cry "Never again!" and resolve that they will evermore be peaceable. Any of the Gadarene swine who escaped destruction, must have decided to remain henceforth at sea level, where the fury of the evil spirits which possessed them would have less dangerous consequences than at higher altitudes. War, like lust, is

> Past reason hunted; and no sooner had,
> Past reason hated, as a swallow'd bait,
> On purpose laid to make the taker mad.

When it is over, it seems inconceivable that it should ever recur; but as time passes, and passion revives, the same fury resumes its old possession of once chastened hearts. "Peace! peace!" when there is no peace yields place to "War! war!" when there is no war, and then comes war.

In the first decade after the War, no country in a position to wage a war, desired one; and French diplomacy was consistently exerted to secure a continuance of this fortunate state of affairs. As the possibility of at any rate a major European war [1] was removed, peace seemed delightfully

[1] A major European war may be defined, from the English point of view, as one which involves England; perhaps, even, as one fought in France.

easy of attainment. All that was needed was that the League Covenant, guaranteeing the status-quo, should be observed. Geneva became, at once, the centre of French intrigues and of pacifist hopes. There took place many shady conversations, and many exalted expressions of pacifist sentiment. It was the headquarters of a flourishing peace industry, greatly productive of travelling expenses, with ramifications in all parts of the world, and many subsidiary enterprises, some amateur and some professional. Thither journeyed all who loved mankind, and had envisaged means whereby their hard lot here on earth might be ameliorated— as, by inducing them to speak Esperanto, reform their calendar, adopt a decimal coinage, promote intellectual co-operation; all who wished to see with their own eyes these architects of everlasting peace—Briand, MacDonald, M. Laval, Sir Austen Chamberlain, Lord Cushendon, M. Paul-Boncour, Sir John Simon, M. Politis, M. Titulescu, and many another.[1] At the International Labour Office, under the energetic direction of Albert Thomas, international labour legislation was formulated and sometimes adopted, and large quantities of statistics and other data bearing on labour conditions, accumulated. White slave- and drug-traffickers had to suffer the humiliation of having their activities discussed by international bodies in the very town they had chosen for their headquarters; and armament manufacturers, unless they happened to be League delegates

---

[1] To those who have been at Geneva in a professional or wage-earning capacity, it may seem strange that many should have voluntarily participated in League and related activities there. Yet such was the case. Winifred Holtby, for instance, used regularly to attend meetings of the League Assembly at her own expense, and for no other reason, presumably, than that she liked it. See *Winifred Holtby As I Knew Her* by Evelyn White.

themselves, were made momentarily apprehensive by resolutions in favour of disarmament.

Like a reformed drunkard eagerly reiterating his renunciation of drink whenever an opportunity offers, the European Powers continued to assert their pacific intentions, and
jointly and severally to swear solemn oaths that they would
never under any circumstances again resort to war.

Parliamentary candidates vied with one another in proclaiming their enthusiasm for the League of Nations;
clergymen made League activities the burden of their
sermons and addresses, and sometimes prayers, and the
League of Nations Union had on its governing body distinguished Conservative, Liberal and Labour politicians, as
well as archbishops and bishops, professors, peers, and
other eminent persons. A large amount of propaganda was
carried on, mostly well-intentioned, whose effect was to
persuade the public that by supporting the League they
would prevent the necessity ever again arising of having to
shed their blood in defence of what blood had been shed
to gain.

The League came to seem like one of those much advertised life insurance policies which the prudent take out to
guard against finding themselves in old age forlorn and
destitute. Improvident nations which neglected thus to in-
sure against the contingency of war, might have to endure
another Armageddon; but the provident ones had their
policy, stamped and witnessed and paid up to date, their
Covenant, to procure their exemption.

It was obvious that, if the League Covenant really was
a safeguard against war, armed forces were scarcely necessary; a traveller who, having insured his baggage, still kep

his eyes glued anxiously on it, was behaving unreasonably. Governments, it was felt, which had repeatedly pledged themselves to eschew war, and repeatedly stressed their allegiance to the League, ought to disarm; yet, though they often proclaimed their intention of doing so, when it came to the point their enthusiasm for disarmament only stretched to advocating the abolition of the weapons they most feared and the retention of those which in the past they had found most serviceable.

All were for peace, all were for disarmament; but none found it convenient to relinquish any of the spoils of previous wars, or appreciably to reduce their armed forces.

France remained heavily armed; England, even under a Labour Government, continued to spend £100,000,000 annually on the army, navy and air force; and the nations which had been compulsorily disarmed, found surreptitious ways of manufacturing armaments and training personnel.

Hopes of serious disarmament were centred on the Disarmament Conference, which after several postponements was due to open at Geneva on February 2, 1932. Various preparatory activities organized by non-official bodies, were intended to promote its success.

A disarmament petition obtained over two million signatures, and was ceremonially loaded on a lorry to be dispatched to Geneva while a band played appropriate music; and a great peace rally was held in the Albert Hall and addressed by political and other leaders.

The Conference was attended by representatives and military experts from sixty-four countries, as well as by an

American observer, and was frequently described as the
greatest conference the world had so far seen. A special
building provided with a rubber floor, and costing 1,000,000
Swiss francs, had been erected by the Swiss Government to
house it, Geneva hoteliers had made ample provision for
accommodating delegates and their staffs, journalists, peti-
tioners, representatives of armament manufacturers with a
watching-brief and funds at their disposal to be used if
required, all who were interested, financially, profession-
ally or emotionally, in the Conference's proceedings; and
each official delegate was presented with a gold medal struck
by the League in honour of the occasion.

The President, Henderson, looked down sadly on the imposing assembly which awaited his presidential address. He
came fresh from an unprecedented electoral defeat; the
party he had been largely instrumental in building up, was
in ruins; where he had expected to see a friendly, or at any
rate familiar, countenance, he saw the forbidding features
of Sir John Simon. Hope in such circumstances was not
easily summoned up. His occupancy of the centre of the
world's stage to which he had been looking forward, had
somehow lost its glamour, and his words when he began to
speak, though they were ostensibly sanguine, fell coldly
from his lips. He might have been addressing a brotherhood meeting in Coventry on the Todpuddle Martyrs.

Altogether twenty-seven disarmament plans were laid
before the Conference. M. Tardieu, who cleverly got in
first by producing his plan at what was intended to be a
preparatory session, suggested the creation of a super-
national armed force capable of defending signatories of
the League Covenant against unprovoked attack. Sir John

Simon proposed the total abolition of submarines and poison gas, and M. Litvinov, the total abolition of all weapons, whether technically offensive or defensive. This proposal, repeated at intervals, and after its novelty had worn off, greeted with laughter, led Señor Madariaga, the Spanish delegate, to tell an instructive parable. Birds and animals, he said, came together for a disarmament conference. The lion suggested to the eagle that it should dispense with its talons, the eagle appealed to the bull to give up its horns, the bull appealed to the tiger to abandon its claws. Finally, the bear suggested that all should disarm and join him in a universal embrace.

Technical committees were set up and discussed at length the difficult and delicate question of distinguishing between offensive and defensive weapons; experts met and considered, for instance, whether permitted guns should be of 100 mm. or 150 mm. calibre; the relative merits of qualitative and quantitative disarmament were exhaustively debated, and great ingenuity was displayed in formulating an acceptable definition of an aggressor. All the Conference's energies were expended on skilfully avoiding issues which might force it to go into liquidation. It became an institution, adjourning, re-assembling, again adjourning; at each adjournment speeches being made and leading articles written to the effect that, though perhaps no definite conclusions had been reached, much useful work had been done, and that the adjournment of the Conference did not at all mean the adjournment of work for disarmament, rather the very opposite. A British Draft Convention provided material for discussion when the twenty-seven plans had been translated, noted, tabulated, and circulated to delegates, who carried them for a while to and from Conference meetings in leather satchels, and then discarded them, arms wearying of carrying them, eyes wearying of catching a glimpse of them when, for some reason or other, or for no reason, satchels were opened and their contents outspread.

Though the British Draft Convention was accepted as providing a basis for discussion, no vote was taken on it, in case it should be defeated and the Conference find itself left with nothing to discuss and no reason for continuing. Each article, as meeting succeeded meeting, acquired amendments, many pages of them, until the whole became visibly swollen. Between sessions, Henderson went to Paris, London and Berlin, engaging in conversations which might prepare the way for better progress when the Conference reassembled; one of the many who had made, and were to make, this hopeless pilgrimage.

The presence of a disarmed Power, Germany, at the Disarmament Conference was as embarrassing as the presence of a starving man at a conference of medical experts assembled to investigate malnutrition. For the armed to discuss disarmament was innocuous, since none seriously intended to lay aside their weapons; but the re-armament of the disarmed was fearful to envisage. When the suggestion was made that Germany should be granted a theoretical equality of status, and the right to have token specimens of weapons forbidden by the Treaty of Versailles, a sudden liveliness possessed the Conference; like jovial drinkers in a bar suddenly called on to pay their reckoning, count their change. Token tanks manned by token Germans, unlike permitted guns of perhaps 100 mm. calibre, perhaps 150 mm., would be real, would exist; not susceptible to amendment, providing no basis for discussion, nor conveniently carried in leather satchels. Discussing disarmament, the armed trembled before the disarmed, and were more than ever inclined to go on arming when proposals for disarming were seen to involve the re-arming of a once dangerous enemy.

There should be no equality of status, no token weapons, it was tremulously decided; then, when a deadlock resulted, the decision was tremulously reversed. Admit equality of status, perhaps even allow token weapons; but let there be a period of probation, say of five years, better still of eight years, during which a system of armament supervision would be tried out, and arms be progressively destroyed, year by year so many, until at the end of the probationary period all, like Germany, would have only token weapons, token generals and admirals, token submarines and bombing planes, token whiffs of poison gas. In such a case, surely there was no point in Germany arming only in order to disarm, building battleships only to take them, along with French and British and Italian ones, into the middle of the ocean and sink them there.

It was too late for this tremulous concession, probably had always been too late. The German delegation withdrew finally from the Disarmament Conference, and Germany's withdrawal from the League was announced, Henderson being heard to mutter from his presidential seat, "It's a bit awkward," as, indeed, it was. The Conference found it impossible to continue any longer with its faint struggle to go on existing. It gave up the ghost. Even M. Litvinov was disinclined again to propose total disarmament; even the technical experts, though provided with salary and expenses, lost interest in their interminable discussions; even the secretarial staff shut up their typewriters and dictionaries, turned their attention to crossword puzzles, and considered the possibility of other employment.

On April 13, 1935, three years, two months and eleven days after its opening, the Conference met for its final plenary session. "We are determined that the Conference shall not die," Henderson said. "I have read many obituary notices in many languages and in many countries, but the Conference is still a living thing." Then he announced the Conference's adjournment, not long afterwards himself ceasing to be a living thing, probably by that time ready enough to die; his course from Liberal election agent to Disarmament Conference President, run.

The Conference stands adjourned still, and is likely to remain so. Its failure has been much debated, attempts being made to fasten the blame on such an individual,[1] or such a Government, or such a mistake in tactics. It may be doubted, however, whether in the circumstances there was ever any possibility of the Conference succeeding, and whether, if it had succeeded in reaching an agreement, that agreement would have proved of any greater worth than, for instance, the Kellogg Pact. The Philistines might have discussed laying down their weapons while Samson's head was still shorn, but without ever agreeing to do so, since each would have known in his heart that hair inevitably

[1] For instance on Lord Londonderry, who when he was Air Minister, attended the Disarmament Conference as a British delegate, afterwards remarking that he had with difficulty retained for Great Britain the right to make use of air-bombardment in subduing hostile tribesmen on the Indian North-West Frontier. Even if this meant that, but for Lord Londonderry's reservation, an agreement abolishing air-bombardment would have been concluded, it is highly improbable that, in view of subsequent developments, such an agreement would ever have become operative. At most, Lord Londonderry's guilt may be compared to that of a small boy who, seeing a gang of men bent on setting fire to a house, allows them to strike a match on the sole of his shoe.

grew again, however closely cut. And when Samson's shorn
head began visibly to sprout, how anxiously would they
not have sharpened their swords and reckoned up their
numbers.

II

While the Disarmament Conference was in session, in a
near-by building the League Assembly discussed Japan's
invasion of Manchuria. A policy-holder had come forward
to claim the benefits promised, and the board of directors
met to consider what was to be done about it. The policy-
holder concerned was unimportant and in arrears, it is true;
but the validity of the claim presented could not plausibly
be questioned. One League member had infringed the territorial integrity of another, and by the terms of the
Covenant, of which both were signatories, should be repri-
manded; if reprimands proved unavailing, forced to withdraw from the territory wrongfully occupied.

Laboriously, the League machinery was put in motion.
Resolutions were adopted, and a Committee of Twelve set
up, presided over by Briand, this being almost his last task
of the kind, exhaustion causing him sometimes to fall asleep
even while one of the Twelve urged Japan to be moderate,
China to avoid provocation; large, untidy head lolling, tired
eyes unseeing, thoughts withdrawn from this so familiar
scene—faces ranged round a littered table while one spoke.

The Twelve's business was to prevent war; and as they
saw no means, and were even, perhaps, little inclined, to
prevent Japanese and Chinese from killing one another,
they achieved their object by beginning, like a Euclid proposition, with an assumption—let there be no war. In making
this convenient assumption they were assisted by the fact

that no declaration of war was made by either side. If the League has prevented no wars, it may at least claim to have prevented declarations of war. The word "war" was scrupulously avoided; the nearest approach made to it being a declaration that "there was a very considerable military element in Japanese activities." Tension, yes, conflict even; but never that terrible word—"war," whose use would have had as devastating an effect on their proceedings as the small boy's cry, "He's naked!" in the fairy story about the vain emperor who thought he was exquisitely clothed in garments only visible to the righteous.

The tension or conflict was in any case far away, and seemed to affect little the interests of the Twelve who had been entrusted with the task of settling it. They preferred to let events take their course, confining their efforts to occupying the intervals between one decisive event and another with suitable discussions and proposals. These delaying tactics were furthered by Mr. Matsuoka, the Japanese delegate, who showed great ingenuity in raising technical objections to whatever was proposed, falling back occasionally on the simple but effective device of unexpectedly making a speech in Japanese, and who was tactful enough even to insist that the Government he represented had no wish but scrupulously to maintain "the principles of the Covenant and the Kellogg Pact," that "Japanese military action in Manchuria was an act of self-defence," and that "the League had no more loyal servant than Japan." [1] His

[1] It might be supposed that such assertions, while accepted at Geneva as evidence of tact, would have met with a sceptical reception elsewhere. On the contrary, Japan's case was sympathetically stated by Conservative newspapers in England (for instance, the *Times*—"The Japanese plan is undoubtedly intended to provide Manchuria with an efficient Government and an honest financial administration. . . . And it would probably

sense of the righteousness of his position led him on one
occasion to compare his country to Christ on the ground
that "Japan was ready to be crucified for her opinions, and
risk incurring the severest sanctions of the League rather
than alter her standpoint in Geneva." As a Calvary, League
sanctions, even the severest, are not impressive.

The Twelve were succeeded by the Nineteen, the Nine-
teen by the Nine, and dead Briand by living Hymans, a
Belgian, and still it went on; in Geneva, words, in distant
China, deeds—Shanghai attacked, even the International
Settlement endangered, and Manchuria vanishing to reappear faintly disguised as Manchukuo, whose sovereign,
Mr. Henry Pu-yi, former Manchu Emperor, had been kidnapped in Peking and set reluctantly upon his new throne.
Before recommendations could be made, it was decided, all
the relevant facts must be made available. Who knew but
that Mr. Matsuoka might be right, and Japan cruelly
wronged? At any rate, as Sir John Simon pointed out several times, the proper judicial attitude was to suspend judgment until all the circumstances of the case were known.
With relief, a decision was taken to appoint a Commission
of Enquiry and await its findings. Difficulty was experienced in securing a suitable Chairman; but after several
refusals, Lord Lytton consented to act, and the Commis-

---

be erroneous to suppose that the scheme is a deliberate attempt to annex
Manchuria"); and for a time a large section of the French Press was enthusiastically pro-Japanese, though in this case the suddenness and thoroughness of the conversion suggested financial stimulation. An indication of a
not uncommon attitude of mind is given by this remarkable assertion, contained in a letter published on the *Times* leader-page shortly after a protracted bombardment of a Shanghai residential suburb by Japanese planes
—"Such loss of life as has occurred among the Chinese civilian population
(many of whom were soldiers in disguise) has been unavoidable or acci-
dental, and, we are convinced, is regretted by no one more than the
Japanese."

sion set off for the scene of its labours, prevented, owing to
the objections of the Japanese Government, from proceeding by the Trans-Siberian, the nearest route, and therefore
obliged to go via the United States, arriving in Tokyo on
March 1, 1932.

The Commission remained for some time in Japan, in
Osaka, "meeting leading industrialists," and then went to
Shanghai. By the first week in April it had reached Peking,
there receiving from the Japanese Government a welcome
assurance that its safety would be provided for when it
passed into Mr. Pu-yi's domains, and from the *Times* a welcome assurance that it was "pursuing its labours courageously and perseveringly." Its Report, comprising 400
pages and 100,000 words, was published on October 1, the
finishing touches being added by Lord Lytton in the German Hospital in Shanghai, where he was recovering from
an illness. At Geneva, consideration of the Report was delayed for six weeks, since the Japanese Government had
expressed the wish to send a special delegate for the occasion. When it was considered, its main recommendations
—that all armed forces should be withdrawn from Manchuria, and international co-operation be invited for recon-
struction purposes—were approved, though a specific
condemnation of either party to the dispute was avoided,
thereby ensuring that there should be no question of instituting sanctions as provided for in Article 16 of the Covenant. "I am very happy to think," Sir John Simon said in the
House of Commons, "that British policy to-day, whatever
may be its shortcomings and imperfections, at any rate is
a policy which has kept us on terms of perfectly friendly
relations both with China and Japan"—like an eminent
counsel lunching after a case with his learned friend who

had appeared for the other side, recalling points they had scored against one another, enjoying a discreet joke at the Judge's expense, perhaps even comparing fees and refreshers received, having an amiable dispute about who should pay for the lunch, each insisting; but perfectly friendly.

Having been written, published and approved, little more was heard of the Lytton Report. It had served its purpose, and might now conveniently be forgotten. The League also had served its purpose, and was no more necessary to Japan, whose withdrawal from the League, though not from the Disarmament Conference, took place five months after the publication of the Lytton Report. An invasion of Jehol by Japanese troops aroused a faint reaction at Geneva; the large-scale invasion of China which followed some years later, none at all, not even being discussed there. By that time public opinion had become accustomed to invasions, and to make them palatable, did not require Mr. Matsuoka's assurance that Japan would never infringe obligations solemnly undertaken, Sir John Simon's admonitions to suspend judgment until all the facts were known, a Lytton Commission courageously and perseveringly to pursue labours productive of 400 pages, 100,000 words. Sir John by that time had left the Foreign Office; Lord Lytton had found in art, particularly the promotion of a National Theatre, a more congenial field of activity than the Far East, and the French Press other sources of income than Japan; and Mr. Matsuoka—who knows or cares what had happened to Mr. Matsuoka?

Japan's slow conquest of China became in time accepted, if not acceptable. Some denounced it, but most took it for granted; and only desultory attempts were made to reinvoke the League Covenant. It was all happening far away;

China was huge, and would take long to consume, longer
still to digest; might even prove indigestible. Even when
British subjects were molested, their trousers removed, and
made to expose bare shanks to interested Chinese coolies,
the indignation caused was shrill and ineffectual. Mr. Chamberlain remarked that such insults were intolerable, and
made his blood boil; but his intolerance of them did not
prevent their occurrence, nor his boiling blood have any
evident consequences. A Japanese general explained to a
gathering of journalists that his soldiers were simple peasants, who lacked the civilized man's shame at exposing their
nakedness, and who therefore found inexplicable the resentment aroused when they deprived Europeans of their trousers. Although not a simple peasant himself, he offered to
strip publicly then and there; but the offer was not accepted.

Considering the tenacity with which British interests and
prestige had formerly been defended, it was surprising that
now they should be so unresistingly sacrificed. Nerveless
seemingly were the hands which exercised authority, feeble
the response when authority was challenged. Empires, like
crops, must constantly be rotated; they flourish only to
languish, arrogance and rapacity soon losing their momentum, giving place to a craven desire to keep what has been
won; then to a readiness for the sake of peace and quietness, to disgorge, though by that means peace and quietness
are never attained, only their opposites—strife and disquiet.
The sun seemed to be setting on the great British Empire
on which it never sets.

III

Rats, when they find a carcass, take watchful bites at its
extremities; then prudently withdraw to see whether any

ill consequences follow before attacking the main portions. In the same way, when it became apparent that Japan's conquest of Manchuria had not been appreciably impeded, other predatory designs, more daring, less distant, were envisaged. What could be done with impunity in the Far East, might likewise be done in Africa, in Europe even. A frontier incident at Wal Wal provided the occasion for the Italian Government to demand territorial and other concessions from Abyssinia; before the League's attempts to deal with one recalcitrant member had quite expired, another potential conflict required attention.

The same procedure as in the previous case was followed. There were Committees of Seven, Five and Thirteen, and a Conciliation Commission, appointed to investigate the circumstances of the Wal Wal incident, which cautiously but unhelpfully reported that "neither the Ethiopians, acting from a national standpoint, nor the Italians, acting from a colonial standpoint," could be held responsible for it. Who, if anyone, was responsible, was not stated. If the various meetings of the League Assembly and Council called to discuss the Italo-Abyssinian conflict were characterized by greater earnestness than those which discussed the Sino-Japanese conflict, this must largely be attributed to the fact that the British standpoint was usually explained by Mr. Anthony Eden, who had been appointed Minister for League Affairs, rather than by Sir John Simon. Where Sir John was chilly and judicial, Mr. Eden was ardent and tireless; where Sir John's pursuit was a formula, Mr. Eden's was a resolution.

In Mr. Eden, admirers of the League found their perfect champion. They fixed their hopes on him with an almost pathetic fervour. He was young, he was handsome, he was brilliant and enthusiastic; above all, he believed in the League. Elderly politicians seemed flat and unprofitable beside him; ideals fell coldly from their lips, but from his were full of fire. He embodied in his person, in the delivery and substance of his speeches, what was hoped for the future—a world whose rulers would look like film-stars, speak like B.B.C. announcers, think like Professor Gilbert Murray; and where passion would be expended in conciliatory words and gestures, never in bloody deeds. Resolved that henceforth no blood shall be shed; any dissentients? no; carried unanimously.

Mr. Eden threw himself into the Italo-Abyssinian conflict almost as energetically as Mussolini. When a decision was taken at Geneva to investigate its origins, he bravely announced that, if necessary, they would trace it back to the Flood—a proposal which, if Mr. Matsuoka had been concerned, might have been readily accepted. No effort would be neglected which offered a hope of a settlement; no pains were excessive when peace was the prize. With M. Laval Mr. Eden spent many hours—a strangely assorted couple; Sir Galahad and friend, with, as later transpired, somewhat different conceptions of the Holy Grail in question. Mr. Eden also visited Mussolini, conveying to him an offer of a strip of desert in British Somaliland, along with the port of Zeila, which might be ceded to Abyssinia as recompense for concessions to Italy. This offer was scornfully rejected, the already prominent Signor Gayda suggesting that one reason for its rejection was that Gandhi's assent had not been obtained.

While the League and Mr. Eden continued with their efforts, Mussolini proceeded with his military preparations, until on October 2, 1935, a telegram was received at Geneva from Haile Selassie announcing that Italian troops had crossed the Abyssinian frontier. Once more a policy-holder came forward to claim benefits due, and once more the directors met to consider the claim, this time unable to resist, or for long delay the conclusion that "the Italian Government had resorted to war in disregard of its obligations under Article 12 of the Covenant of the League of Nations." Newsboys appeared in the streets with bills announcing the forbidden thing—"War!"; this time the forbidden word was spoken, no incident, or conflict, or embroglio, or tension, but authentic War.

Even so, it was a minor war, involving black men, not white; in Africa, not Europe. An army of journalists descended upon Addis Ababa, where they lived, quarrelsome and restless, in a single hotel, looking for news and finding little, or none; occasionally attempting to visit the fighting zone, and rarely succeeding. They were like high-mettled steeds expecting a battle-charge, and left tediously grazing; among them one old war-horse, Sir Percival Phillips, who alone, to their, and perhaps his, surprise, covered himself with glory by exclusively reporting the only sensational item of news which emanated from Addis Ababa. To the Abyssinian capital, inevitably, flocked many with arms to sell, loans to negotiate, concessions to acquire; on the whole a shady crew, who, acting on the assumption that where blood flows money will also flow, are always to be found in war's precincts. So many coming and going, getting or not getting the interviews they sought, left the journalists off their guard; and it was only Sir Percival who detected a special significance in the mission of Mr. F. W. Rickett, envoy of the African Exploration and Development Corporation, a subsidiary of the Standard-Vacuum Oil Company. He took the precaution of seeing Mr. Rickett off at the station when he left Addis Ababa, and there learnt that he had succeeded in obtaining for his company an important concession of oil and mineral rights in Abyssinia.[1] Sir Percival's cable that evening to the *Daily Telegraph* was a source of deep grief and chagrin to his fellow correspondents, who found themselves in the position of youthful warriors worsted by the cunning and experience of an aged adversary.

At home, experts on military and naval strategy left their retirement, enforced since 1918, and began business again, mostly demonstrating that Mussolini had undertaken a difficult, if not impossible, task, and that circumstances favoured the Abyssinian side. Others, following their lead, wrote knowingly of the rains, which when they came would assuredly prevent Italian military operations; and an illustrated newspaper published Mr. G. D. H. Cole's plan for stopping Mussolini. Haile Selassie [2] became a familiar figure, bearded and cloaked, in white breeches and approximate bowler. There was a Friends of Abyssinia Society, as, later, of Czechoslovakia, Albania, Poland and other disappearing countries. The enlightenment, at any rate latterly, of Haile Selassie's rule was stressed; his determination to abolish the slave trade in his dominion, admired, and Abyssinia's Christianity discovered by many who had for-

[1] The concession was soon cancelled as a result of pressure from the American State Department. Mr. Rickett's subsequent movements continued to arouse journalistic interest for a little while, but this belated attention proved unproductive.

[2] He was variously designated—by sympathizers, usually as the Emperor; by those who anticipated, or hoped for, an Italian victory (for instance, Mr. Garvin), as the Negus or, ironically, as the Lion of Judah. Neutral commentators kept to Haile Selassie, which suited equally a reigning and an exiled monarch.

merly assumed its non-existence. Lake Tsana came into the lives of the more assiduous newspaper readers; and some transient excitement was caused by the publication in the *Giornale d'Italia* of the confidential Report of an Inter-Departmental Committee, presided over by Sir John Maffey, which had been set up in the spring of 1935 to investigate the extent to which British interests would be affected by the realization of Italian aims in Abyssinia.[1]

The Italo-Abyssinian War faced the Government with a serious dilemma. Its natural impulse was to react to it as to Japan's invasion of Manchuria; to exhibit a dignified but tepid disapproval, and to let events take their course, afterwards dealing with the resultant situation as seemed best at the time. Against this, was the enthusiasm of a large and important section of the electorate for the League and its Covenant. "The League of Nations is the keystone of our foreign policy," Mr. Baldwin had said and often repeated, thereby ensuring the support of many voters who might otherwise have turned away their faces from him. If the League was the keystone of our foreign policy, then, clearly, some attempt must be made to demonstrate its efficacy in preventing one League member from forcibly taking possession of the territory of another; if an embroilment with Italy was to be avoided, then, equally clearly, Mussolini's designs on Abyssinia must not be seriously impeded. It was another case for a Doctor's Mandate.

As Foreign Secretary, Sir John Simon had not enhanced his reputation. The post was a difficult one, and grew ever more difficult as European tension increased. Sir Austen

[1] The Report's conclusion was that no important British interests were endangered, with the exception of Lake Tsana, the waters of the Blue Nile, and certain tribal grazing rights.

Chamberlain had cracked under the strain, and resigned, recovering to fill the•less exacting role of an Elder Statesman; to the last delivering solemn pronouncements upon public affairs, and when he died in 1937, respectfully mourned as "one who had achieved pre-eminence in recent years among those Elder Statesmen, ever required, and ever ready to give the fruits of their great experience in their country's service." No breakdown terminated Sir John Simon's occupancy of the Foreign Office; still sound in body and in mind, he moved unwillingly across to the Home Office. The difficult task of, at the same time, making the League the keystone of our foreign policy and neglecting to fulfil the obligations assumed by signatories of the Covenant whenever fulfilling them might exacerbate relations with other Powers, required someone more supple and dexterous than he. Sir Samuel Hoare seemed a suitable choice; as he had succeeded in framing an Indian Constitution which purported to satisfy Indian nationalist aspirations without alienating those who regarded their satisfaction as calamitous, it was reasonable to suppose that he might succeed in framing a foreign policy which purported to satisfy the League of Nations Union without alienating those who abhorred its activities.

As far as the former of these requirements was concerned, Sir Samuel scored almost at once a resounding success. He delivered a speech at Geneva which eloquently and vehemently asserted the British Government's determination to maintain its support of the League and its ideals as the most effective way of ensuring peace: "the ideas enshrined in the Covenant," he said, "and in particular the aspiration to establish the rule of law in international affairs, have appealed with growing force to the strain of idealism

which has its place in our national character." Such a sentiment was bound to give widespread satisfaction; the *Morning Post* alone, its doom already upon it,[1] objected that
strains of idealism were better left unmentioned by their
fortunate possessors, and for others to detect. From the
Times to the *Daily Herald* rose a chorus of praise. At last
England had a foreign policy, and a Foreign Secretary with
the vision and ability to execute it. Mr. Eden who, when
yoked to Sir John Simon, had often seemed to be dragging
him along, was momentarily quite outstripped by his new
chief. It was true that the principles enunciated by Sir
Samuel were no novelty; his advocacy of them might, indeed, be compared to that moment in the Litany when,
after many long prayers, the officiating clergyman ex-
claims: "Let us pray!" Yet, though familiar, they acquired
a freshness from the resolute and unequivocal manner with
which Sir Samuel stated them. This time he really was going
to pray.

Having delighted the League of Nations Union, it remained to ensure that no ill-consequences should result; a
drunkard who in the excitement of a revivalist meeting publicly takes the pledge, may still on the way home surrepti-
tiously replenish his pocket flask. Sir Samuel Hoare and

---

[1] Its circulation steadily dwindled after the War; and as its patrons died
off, there were none to take their places. Its point of view was unfashionable, and the honesty with which it was stated, uncongenial. In its last
years, before its absorption by the *Daily Telegraph*, it was a stranger in a
strange land; with no ideological affiliations, finding MacDonald as unpalatable after he had formed the National Government as before, Hitler
as unpalatable as Stalin. Its correspondent was among the first to be
expelled from the Third Reich. With a final burst of energy, it attacked
Sir Samuel Hoare's Indian Bill, and the subterfuges adopted to gain
support for it, and then expired. Its lonely but spirited existence in a
world in which Colonel Blimp was funny and Litvinov on the side of
the angels, could not be protracted.

M. Laval worked out a plan which, while it left Haile
Selassie with a fragmentary kingdom connected with the
sea by a slender desert strip, gave Mussolini effective control of most of Abyssinia. The arrangement was intended
to be secret until its practicability had been tested, and
ultimately to be submitted to the League Council, whose
approval its architects presumably thought might be obtained; but a leakage in Paris led to its premature publication. At first the version of it which appeared in the
French Press was officially dismissed as inaccurate and misleading. This attitude was difficult to maintain when what
had been published was largely authentic; and at last it was
reluctantly admitted that Sir Samuel and M. Laval had,
with the best possible intentions, tentatively drafted what
they thought might provide a basis for an Italo-Abyssinian
settlement.

At once a great storm broke. Sir Samuel, from being the
most righteous of Foreign Secretaries, became the most
execrated; pacifists of all varieties rose up in their wrath, a
formidable company, and even National Liberals breathed
defiance. When the *Times* turned on its own, what could
poor Sir Samuel do but resign? *Et tu, Brute!* His tenure of
the Foreign Secretaryship, which had begun so gloriously,
ended thus sadly, with almost universal blame. In one of
those scenes dear to politicians and journalists, when reserve
is broken down and the man emerges from the statesman,
when Cabinet Ministers may weep [1] and Under-Secretaries
of State show that they too have hearts, Sir Samuel explained
to the House of Commons the circumstances of his resigna-

---

[1] Men of action are often tearful. Cromwell was given to weeping. ("To
render his persuasions more efficacious, he avails himself of tears, weeping
more over the sins of others than his own"); Mr. Winston Churchill and
Mr. J. H. Thomas have tears and are prepared to shed them.

tion. He had acted as he thought for the best; to become Foreign Secretary had been his life-long ambition, realized only to be disappointed; if his career was broken, he had no regrets; he had tried to do his duty, and it was for posterity to judge whether his policy was sagacious or mistaken. These noble sentiments, delivered with dignity, and sometimes with palpable emotion, were sympathetically received. In the sanctity of martyrdom, he withdrew for a recuperative trip to Switzerland, not long afterwards reappearing in the Cabinet as First Lord of the Admiralty, his broken heart and career both, it seemed, mended, with no visible mark of the rupture they had suffered.

Before Mr. Eden was appointed to succeed Sir Samuel, there was some delay, during which Lord Halifax acted as Foreign Secretary. He, too, had survived a temporary setback in his fortunes; the Irwin-Gandhi Pact had damaged him as the Hoare-Laval Pact had Sir Samuel. Now, his Viceroyalty forgotten, he was being carried along from office to office, propelled more by the inevitability of his advancement than by his own ambition or conspicuous ability. English politicians, unless they are Jews, to succeed must look and speak like bookies or like clergymen. Lord Halifax was of the clergyman variety; his speeches were earnest but not very lively sermons, his manner that of a country vicar proceeding along a village street, genially greeting each of his parishioners with a smile and a suitable remark. Thus equipped, he was bound to succeed. Reputations rose and fell, but his went on forever; for the moment an Eden filled the firmament, but when that brilliance had subsided, his quiet glow would remain.

Many clamoured for their Eden, and when they got him, rejoiced. He was, the *New Statesman* exulted, "Mr. Bald-

win's Christmas present to the nation," and no gift could
have been more acceptable. His zeal for the League was
beyond question; he was still youthful, and vigorous and
idealistic, with no roots in the old, unhappy past; a child of
enlightenment, young Master High-Mind. He would not
conclude questionable deals with M. Laval, truckle to Mr.
Matsuoka or Mussolini, desert Haile Selassie in his hour of
need. The Goliath of ruthless, overbearing force would be
laid low by this spirited David with his accurately aimed
pebble sanctions.

Sanctions, which had already been in operation for some
months, had proved somewhat disappointing; and it was
hoped that Mr. Eden would impart a new vigour to them.
They represented in the public mind a means of engaging
in warfare innocuously, a play-way or substitute war;
enough war to cover a sixpence. When the aggressor reared
his ugly head, instead of it being necessary to stiffen the
sinews, summon up the blood, and advance against him, his
purposes might be frustrated by peppering him with sanctions. Covenant-breaking Powers would go down before
sanctions like reeds before a wind, and those who applied
them suffer perhaps an inconsiderable pecuniary loss, but
none of life or limb. Sanctions in our time, oh Lord!

The League's cumbrous machinery actually succeeded in
functioning to the extent of inducing most of its members
to put an embargo on trade in certain specified commodities
with Italy; sanctions were instituted, and the institutors
waited, or purported to wait, for the Italian campaign in
Abyssinia to die of inanition. It seemed in practice to be not
much affected either way. Oil, whose deprivation might
have seriously impeded military operations, was, perhaps
for that very reason, not included among sanctionable com-

modities; a self-righteously imposed embargo on the supply of arms to both belligerents left Italy with an overwhelming superiority in war material, and by making full use of aerial bombardment and poison gas, an easy and quick victory was assured, and was hailed by Mr. Garvin as an outstanding and almost unparalleled achievement. "Remember," Mussolini had said, "the Italians have always defeated black races." Though this was not strictly accurate, they indubitably defeated the Abyssinians; and the pride, and perhaps surprise, their victory occasioned Mussolini, was indicated by the manner in which he announced it in Rome. No more momentous or splendid happening, he exulted, had been heard of even in that city, which in its long history had been the scene of so much that was momentous and splendid; Caesar's triumphs were trifles, and St. Peter's martyrdom insignificant compared with the Italian conquest of Abyssinia.

The League was left with sanctions on its hands; and, even with Mr. Eden in charge of British foreign policy, they soon became as embarrassing and unpalatable as yesterday's sardines. What they were to prevent had come to pass; and though this could scarcely be said to provide a reason for calling them off, it equally made their continuance seem rather pointless. They lingered on, few remembering their existence, causing, it was said, a certain shortage of lemons in Covent Garden, until they were finally extinguished by Mr. Neville Chamberlain, who referred to them as "the very midsummer of madness." It was his first pronouncement upon foreign affairs, suitably marked by a misquotation; the prelude to an astonishing performance in that field.

Besides sanctions, the League had also to dispose of Abyssinia, whose delegate persisted in putting in an appearance at Assembly meetings. His credentials could scarcely be challenged in the circumstances; yet as the Government he represented no more existed, its representation created difficulties, especially as the Power responsible for its situation remained a League member. The awkwardness of this situation was intensified when Haile Selassie appeared in person at Geneva, a reproach to his disconcerted defenders; a Dead Soul, with only a paper or Covenant existence; a monarch who had lost his kingdom, but retained his right to participate in the League's deliberations. Even this poor remainder of his former glory, he soon also lost, vanishing into retirement at Bath, where he lived secluded and alone. Lord Halifax proposed, and the others agreed, that Abyssinia should henceforth be regarded as non-existent in the capacity of Sovereign State.

Now the League fell into a decline, its proceedings little noticed, members falling away, contributions collected with difficulty, or not at all; Herr Greiser, President of the Danzig Senate, actually cocking a snook at assembled delegates. An imposing Palais des Nations, planned when prospects were brighter, stood, desolate, by the Lake of Geneva, large assembly halls empty, lavish accommodation for journalists and visitors, unused, a commodious and well-stocked library provided by the Rockefeller Foundation, entered rarely. Perhaps ghosts walked there, but few live persons; perhaps ghosts orated, ghostly voices proclaiming ghostly hopes in the stillness of night, shadows flitting—Wilson, Briand, Stresemann, my frrriends.

Their kingdom, like Haile Selassie's, had vanished and gone; attempts to revive it when it was seen to be languishing, all were fruitless. It was an idea they had raised as their standard, seemingly fluttering proudly, seemingly fluttering; then only a flag-pole with no flag attached. Friends deserted and enemies adhered; the Soviet Government, once confident that the League was a "hypocritical organization whose thin veneer of internationalist cant did not hide from a discerning eye shameless imperialist intentions," sent Litvinov to Geneva, where he soon was regarded as the Covenant's most faithful adherent, perhaps its only true one. In time, even he came no more; a suggestion made when he resigned his post as Commissar for Foreign Affairs, that he might be appointed "a roving ambassador of good-will," not fructifying; no more good- or ill-will emanating from this plump Jew, once Mr. Harris with lodgings conveniently near the British Museum, no more ambassadorial appointments for him, roving or stationary; on the rare occasions that he appeared at public functions in Moscow, the chairs on either side of him ostentatiously unoccupied.

Bearded Scandinavians, Titulescu, Politis—Geneva knew them no more. The last agenda discussed before Swiss frontiers had to be hermetically sealed with blasts of dynamite, "included items relating to nutrition and the unification of signals at level-crossings." Then only the Secretariat remained, indestructible, but under instructions that they might be required at short notice to remove themselves to Vichy, presumably with essential documents and cash reserves, if any.

IV

As he walked away from signing the Treaty of Versailles, Clemenceau mournfully remarked: "I fear a peace without victory, just as we had a victory without peace," in that showing a clear understanding of the impossible task which had been set—to establish peace on the foundations of a

victory, to safeguard a victory without jeopardizing peace.
The two—peace and victory, were incompatible and
mutually destructive. What strengthened the one weakened
the other, and *vice versa*. Put together, they made an explo-
sive mixture, which, exploding, must destroy both; leave
neither peace nor victory.

The League was intended to make possible everlasting
victory by ensuring everlasting peace. Other associated
devices with the same objective, were suggested or tried out
as its weakness became apparent. Briand circulated to all
European Governments a project for a United States of
Europe, his communication being in each case politely
acknowledged; and Litvinov indefatigably laboured at con-
structing a system of non-aggression pacts; some of these
being actually concluded and ceremonially signed. Occasionally the President of the United States or a member of
his Administration participated, sending across the Atlantic
to all heads of States messages calling upon them to live at
peace as good neighbours should; and an American journalist, Mr. Clarence K. Streit, disillusioned by some years of
reporting the League's activities, put forward a proposal
for a federation of democracies,[1] which, according to Sir
Norman Angell, Mr. Lionel Curtis and others, marked a
milestone in history, and which left a small deposit in the
shape of an organization called Federal Union, with an
office and officers and headed notepaper, one among many
such. Like a jig-saw puzzle, pieces signifying victory were
fitted together in the expectation that they would signify
peace; and when the pattern was completed, and all who
abhorred war were ready to rejoice, still it signified victory.

Among pacifists, there was much heart-searching, pro-

[1] See *Union Now* by Clarence K. Streit.

ductive, as heart-searching usually is, of debates, lectures, loud-speaker vans, processions, books, letters to newspaper editors, symposiums, banners, and protracted fireside talk, as well as, surprisingly, some heroic machine-gun units; "the pacifists from the English universities make excellent machine-gunners," a *Manchester Guardian* special correspondent reported from Spain. Belief in the desirability of disarmament did not expire with the Disarmament Conference; nor was hope in the League utterly dashed by its failure to prevent Japan's conquest of Manchuria and Italy's of Abyssinia. A cripple in a wheel chair usually to be found outside meetings with a Leftwards tendency, shrilly declaiming: "Penny *No More War!* Penny *No More War!*" continued to put in an appearance and to declaim. The League of Nations Union went on increasing its membership, later impressing politicians by organizing a Peace Ballot in which eleven millions voted that they were opposed to war [1] and in favour of collective security. In the same way, they might have voted that they were opposed to misery and want, opposed to death even, and in favour of collective

[1] "You Shall Decide Peace or War," a poster used by the organizers of the Ballot announced. The questions put were: (1) Should Great Britain remain a member of the League of Nations? (2) Are you in favour of an all-round reduction of armaments by international agreements? (3) Are you in favour of an all-round abolition of national, military and naval aircraft by international agreements? (4) Should the manufacture and sale of armaments for private profit be prohibited by international agreement? (5) Do you consider that if a nation insists on attacking another, the other nations should compel it to stop by (a) economic and non-military measures, (b) if necessary, military measures? To all except 5b (the only question which might involve personal obligations and risks), the answers given were overwhelmingly affirmative. In the case of 5b, there were 6,784,368 "yes" votes, 2,351,981 "no" votes, and 2,422,816 abstentions and doubtful answers. What proportion of the "yes" voters were male, and of them, what proportion were of military age and prepared to undertake military service, was not stated.

happiness, collective prosperity, collective deathlessness; afterwards, perhaps, wondering why it was that despite so impressive a demonstration of their wishes, sufficient to turn an election, make or break a government, they still suffered, still groaned with unsatisfied desire, still at last breathed no more.

Pledges were earnestly registered never in any circumstances whatsoever to take up arms; Nobel Peace Prizes were awarded, to Henderson, Sir Austen Chamberlain, Sir Norman Angell, almost, in 1933, to Mussolini, and in France a Golden Book of Peace was inscribed with several million signatures. The Oxford Union carried a motion favouring a refusal to fight for king and country if requested so to do, and some, taking literally a remark of Professor Einstein to the effect that if only four per cent of humanity were resolute in refusing to go to war, Peace would be assured, decided to constitute themselves that four per cent, and wore badges indicating the same. Mr. C. E. M. Joad wrote a book entitled *Why War?*, when war came none the less, perhaps wondering, "Why Joad?"; and Mr. Aldous Huxley derived comfort from the thought that "most zoologists are now of the opinion that man's ancestor was not a gorilla-like ape, but a gentle, sensitive creature, something like a tarsier." [1] At a Wembley Hospital fête a Peace Balloon Race was organized; Mr. Lansbury, seen off at Victoria Station by a little band of enthusiasts and there presented with a sprig of white heather to wear in his button-hole, made a round of visits to European statesmen, after some hours with Hitler remarking that he and the Führer had had "a friendly discussion on the entire international situation"; and postcards were dispatched to addresses chosen at random from

[1] See *An Encyclopaedia of Pacifism* edited by Aldous Huxley.

German directories, stating that the writers of them were resolved in all circumstances to practise non-resistance, surprise being expressed that these communications were duly delivered, though it is difficult to imagine any which would give greater satisfaction to the authorities in Germany responsible for examining correspondence from abroad.

Many and varied were the suggestions made (among them one for the enthronement of a League of Nations monarch, who would hold his court with suitable pageantry at Geneva [1]), many and varied the enterprises launched, great the expenditure of energy and of passion, enormous the area of paper covered, heartfelt the vows taken,[2] undeniably sincere the words spoken. The pacifist ranks included disciples of Gandhi who held that life was sacred and should never be put out, as well as Marxists bloodthirstily eager to exterminate the bourgeoisie and establish a dictatorship of the proletariat. There were those who followed Lord Davies in advocating an international force which would fall upon Covenant-breakers as efficaciously as policemen upon housebreakers, and those who, like Dr. Maud Royden, wanted a peace-army engaged to march between belligerents, forcing them either to suspend hostilities or shoot down unarmed and unresisting civilians. Women were advised, sometimes by men, to refuse to bear children as long as the possibility of war remained; conferences were held and demanded; petitions were frequent, and armament manufacturers boldly denounced both in prose and in verse.

So great a diversity of pacifists and pacifist-activities inevitably led to clashes, especially as pacifists tend to be

See *Which Way To-morrow?* by Noreen Blyth.
For instance by members of the Peace Pledge Union—"We renounce War and never again, directly or indirectly, will we support or sanction another."

somewhat aggressive in temperament. The violence in action which they abhor appears to get transferred to their opinions, as ascetics who renounce sensual pleasure sometimes find it necessary to indulge in sensual pain. Peace demonstrations were often more vehement than recruiting meetings; the course of the League of Nations Union proved more troubled than that of the Navy League, and an international gathering of pacifists held in Paris in November 1931, ended in angry disputes, and at last in fighting so violent that the police had to be called in.

Apart from hopes of ensuring peace by some particular device, there was always the general feeling that war had become too terrible to happen. Governments would recoil, it was thought, from precipitating a conflict whose consequences would be so disastrous for all. Before aeroplanes and poison gas and high explosives it was all very well, but these horrors had fundamentally altered the situation. What Mr. Harold Macmillan has called with deep feeling the "modern foul ubiquity" of war, made it inadmissible. When the victims could be selected and the scene of their suffering localized, it was understandable that wars should be lightly even uproariously, entered upon; but a foully ubiquitou war, a war which might as easily demolish the Bank of Eng land as Rheims Cathedral, and as easily decapitate an Arch bishop of Canterbury as one of his parishioners, was not t be endured.

With pathetic tenacity men cling to the belief that chang ing circumstances change life. Can a world in which aero planes travel at 400 miles per hour, they ask themselves, b the same as one in which there were only steam-engine laboriously attaining their mile a minute? If a voice may b carried across a wide ocean, is it conceivable that the word thus transmitted should have no greater significance than if spoken across a tea-table? "The world of everyday life is now so radically different from the world of the Gospels," a clergyman writes,[1] "and the effort required to interpret the universal truths that derive from the Gospel, in terms that mean anything in a world of intricate social organization is so immense, that the whole thing appears remote from life as it has to be lived," not, perhaps, reflecting that the Roman Empire's "world of everyday life" was also radically different from the world of the Gospels, yet not, for that reason, blind to their significance. War has always been brutish and unprofitable, but not so brutish and so unprofitable as now; therefore, the angry passions which formerly brought it to pass, must have given place to a more reasonable temper. The pursuit of power has for many centuries been recklessly undertaken, without counting the cost in life or in treasure, nor deterred by the monotonously repeated demonstration of its inevitable failure to bring satisfaction; yet when it involves millions dying where previously thousands died, an expenditure reckoned in milliards instead of in millions, then, surely, it must be abandoned. Machiavelli's cynical precept that, though "everyone admits how praiseworthy it is in princes to keep faith and live with integrity and not with craft, our experience has been that those princes who have done great things have held good faith of little account," may hitherto have been borne out by experience, Mr. Eden argues, but has now been invalidated by "the greater interdependence of the modern world, the constant contacts, the reduction and indeed the virtual elimination, of the problems which distance once created." In the same way, it might be argued

[1] *The Crisis and Democracy* by the Rev. Eric Fenn.

that whereas hitherto it was legitimately complained that the
wicked prospered, non-stop electric trains between Brighton
and London have rendered such a complaint obsolete; or
that though it unquestionably used to be foolish to lay up
treasure on earth for rust to corrupt, the invention of stain-
less steel has made it foolish no longer. In 1139 the Lateran
Council pronounced the cross-bow "too murderous a
weapon for Christians to employ against one another"; and
doubtless there were Christians who, in the light of this
pronouncement, looked forward to a quiet life in the enjoyment of whatever possessions an unscrupulous use of the
long-bow had procured for them. If so, they were disappointed. Similarly, when during the Crimean War the War
Office rejected a proposal to make use of sulphur fumes in
attacking Sebastopol, on the ground that "an operation of
this nature would contravene the laws of civilized warfare,"
some may have assumed that the use of poison gas in war
need not be dreaded. The use of each new weapon seems
inconceivable, until it has been used long enough to become
familiar.

The fact that in contemporary warfare the home front is
as perilous as any other, has certainly led to an abatement
in martial ardour among those who formerly had a reasonable expectation that in the event of a war their lives would
be regarded as too precious to be endangered. Kipling's
popularity has waned as air-raids have become more dangerous, and imperialism lost much of its appeal since the Strand
became an outpost of empire. Few take pleasure in reading
about, for instance, the British conquest of India, when
doing so only serves to recall episodes which were glamorous
until their like in Abyssinia and elsewhere threatened a
European war and a possible bombardment of London.

"The English have seen my country, therefore I have lost it," [1] an Indian potentate wrote to Sir Charles Metcalf when he learnt that an Englishman had travelled through his territory. His plight is now too reminiscent of Haile Selassie's for its recollection to afford any satisfaction. Imperialism, like Splendid Isolation, flourished when the channel was an effective safeguard against invasion; when we sing "Wider still and wider shall thy bounds be set," Mr. Eden has explained, that "does not indicate any desire for more territory," though without explaining what it does indicate. Perhaps in present circumstances, "Further still and further shall thy bounds be set" would be more suitable. Air warfare has made the Empire seem rather an embarrassing, but still desirable, possession whose origins are better forgotten, than a splendid heritage to rejoice in; and those self-righteous admonitions which were once addressed from London to a turbulent Europe, now emanate in Washington, a wider stretch of water than from Calais to Dover being necessary to facilitate them. The cult of imperialism has moved with them across the Atlantic. It is Hollywood rather than Elstree which delights (as in *The Lives of a Bengal Lancer*) in portraying outposts of Empire and the stern glory of the White Man's Burden.

Peace in our time, is an ancient prayer, devoutly uttered by generation after generation; what is unusual about this generation is that among them the belief has been prevalent that peace was assured. Their desire for peace expressed itself in an institution, resolutions, pledges, a conviction that what they dreaded could not happen; and when the institution proved worthless, the resolutions and pledges of no account, the conviction of no validity, they wondered why,

[1] Quoted in Edward Thompson's *Life of Sir Charles Metcalf*.

many explanations being offered, some indignant, some despairing, and some struggling still to be hopeful. Statesmen were to blame for wrongly interpreting, or wilfully misinterpreting, the will of those they represented. Or, class interest was to blame,[1] leading the privileged to prefer the hazards of war to promoting a universal peace which might jeopardize their privileges; making them acquiesce in Japan's and Italy's acts of aggression, and in Germany's growing strength, for fear that if these countries were frustrated, their Governments would be discredited, and proletarian revolutions result. Or, the League's ideals in the present condition of mankind, had proved too exalted to be practicable, but their application, having once been attempted, would doubtless be attempted again, probably with greater success.

Such explanations, each sufficiently plausible to satisfy some troubled minds, most found inadequate. If statesmen had betrayed the trust imposed in them, all were alike guilty, since all had at different times been entrusted with power; if armament manufacturers and others fearful for their class interests and profits, were to blame, how had a situation been allowed to arise which threatened to encompass their ruin as surely as the ruin of those they preyed upon? A Rothschild in flight from Vienna, and stripped of all his possessions, scarcely suggested that the Anschluss was good for dividends; and the losses sustained by persons with capital invested in the Far East as a result of Japanese depredations there, made it seem unlikely that their interests and Japan's were identical. As for the League's high endeavour, brought to nothing this time by mankind's present moral

[1] An assiduous promoter of this view has been "Vigilantes," a pseudonym which became unnecessary when in 1938 K. Zilliacus, whose identity it hid, left the League Secretariat after being employed for eighteen years in the Information Department. See, for instance, his *Between Two Wars*.

shortcomings, but perhaps meeting with a better response hereafter—that was as may be; only, looking back, more low than high endeavour was noticeable in the League's proceedings.

The great peace debate which went on until, almost without those who participated in it noticing, it had become a war debate, reached no clear conclusions. Again and again, and in a variety of ways, the problem was stated, expounded, elucidated, but still remained intractable—so many desiring peace, and the possibility, then probability, then certainty, of war none the less remaining. It is not the first time that this problem has been considered, nor will it be the last. Many have marvelled that with so deep and widespread a longing for peace, fifty warless years should be a rarity,[1] that peoples tend to look back with most pleasure on the most warlike periods of their history, and that the most beloved leaders are those who summon their followers, not to live, but to die. Has any man of peace in his lifetime commanded the devotion of a Mohammed or a Napoleon? Has any scheme for procuring happiness and security been

[1] See *All in a Maze* by Daniel George and Rose Macaulay, a selection of extracts from the writings of the last 2,500 years which show that there have never lacked impressive expositions of the folly of war and of the excellence and desirability of peace—for instance, from St. Augustine's *The City of God:*

"Whoever gives even moderate attention to human affairs and to our common nature, will recognize that there is no man who does not wish to be joyful, neither is there anyone who does not wish to have peace. For even they who make war desire nothing but victory—desire, that is to say, to attain to peace with glory. For what else is victory than the conquest of those who resist us? And when this is done there is peace. It is therefore with the desire for peace that war is waged, even by those who take pleasure in exercising their warlike nature in command or battle. And hence it is obvious that peace is the end sought for by man. For every man seeks peace by waging war, but no man seeks war by making peace."

as productive of fanaticism and self-sacrifice as war? The
liberal commonly assumes that what men most desire is easy
circumstances, and the pacifist that what they most desire is
to remain alive. Both are understandably bewildered when
they and the benefits they offer are swept contemptuously
aside in favour of one who promises his followers only
privations and death. Seen from a prebendary stall, a *sadhu*
ecstatically reclining on his bed of nails is incomprehensible,
and even the Crucifixion a remote and not very apposite
symbol; yet the *sadhu* receives more veneration than preb-
endaries, and the Crucifixion has caused many wonders to
be performed, and many hearts to be deeply stirred.

It is one of the illusions of Liberalism and all its many
offshoots and affiliations, that the way to men's hearts is to
offer them material benefits. If this were indeed the case,
the triumph of pacifism would be assured, since there is no
material benefit more precious than life, no material catastrophe more awful than death. If, however, men want to
live, they also want to die; and their longing for death is
usually the more ardent and more easily played upon of the
two, because more rarely indulged. It accumulates through
monotonous, disappointing years, a reservoir of death-long-
ing, ready to be tapped, and when tapped, producing wars,
revolutions, and other upheavals. Between the two longings
to live and to die, men fluctuate, making civilizations and
destroying them, formulating beliefs and demolishing them,
bringing order out of disorder and then disorder out of
order, weaving the pattern of their history.

V

Each individual is his own universe, reacting subjectively
to the confused happenings around him, and to the confused

influences brought to bear upon him. Entities are envisaged
—as, public opinion, informed circles, Germany, Peru, the
Workers; but these are largely imaginary. No individual
wholly loses himself in any corporate existence. He remains
alone, a separate particle of life, with eternity before him
and behind, coming solitary into the world, and solitary
departing from it. Even propaganda, whose function it is to
create mass emotions, a heat which makes the tough ego
molten, so that many run together into one brew, cannot
entirely overcome this persistent subjectivity. What is intended to influence, itself takes on the character of what is
influenced. A law-student in the eighteenth century, after
reading *Timon of Athens*, noted down in his diary that its
chief moral was "that prosperity creates abundance of
friends and adversity drives them away again." [1] Such a
view, while it pointed to the law-student in question in due
course becoming Lord Chief Justice (as, indeed, he did),
would have disappointed Shakespeare, who believed that he
was propagating the opposite principle—that prosperity destroys the possibility of friendship. Blake well describes the
technique of all propaganda:

> *This life's dim windows of the soul*
> *Distorts the heavens from pole to pole*
> *And leads you to believe a lie*
> *When you see with, not through, the eye.*

As, however, it is impossible to see only with, not through,
the eye, lies cannot be imposed from without. Lies, like the
Kingdom of Heaven, are within.

A particular event, looked back on, may be adjudged
decisive, or, like Mr. Streit's proposal for a federation of

[1] See *The Diary of Dudley Ryder* edited by William Matthews.

democratic states, as marking a milestone in history; but who knows how it was regarded by this person or that at the time? Who knows even whether, apart from an interested few, it was noticed at all, or if noticed, more than vaguely registered? The keenest nose for news would scarcely have detected any appreciable news-value in the execution, along with two other bad characters, of a seditious Jew, and it is improbable that Shakespeare's obituary notice would have equalled the most insignificant baronet's in length and servility.

Constitutional lawyers were excited by the Statute of Westminster, which drastically modified existing relations between the Dominions and the Mother Country; the acquirement of the Codex Sinaïticus from the Soviet Government for £100,000 delighted antiquarians, led the *Daily Express* to complain that the money might have been better spent, and in Bloomsbury provided amusement at the thought of this perhaps spurious manuscript of the Bible bringing grist to the Marxist mill; Lord Robert Cecil's refusal any longer to represent the National Government at Geneva provided the Opposition with useful ammunition, and the correspondence columns of serious newspapers with letters whose signatories were sufficiently distinguished to justify the use of large type; the discovery in an old croquet-box at Malahide Castle of the original manuscript of Boswell's *Journal of a Tour to the Hebrides*, created some pleasurable anticipation at the prospect of knowing at last what precisely were the "variety of degrading images of every one of which I was the object" which Boswell called down on his head by laughing when Johnson remarked that he had often thought that if he "kept a seraglio, the ladies should all wear linen gowns or cotton; I mean stuffs made of vegetable substance." [1] Yet what proportion of those passing over London Bridge each morning, were troubled about the Statute of Westminster, gratified at possessing the Codex Sinaïticus, disturbed that Lord Robert Cecil should no longer represent them at Geneva, relieved that the Malahide Castle croquet-box had been opened before its precious contents were indecipherable? A little procession, it is true, moved past the Codex Sinaïticus when it was displayed at the British Museum, glancing through glass at its incomprehensible characters with forlorn wonder, and respectfully disposed towards a manuscript which had cost £100,000; but this momentary curiosity was soon satisfied, and the Codex Sinaïticus put away, few knew or cared where. Parliamentary denunciations of the Statute of Westminster by politicians out of office (among them, Edward Majoribanks, whose ambition showed outwardly in a Disraelian curl arranged to fall over his forehead, and who, after completing one volume of a Life of Carson, surprisingly shot himself), statements by politicians in office to the effect that it marked the beginning of a new and more blessed era in imperial relationships, are unlikely to have caused any loss of sleep, except perhaps to the politicians concerned.

Public events, however portentous, trouble little the great mass of mankind, who feel with reason that they are power-

[1] "To hear Mr. Johnson, while sitting solemn in arm-chair, talk of his keeping a seraglio and saying too, 'I have *often* thought,' was truly curious. Mr. MacQueen asked him if he would admit me. 'Yes,' said he, 'if he were properly prepared; and he'd make a very good eunuch. He'd be a fine gay animal. He'd do his part well.' 'I take it,' said I, 'better than you would do your part.' Though he treats his friends with uncommon freedom, he does not like a return. He seemed to me to be a little angry. He got off from my joke by saying, 'I have not told you what was to be my part'—and then at once he returned to my office as eunuch and expatiated upon it with such fluency that it really hurt me. He made me quite contemptible for the moment."

less to influence them, and in any case must endure their consequences. An aching tooth is more woeful than Hitler, a cold in the head of greater concern to the sufferer than the annexation of Albania. What turns a Foreign Secretary grey and haggard in a few months, leaves unperturbed the half-million who assemble to watch the Derby. His egotism is involved, but theirs is not, though later the decisions he takes may cost them wounds, bitter separations, their lives even. Until this happens, the fortunes of the horse in which they have invested a few shillings, are of greater moment than proposed alliances, fallen dynasties, and persecuted minorities. Power, the raw material of politics, is a specialized taste; most find money and fornication and snobbishness more alluring. Those who are preoccupied with power—politicians, dictators, revolutionaries, reformers, to inflate their own importance try to create the illusion that others share their preoccupation, or rail against them for not sharing it, complaining that when civilization is endangered the foolish multitude goes on its way, unheedful of them and their prognostications, too apathetic to read or listen to what they have to say, or to register votes for or against them. Such apathy cannot be wholly obscured even in dictatorial states, with all their propagandist and coercive resources. Though apathy is made a crime punishable with imprisonment or death, still it exists; perhaps more than ever. How stupendous must be the apathy of one who has for the hundredth time processed with a banner past Lenin's tomb, or roared his salutation to Führer or Duce; for the thousandth time opened his *Pravda* or *Angriff* or *Popolo d'Italia* to find there a glowing account of his rulers' achievements. Flags are obediently displayed, slogans obediently shouted; yet somehow the result is not convincing. A football match, a photograph, an almost nude beauty chorus, the announcement of lottery winners, evokes more authentic enthusiasm.

Newspapers with large circulations reflect public tastes and interests more surely than politicians' speeches or leading articles in the *Times* or *Manchester Guardian*. Their so ardent pursuit of news has to be based on the single consideration of what will interest their readers. If their readers are indifferent to soil erosion, so are they; if their readers find the Rev. Harold Davidson, Rector of Stiffkey, more enthralling than Lord Robert Cecil, so do they. Where the space devoted to soil erosion or Lord Robert is measured in inches, that devoted to the Rev. Davidson is measured in columns. He strikes a responsive chord, whereas the others are worth at most a casual, forgetting glance. For days on end millions are absorbed in his adventures, copy arriving in newspaper offices, precious copy, scarcely needing attention from sub-editors, sent straightway to be set, with only easily devised headlines and sub-headings added to attract the eye, and a bill printed—"Rector in the Box"—to be waved in the faces of passers-by, hoarsely shouted in their ears, lest they should forget what is available for them.

The Rev. Davidson appeared before the Norwich Consistory Court charged with immoral practices. Such a charge was certain to arouse interest, especially as, since the passing of legislation which forbade the reporting of divorce court proceedings, newspapers had been deprived of a valuable source of salacious matter. The fact that a clergyman was concerned, added to the interest; and the Rev. Davidson's obvious delight in the publicity accorded him ensured that the Court's proceedings should be lengthy and colourful. Lawyers pieced together the tale of his misdemeanours, questioning, producing witnesses and exhibits; among these a recently taken photograph of the Rector and a female acquaintance, apparently naked, whose effect was scarcely offset by a letter from the Bishop of London commending the Rev. Davidson's missionary zeal. Each word was precious; eagerly recorded, telephoned, and soon available ·to relieve the tedium of a homeward journey, or to enliven a quiet hour with a pipe after supper. Between the Court's sittings, interest shifted to Stiffkey, where the Rev. Davidson still conducted services, char-a-bancs bringing a large addition to his usual congregation, and flashlight photographs being taken of the Rector in his pulpit, in hood and surplice expounding his text.

His own evidence was spirited, but failed to undo the damaging impression produced by that of Miss Barbara Harris, a girl he had known, and, it appeared, referred to affectionately as "Queen of my heart." When asked if he had made any reference to religion in the course of their many conversations, Miss Harris said the single instance she could recall was an, in the circumstances, unfortunate reference to God not minding sins of the body, but only sins of the mind; and though he had recommended her to read "good books and Shakespeare," the only good book specified had been *Damaged Goods*. Perhaps the public attitude to the Rector, after digesting his own and others' testimony, was best expressed by a publican who, according to one witness, had greeted him when he came into his bar with: "Hullo, you old thief. Still getting cash? How are all the girls?"

The unfrocking of the Rector of Stiffkey proved a long and expensive process, beneficial to newspapers and lawyers, but distasteful to his fellow clergy, who understandably resented the publicity which attended the exposure of one black sheep when their own virtuous labours passed largely unnoticed. Nor was the Rev. Davidson wholly forgotten when deprived of his Holy Orders. For some months he appeared at cinemas in various parts of the country. Wearing ill-fitting evening dress, he came in front of the screen between one film and another; made a short speech about the wrongs he had suffered, and then gave a recitation, usually humorous, of a type once popular at amateur concerts, but now seldom heard. When this resource failed him, he found other means of making a living out of his notoriety; as by starving in a barrel on Blackpool beach, in the hope of thereby diverting holiday-makers, who were invited to pay sixpence for the privilege of being admitted to his presence. Such activities, if they kept his name before the public, provided only a precarious livelihood, and sometimes got him into trouble with the police. He found, as many others have, that fame is dearly bought; and he must have occasionally looked back regretfully to his obscure, but comfortable Stiffkey days, when he enjoyed the assured income and social position of a beneficed clergyman.

In the end, like the early Christians, he was thrown to the lions. A travelling menagerie announced as an additional attraction that the famous Rector of Stiffkey would appear with the lions in their cage. At first the lions gave no sign of resenting his presence among them, and then one day in a fit of petulance mauled him so severely that he had to be taken to hospital, where he soon died. A large crowd attended his funeral, and after he had been interred, struggled to get handfuls of the earth which had been piled on his coffin, in their eagerness pushing against one another, so that some swooned.

VI

Sex, which carried the Rev. Davidson to fame, was the commonest ingredient in curiosity's daily fodder; often enriched by violence and bloodshed, with money to sweeten it, and social position to make it fragrant. It called down from posters, sparkled when night came in innumerable coloured lights, permeated cinema darkness. Loud-speakers and gramophones roared or crooned it, books and newspapers and illustrated periodicals made it their concern. Sex was the spur that the clear spirit did raise (that last infirmity of noble flesh) to scorn delights and live laborious days.

Like gold-prospectors looking in their sieves for the minutest particle of precious ore, the faintest gleam amidst dull mud, each day's happenings were painstakingly searched for their sex-deposit. Crime provided a rich yield, misery and despair were not to be neglected. Here a man found in pyjamas in a gas-filled room. Pyjamas entitled him to one day's fame; six lines of print between an under-secretary's speech at a prize-giving and bankruptcy pro-ceedings. Here a woman picked up, naked, from the sea. Her nakedness deserved a mention, at any rate in early editions. Clothed, she had been nothing. Even the Royal Academy was worth a casual glance in case it should contain a suitable nude; and in denouncing books as indecent, their indecency might be displayed.

Honour Slaying in Honolulu was fool-proof—warm, indolent nights, and rape; a cruelly ravished wife cruelly avenged. Mrs. Barney kept the wires busy and typewriters tapping when her youthful lover was found shot dead, and a tale unfolded of love and debauchery—photograph circu-lated, taken long ago when her life was new and in the spring; eminent counsel briefed, and special reporters active, among them Mr. Gilbert Frankau, who expatiated upon the great beauty of Mrs. Barney's neck, his admiration for which led him to describe her as "Almeira of the marble neck"; at last an acquittal, this enabling her to make her own small, belated contribution towards satisfying the curiosity she had aroused.

A sentimental judge might unknowingly help sub-editors in their daily search for what would warm the blood a pennyworth. Mr. Justice McCardie, hearing a case in which Mr. Dover Place, a grocer's assistant, sued Dr. Charles Searle for damages for the alleged enticing away of his wife, compared Mrs. Place to Helen of Troy. Henceforth it was the Helen of Troy case, and worth headlines, posters even. Mr. Justice McCardie's poetic imagery, though appreciated in Fleet Street, met with the disapproval of his fellow judges; in allowing an appeal against his verdict in favour of the defendant, Lord Justice Scrutton remarked tartly that it was no part of a judge's business to air his views about, for instance, underclothing, especially when, like Mr. Justice McCardie, he was unmarried, and might therefore be assumed to have no more than a theoretical knowledge of such matters. Mr. Justice McCardie retorted by stating publicly that if another appeal against any verdict of his came before Lord Justice Scrutton, he would decline to let him have the use of his notes. With some difficulty their unseemly quarrel was patched up, and any possibility of its renewal removed when Mr. Justice McCardie took his own life. In his lifetime he provided much suitable material for newspapers, and crowned this service by the manner of his death, which was amply reported, and sustained its interest even until the funeral—wreaths and mourners eagerly examined; sobs, tears, anguished looks, all recorded, and indignation expressed when, some weeks later, the chair in which he was sitting when he shot himself, was knocked down for a paltry sum at an auction of his effects.

Like a dark octopus with many quivering tentacles, curiosity hungered, and in being fed, hungered the more. Protests were lodged against its rapacity, but they were unavailing. Cameras were all-seeing eyes, and telephones all-hearing ears. "Mother who starved for her Children— Pictures." She must be seen, lean and desolate and heroic. The wife's kiss, the widow's tear, the murderer's terror, the lover's desire—these must be made palpable to feeling and to sight. Words lost their force; leaded, staring, becoming ever bigger and ever fewer. It was the eye which required, and was given, sustenance.

In America Colonel Lindbergh's baby was kidnapped. What a concentration of attention on this melancholy happening, hearts panting after news of it like the hart after the water-brook; newsmen descending, a resolute army not to be gainsaid, coming on foot, in motor-cars, aeroplanes even; no detail too small to escape their attention, no scene too poignant to abash their restless pencils. Breathlessly the sequence of events was followed—dollar-notes tossed over a cemetery wall, the help of underworld characters invoked, a curious retired schoolmaster, John F. Condon, purporting to act, under the pseudonym "Jafsie," as intermediary between the kidnappers and Colonel Lindbergh, and momentarily famous, his tight-lipped mouth and dull features easily recognized. When the baby's remains were found, interest waned, and Colonel Lindbergh and his wife decamped to

Europe, hopeful that there they might escape the publicity which had become distasteful to them.[1]

Like T. E. Lawrence, Colonel Lindbergh shrank from his own legend, and in escaping notice became mysterious, thereby attracting it the more. Truly those that take to publicity must perish by publicity. The craving to be known, like all other cravings, is its own undoing, since it is soon apparent that the multitude stares as intently at murderers as at heroes, at monstrosities as at saints. Cromwell riding beside Lambert at the head of his army remarked of the cheers which everywhere greeted them, that the same noises would come from the same throats if he was on his way to be hanged.

Lytton Strachey died, but his spirit went marching on, leaving a trail of biographies in his manner; one after the other old idols pulled down, until so many littered the earth that the fashion began of standing them up again, somewhat chipped and battered from their recent overturning, but still once more upright. Queen Victoria had her fame renewed, perhaps because of a longing for the stability she seemed to symbolize; perhaps because, when homosexual tendencies were so prevalent, she had the appeal of a woman with little or no expectation of being seduced. Books about her continued to appear; her letters were published; and, when the Lord Chamberlain's ban was lifted, Mr. Laurence Housman's *Palace Plays* enjoyed great popularity. Victorian furniture and bric-à-brac, formerly unsaleable, began to be eagerly acquired, chromium plated chairs and mathematical

[1] They decamped back to America when war broke out, finding even publicity more bearable than it. Colonel Lindbergh celebrated his homecoming by a broadcast advising his fellow-countrymen at all costs to preserve their neutrality.

vases were discarded, to give place to pianos tied with bows
of ribbon, and minutely carved sideboards. The Victorian
Age, so confident of its own greatness and solidity, had been
regarded successively with horror, sniggering amusement,
and now with romantic esteem.

A rebellion in Dartmoor Prison disturbed the quiet of a
Sunday afternoon, and provided the occasion for a journalistic feat. Within a few hours of the outbreak, special
editions of Sunday newspapers were available containing
an account of it, and photographs of the prison in flames.
This sombre, lonely edifice, whose existence and occupancy
had been taken for granted, became suddenly of present
concern, when accounts were read of enraged prisoners
beating at their cell-doors, refusing to return from exercising
in the courtyard; like revolutionaries, aiming first at burning
the paper records of their subjection, as though when these
were gone they would be free. "The public," the *Times*
wrote, "will read of these events with amazement. They
seem to belong to another age, or at least to some other
country." Later, they would have seemed less amazing,
dwarfed by larger conflagrations; less remote, when institutions more substantial even than Dartmoor Prison showed
signs of cracking. Anxiety continued after the rebellion had
been suppressed, and rumours were current that another
concerted escape might be attempted, this time with outside
help. Local inhabitants stayed, frightened, at home, and
soldiers equipped with machine-guns and searchlights
guarded the prison, until, gradually, the tension eased, and
Dartmoor Prison was again forgotten. A Commission of
Enquiry subsequently condemned it as "unsuitable for
criminals of the dangerous modern type"; the leaders of the

rebellion were severely punished, and those who had been "loyal," [1] rewarded.

The opening of a new Shakespeare Memorial Theatre at Stratford gave an occasion for one of those functions which delight equally politicians, professors, clergymen, aspiring knights and caterers, bringing them together in one common enterprise, objectionable to none and profitable to all. The politician has an opportunity to demonstrate his culture, to convey an impression of himself turning with relief from wearisome and often distasteful public duties to celebrate higher things; the professor or clergyman is exhilarated by making personal contact with the great and the famous; the aspiring knight associates himself with a cause which, perhaps helped out by a contribution to party funds, has often received recognition in Honours' Lists, and the caterer caters. They march in procession, make speeches, pay one another compliments, easily finding in the poet they are celebrating lines to their purpose, making him sportsman,

---

[1] A certain uneasiness about the use of the word "loyal" in such a case was manifested by some newspapers putting it in inverted commas. Others, however, used it without this mild qualification, reassuring themselves, perhaps, by the reflection that if a politician who votes against his principles in obedience to party orders, may be described as loyal, why not a prisoner who upholds the authority of his gaolers? Inverted commas provide a small, but accurate, register of the fluctuation of values. Until his last years, the founder of the Salvation Army appeared as "General" Booth in the columns of the *Times*. When the inverted commas were dropped, his reception at Court was only a matter of time. Left-Wing writers used hopefully to refer to the Nazi "Revolution," but most of them have now ceased thus to question the authenticity of Nazi revolutionary pretensions. The abandonment of sanctions at the end of the Italo-Abyssinian War was heralded by their sudden appearance as "sanctions," a change which should have relieved Mussolini of any anxiety he may still have had about them. If the *Times* ever begins to refer to the "King" or the "Archbishop of Canterbury," a revolution may be confidently assumed to be imminent; if to the "Times," some cosmic catastrophe.

countryman, patriot, gentleman, democrat, according to the exigencies of the moment. Flags are unfurled, wreaths carried and deposited; top-hats gleam in the sunshine, and dull applause resounds when large meals have been eaten.

Each generation gets, as well as the Government, the Shakespeare it deserves. He is assimilated by each successive phase of human folly; a process which is facilitated by the fortunate chance that little is known about his life, and that his works are so comprehensive that even temperance reformers can find sustenance in them. To Victorian critics like Dowden, he had every Victorian virtue, including financial and social success; when he died, Anne Hathaway "smoothed the pillow beneath his head for the last time, and felt that her right hand had been taken from her." With the publication of *The Portrait of Mr. W. H.*, the Sonnets came into their own, and homosexuals were heartened to feel that there was no *prima facie* reason why they should not have written *Hamlet*. In the heat of 1914 a professor indignantly asserted that Germans might occupy Belgium, but "Shakespeare shall never be theirs"; when this heat was spent, pacifists claimed him, though without endorsing Falstaff's statement of their case—"What is that word honour? air, who hath it? he that died o' Wednesday." Falstaff's pacifism, like Rabelais', was too unlike Professor Gilbert Murray's to be congenial. After Freud, it was inevitable that the serenity which Dowden had detected in *The Tempest* should be looked for, and found, in *Antony and Cleopatra*. This serenity, the authors of a recent volume of Shakespearean criticism [1] contend, may clearly be attributed to the fact that Shakespeare had "met a woman in

1 *The Voyage to Illyria* by Kenneth Muir and Sean O'Loughlin.

whom his desire and affection could reunite," thereby solving "the sex problem of his own life." Their only complaint is that his "conclusions on sexual love are for us a little strained by his irritating insistence on pre-nuptial chastity." With Dowden it was the other way round; pre-nuptial indulgence proved his stumbling-block. If Shakespeare fitted Freud like a glove, Marx presented some difficulty. The easiest course would have been to argue, like Mr. Wells, that since Shakespeare had formulated no ideas, made no contribution towards human progress, he was historically negligible. Elaborate productions of *Hamlet*, and even *Romeo and Juliet*, in Moscow, made such an attitude heretical, and Marxist critics were able to demonstrate that Romeo and Juliet was "litmus paper registering the social currents of their time," and Caliban Shakespeare's contribution to the problem of colonial exploitation; that Shakespeare, "standing on the watershed between mediaevalism and capitalism . . . dealt with the relation between centrality of power and the confused rivalry of feudalist nobles . . . was emotionally dominated by the contradictions of emerging capitalism." [1]

The Shakespeare industry throve despite changing conditions; ideologues laboured upon him as once theologians had, and on several important occasions Mr. Neville Chamberlain took his name not in vain. *Richard II* provided the *Daily Express* with a middle-article on the occasion of King Edward VIII's abdication, and *Coriolanus* cost the director of the Comédie Française his post. An expensive, all-star production of *A Midsummer Night's Dream*, directed by

[1] See "William Shakespeare." An essay by Jack Lindsay published in the *Left Review*.

Mr. Max Reinhardt, proved popular, cinemas at which it was showing being furnished with small plaster-of-Paris busts of the Bard for publicity purposes.

VII

While such matters were preoccupying few or many minds for some minutes or hours or days, but mostly minutes, the inexorable process of change continued. Inside the doors of imposing mansions, now become shabby, bells multiplied, and in Piccadilly Circus, electric signs—fiery words written on darkness, some moving, spelling out a meaning which all who strained their eyes upwards, might read. London kept growing, ever larger, houses springing up on its outskirts, frail and wonderful, with shops to meet all needs, vehicles to fetch and carry, banks to disburse money, cinemas to give delight, but little or no provision made for any who felt constrained from time to time to confess themselves miserable offenders and lift up their hearts. Into London, derelict industrial areas and a derelict countryside emptied their surplus or restless population, who found accommodation where they might, some reduced to taking shelter in the crypt of St. Martin-in-the-Fields, made available for the purpose by an enterprising Vicar, there at least a congregation never lacking. Large blocks of flats came into existence, housing many couples and solitary residents, each provided with partitioned-off living-space, where they might eat and sleep and struggle with the tedium of time according to their varying capacities; newspapers delivered at each door to tell of the world's doings, who's in, who's out, who loses and who wins; radio sets to give instruction and music, sometimes played the livelong day, a rhythmic murmur, underlying all other sounds, and constant as the sea's wash; cosmetics to keep lips red and cheeks smooth, to kindle desire, and contraceptives to sterilize its anguish.

Dog-racing tracks, skating-rinks, amusement arcades, increased; on bright Sunday mornings the throng of vehicles on roads leading away from London, grew denser, an unending procession, slowing down when it passed through towns and villages, then springing forward again; in the evening returning along its course, faces two by two, one at the wheel intent, others relaxed; after nightfall only lights sweeping the road, and modestly dipping when against one another. Movement exhilarated more than direction—just to keep moving, to move faster, air whistling by, and a foot languidly, effortlessly governing the acceleration. The toll of life taken, slowly mounting, caused little anxiety. Speed required its sacrifice like any other deity, though the placid acceptance of the inevitability of this sacrifice may surprise posterity more than larger and more passionate carnage. Petrol-pumps, brightly coloured, and Belisha beacons to mark pedestrian crossings, blossomed like flowers; dashboards glowed with a dim, religious light; road-houses offered entertainment, dancing and swimming, between instalments of mileage; amidst the dust, baskets of fruit and eggs were humbly offered, held up beseechingly to cars as they passed. How sweet the smell of new leather, how satisfying mudguards' black curves, how exhilarating the sensation of gaining speed—teeth gritted together, one hand free to take and light a cigarette; free to explore and caress, this sensation and the other merged together, the same. With such power at his disposal, the weakest felt strong; the poorest-spirited, formidable. Large cars swept past, gleaming and swift and lordly, imperiously demanding that the way before them should be cleared of all lesser things; smaller and more decrepit cars clattered along, leaving behind them a trail of fumes and stench.

"Buy British" was a slogan; across the blue sky "Bile Beans" was written in smoke, some objecting and others detecting progress in this innovation; finger-nails, and sometimes toe-nails, were crimson, eyebrows plucked out and black symmetrical lines traced where they had been. Children were fewer, and suicides more numerous, a convenient method of self-destruction being found in motor-car exhaust-pipes; death eagerly sucked from them by those thirsting for death. Smash-and-grab raids became frequent; female figures needed to be slim, even though it meant break-fasting on orange-juice and lunching on green salad, and otherwise mortifying the flesh. Waistcoats were double-breasted, American slang much in use, Negroes much sought after, beards grown on youthful chins, and two Woolworth's made to grow where only one grew before. Char-a-bancs penetrated to hitherto remote and inaccessible places, quite filling country-lanes; petrol-fumes mingled with spring and summer scents, and even rabbits became traffic-conscious, waiting their chance to cross from one burrow to another. Fields were neglected, tall thistles showing above the golden corn; farmhouses and cottages, cleared of farmers and labourers, acquired central-heating and garages, and put on a new prosperity, their occupants champions of preserving the countryside's amenities, though not its utilities; money subscribed for this purpose, and tracts of country bought to prevent them from being built upon.

If the Preservation of Rural England was a cause which attracted adherents, and sometimes money, the Productivity of Rural England aroused little concern. The Ministry of

Agriculture was the grave of the political expectations of its successive occupants.[1] Quotas and bounties and, later, marketing schemes would not make the soil increase its yield. Their harvest was largely pensionable officials, of these a fine crop. Even where the main spring of urban prosperity had dried up, and towns were left derelict, like ports where the sea had receded, still their dwellers remained together, clinging to one another and to their corporate hopelessness. If they moved, it was to other towns; to London, greatest of all. Silence and solitude were too like Eternity to be comfortable; and there was desolation where no trams ran. More returned from Canada, Australia and New Zealand than went there; and those who went could rarely be persuaded to endure the absence of the sounds and anonymous human companionship which had become necessary to them.

Like a magnet, cities attracted to themselves individuals, separate particles of life which had no other cohesion. The Godless must stay together; alone, their condition is unbearable—solitary ego in its nest of decaying flesh, counting the hours as they pass. Fear coagulates them, and only a greater fear will scatter them again; fear of sudden destruction rained from the skies, this sending them scampering in every direction, carrying what belongings they may, now intent only on leaving behind them what had formerly drawn them together. The prospect of war in September 1938 proved more efficacious than Christian's prophecies of wrath to come in evacuating the City of Destruction; and when war

[1] Both Mr. Walter Elliot and Mr. W. S. Morrison were regarded as lively, and set for rapid promotion, perhaps for the Premiership, until they were put in charge of Agriculture. Then their careers wilted, and would not afterwards be revived. General Bramwell Booth was in the habit of putting too energetic officers into what was called the "freezer"—that is, sending them to remote and unexciting posts where their ardour would soon cool; the Ministry of Agriculture was Mr. Baldwin's "freezer."

actually came, millions were evacuated to rural areas, the towns they, mostly gratefully, left behind them, darkened, cinema-less, deserted, sand-bagged, and expecting the siren's shrill call.

If agriculture languished, on by-pass roads out of London new factories, frail and hygienic, made their appearance; building societies and insurance companies accumulated impressive reserves, bank-directors were able to announce a gratifying increase in the amount of money entrusted to them, and the spread of instalment-buying gave an impetus to retail trade. Mr. J. Gibson Garvie, managing director of the United Dominions Trust, went so far as to express the hope that "the principle of instalment-buying would eventually prove the spearhead of an advance to a fuller civilization." If his expectations have not been wholly realized, the spearhead has continued to thrust energetically, enabling many to acquire radio-sets, bicycles, dentures, dress-suits, dictionaries, which they would otherwise have lacked. A trifling weekly payment seemed a small undertaking in return for furniture to set up house for the first time; but as the weeks passed, and bliss, as it must, evaporated, the payments became more onerous, like a soldier's pack on a route-march. A spell of unemployment, or some other misfortune, might make their continuance impossible; and then all was lost—bliss, furniture, and expectations of an advance to a fuller civilization. The severity of this process was mitigated a little by a private member's Bill, promoted by Miss Ellen Wilkinson, which made it obligatory for defaulting instalment-buyers to be partially reimbursed for payments already made before what they had been in process of paying for could be seized.

In the restless determination to extract ever more material

satisfaction from life to compensate for other satisfactions which were lacking, ever heavier drafts were drawn on the future. Expense of shame in a waste of passion; gather ye rosebuds while ye may—even in winter, before any have bloomed. Advance to a fuller civilization was made on the easy-payments system, with soon the haunting fear of default, when all that had been acquired—votes, education, peace, many amenities, delivered, as guaranteed, in a plain van—would suddenly be taken, without even the reimbursement provided for in Miss Wilkinson's Bill.

Perhaps more conducive even than instalment-buying to a fuller civilization was publicity, whose ramifications were constantly being extended. Large numbers of copy-writers were engaged in devising new slogans likely to increase the sale of particular commodities; artists devoted their talents to the same purpose, and it was possible to earn a guinea or so just for lending an anonymous radiant countenance to a display advertisement. Celebrities were able to augment their incomes by publicly acknowledging their taste in face-cream or in cigarettes; science, learning and art, all were utilized in the great task of persuading the public to eat more, drink more, smoke more, wear more, consume more. Bread, whose popularity might have been thought assured, was worth a campaign; milk had its advocates, and six athletic girls performed gymnastic feats at seaside resorts in the expectation of thereby stimulating the consumption of potatoes. How misfortunes like constipation or body-odour might be overcome was delicately explained; and pictorial representations of the advantages of correcting night-starvation and other ills, impressed many.

Nor was all this effort without its idealistic side. As MacDonald put it in his speech at the opening of an advertising

Convention: "Your advertisements should appeal to the public, not merely for the satisfaction of what you might call the lower appetites, but you should endeavour to make the public buy with some kind of idealism, to awaken some of the higher needs of the human body, the human mind, and the human soul." The higher needs of the human body, the human mind and the human soul, were duly awakened. A Recall to Religion, initiated by the Archbishop of Canterbury, was recommended to the public by a picture of a well-dressed man seated at a desk, with telephone and other office appurtenances before him, and looking up wistfully at a window through which came a shaft of light, this, presumably, symbolizing his impending conversion. Among other higher needs publicized were, loving-kindness, promoted by suitably decorated greetings-telegrams at reduced rates; knowledge, in the form of dictionaries and encyclopaedias, available for a small payment to newspaper subscribers; truth, as proclaimed by the *Daily Express* and other publications; health and beauty, whose secrets were brought within the reach of the poorest in the land. A Fitter Britain was assiduously recommended, and Youth and Beauty held up to women of all ages, and at all stages of decrepitude, as a worthy and realizable aspiration.

Publicity became a mighty industry, whose annual turnover ran into millions, whose captains were knighted, and in other ways honoured; a cult, almost a religion, with many devotees. Actresses, politicians, athletes, authors, had their publicity agents, whose business was to make their light shine before men, and keep it shining. Government departments and business enterprises required public relations officers, for the same purpose. Contacts, like time, were money, since they yielded publicity, might be bartered one against

the other, with profit to all concerned. He who had many
contacts was rich, and soon got more; he who had few,
soon lost even those which he had. A contact buried in the
earth was wasted; used, it would multiply. Give us this day
our daily contact. Clubs, bars and grill-rooms were the mart;
smiles, confidences, meals and drinks, jokes, mostly salacious, the medium of exchange; money, the oil which ensured smooth running.

To sell an idea was the concern of many; ideas ripe, ideas
ripe, buy my idea. An American publicist announced that
at one point it would have been possible "to sell a European
war to the Middle-West," though without stating the price
it might have been expected to fetch. Personalities were
sold, sometimes realizing high prices, sometimes knocked
down for paltry sums; hopes were sold, and fears, and
futures, and pasts. Selling them was an art, not a trade; more
like conducting an orchestra than street-hawking—the little
gossip-paragraph and chance reference, as well as large
hoardings and display advertisements, contributing to the
whole symphony; *piano* needed to intensify the *fortissimo*
effects. The orchestra was large, with many players and
instruments; its music varied, its turnover considerable, and
its audience large and appreciative.

THE election was won, the Doctor's Mandate granted, the Post Office Savings Bank deposits secured, Snowden became a Viscount and his place as Chancellor of the Exchequer taken by Mr. Neville Chamberlain; and again the National Government was presented with the unfortunate necessity of doing something. Sir John Simon might insist that the Government "was a happy family with no internal dissensions," and the Prime Minister that he had "never known a Cabinet which works so well together as the present one"; but an unprecedented electoral triumph had not obliterated the divisions which prevented the Cabinet from agreeing on a programme to put before the electorate. Sir Herbert Samuel was still a firm believer in Free Trade, and his Conservative colleagues in Protection; the Prime Minister still called himself an "old-fashioned Socialist," [1] and spoke earnestly of disarmament and the League of Nations; whereas few of the 554 Members of Parliament whose leader he ostensibly was, shared these vague predilections.

[1] MacDonald never disavowed Socialism, though his references to it soon became, in the circumstances inevitably, rare and even for him, vague. On one occasion, in the course of a parliamentary debate on Socialism, a Labour member memorized, and repeated, a speech the Prime Minister had once made in a similar debate. MacDonald was thus put in the position of having to refute his own arguments without admitting that he no longer accepted their validity—a test of dialectical skill which even Jesuits might regard as severe, and which called for the exercise of all his masterly incoherence.

As before the General Election, so after it, the Cabinet found themselves in agreement only on the seriousness of the situation which faced the country, and on their competence to deal with it.

If, however, Cabinet Ministers remained divided, the Conservative Party's preponderance in the new Parliament gave it a preponderating influence in the Government. Sir Herbert Samuel's views might be listened to respectfully, but a threat to resign represented his only means of protest if they were disregarded. His little band of followers could not appreciably influence a division; other Liberals, led by Sir John Simon, had made it clear that there was no conceivable issue which might be expected to lead to their resignation. Like Charles II, they had been on their travels, and now, unexpectedly restored to office, were determined to travel no more. As for National Labour it was an army with no rank-and-file, but only staff officers. The distribution of a few honours would keep sweet its small contingent outside the Cabinet, and those in the Cabinet could be relied on to efface themselves, until death, or some accident like the disclosure of Budget secrets, led to their places being vacated.

The immediate difficulty was Sir Herbert Samuel's conscientious scruples about associating himself with a change in fiscal policy of which he did not approve. For him to resign so soon after the General Election would have been inconvenient; to abandon, or even postpone, the imposition of tariffs would deprive the Government of the only measure a majority of its supporters actively wished to see introduced.

Sir Herbert remained adamant. Useless to point out to him that in a Government like theirs give and take was essential; that no drastic change was proposed, but only an experiment (that persuasive word,[1] made to cover so much; so many experiments—tariff, League, Soviet, Nazi; experimental appeasement, to be followed by experimental war), which, if successful, might be continued, if unsuccessful, discontinued. He would not budge. There is no obstinacy like that of a sheep asked to move from its last corner of pasture, of a guest asked to go when one drink is still in the bottle; of a woman asked to remove one remaining garment, or a politician one remaining principle. If Liberals were not free-traders, what were they?

With this difficult situation, MacDonald was well qualified to deal. Composing differences was his occupation; making the lion (whichever is the lion) lie down with the lamb (whichever is the lamb). He made Sir Herbert Samuel lie down a little longer with Mr. Neville Chamberlain by the simple expedient of an agreement to differ; "Ministers," it was announced, "who found themselves unable to support the conclusions arrived at by the majority of their colleagues on the subject of import duties and cognate matters, were to be at liberty to express their views by speech and vote." Thus Protection, long clamoured for, came to pass without Sir Herbert Samuel having either to signify approval or resign; and the House of Commons was treated to the curious spectacle of one member of the Government Front Bench demolishing another's arguments; directing his attack, not on the Opposition, but on his colleagues.

Though the arrangement was generally pronounced a success, and an interesting innovation, it led to some em-

[1] Its equivalent, in the preceding generation, was "reform." Thus what was called in Joseph Chamberlain's day Tariff Reform, was called in his son's the Tariff Experiment.

barrassment and irritation; and as time passed, and Sir
Herbert Samuel's resignation, from being inconvenient,
became desirable, he found it increasingly difficult to agree
at all with his colleagues, even to agree to differ from them.
He was repeatedly urged by the *Manchester Guardian* and
other Liberal newspapers to cross the floor of the House,
and at last did so, leading away a minute band of followers
and three members of the Government. An act so long de-
ferred, and whose consequences were so insignificant, was
bound to seem unimportant. The Opposition gained no
noticeable accession of strength, the Government was not
appreciably weaker; and after the next General Election,
Sir Herbert went, as Viscount Samuel, to the House of
Lords, there in a position to obey the dictates of his conscience without equivocation, and steadfastly uphold the
principles of Free Trade.

The abandonment of Free Trade was as easily taken for
granted as the abandonment of the Gold Standard had been.
Attempts to revive the strong feelings which the Tariff
Reform controversy had once aroused, signally failed. If no
cry went up, as some Liberals had predicted it would, from
an electorate tricked into accepting a hated imposition, nor
were there any signs of the elation which Lord Beaverbrook and others expected. Writers of parliamentary
sketches did their best to present as historic the occasion on
which the Chancellor of the Exchequer laid before the
House of Commons legislation instituting a general ten per
cent tariff on all imports, with certain specified exceptions;
a note of deep emotion, they wrote, came into Mr. Chamberlain's ordinarily dry voice when he remarked that his
father would doubtless have been gratified to know that
the protectionist legislation he had so strenuously advocated

was to be introduced by one son and in the presence of another. If this deep emotion really did come into his voice, it may be assumed to have stayed there, since it was apparent nowhere else.

With tariffs settled, the Government was urged to revert to its first cause, economy. When Lear consented to reduce his retainers to fifty, it was not long before he was asked to content himself with twenty-five. The economies made in Snowden's emergency budget were all very well, it was argued, but no more than a beginning. Virtue should be persisted in if the National Government was to deserve the praise which had already been bestowed upon it. Various proposals were made for realizing further economies in public expenditure; among them one for the imposition of a Means Test, to be applied to recipients of unemployment benefit. "The financial saving," the *Times* wrote of this proposal, "will be great, and the tonic to public opinion will be strengthening." As a slight palliative to the squeamish, it suggested that Needs Test more aptly described what was intended than Means Test, and drew attention to an instance, "rightly described by Our Correspondent as sinister," in which a family of five were in receipt of no less than 69/-a week unemployment benefit. A strengthening tonic in the shape of a Means or Needs Test was duly administered to public opinion, though only after its conditions as first projected had been drastically revised in face of protests from quarters unappreciative of its tonic qualities.

This victory for economy was offset by a slight reverse. Judges continued to profess "a reasoned scepticism as to the competence of recent legislation, aimed at reducing the salaries of public servants, to affect the remuneration of our Judicial Bench." Nor did their cause go unchampioned.

Professor Holdsworth, for instance, expressed the view that
£5,000 a year subject to taxation was "not sufficient to
induce the ablest lawyers in the prime of life to accept
judicial office"; and the ingenious argument was used that
since judges have every year to try "many cases which
involve enormous amounts of money," and since "a wrong
decision in any one of these may inflict on a litigant the
unmerited sacrifice of a sum which vastly exceeds the annual
saving on all judicial salaries," it was, perhaps, ill-advised to
make them subject to the cuts imposed on other civil servants. The same argument would seem to apply to porters
employed to shift bullion, who might plead, when a reduction in their pay was proposed, that since they had to transport enormous amounts of money, and since any carelessness on their part would involve losses vastly exceeding
what would be saved by reducing their pay, it should be left
intact. "A hundred years ago," a leading article in the *Times*
contended, " £5,500 a year tax free was not thought an
excessive stipend for a puisne judge. Is it not possible that
£2,500 (which is all judges will receive in the present year)
is too little?" Apparently it was, for the judges' sufferings
were soon cut short, and their full salaries restored. In the
controversy which resulted from the attempt to reduce
them, it was disclosed that an Attorney-General might expect to earn in fees, refreshers and other emoluments, an
annual income of £44,500, and a Lord Advocate, about
£11,000. These cases, unlike the one of the family of five
in receipt of 69/- a week unemployment benefit, were not
thought to merit the description "sinister."

As the National Government settled down to its secure
existence, the Prime Minister's part in it became more
shadowy. His health soon showed signs of deterioration;

and though an anxious public were from time to time assured that there was no reason to anticipate being deprived of his services ("The Prime Minister has so steadily gained in strength and public estimation since he took his great decision to face the country that, if any man can ever be called indispensable to the State, he has won that title to-day"), many of the responsibilities which ordinarily went with his office devolved upon the Lord President of the Council, Mr. Baldwin. MacDonald had performed an important service in inducing many Labour and non-party voters to support Conservative candidates; but with 471 Conservative members of Parliament, and five years to run before another General Election, his usefulness was largely exhausted. Trade was improving, unemployment decreasing, and revenue coming in well; the Labour Party was no longer formidable, and unlikely to become so again, at any rate in the near future. What purpose, then, was served by having its former leader as Premier, and listening to his meandering speeches, with the obligation of occasionally applauding sentiments which were only tolerable because incomprehensible?

Someone more substantial was required; still high-minded, still enlightened and with a feeling heart, but whose feet were firmly planted on the earth and who was less prone than MacDonald on the slightest provocation to go up and up and up and on and on and on. The right man was available, as he always is. After Lossiemouth came Bewdley; after simple fisher-folk and a library in which to go "wandering and roaming and dreaming alone," came pigs and a pipe. MacDonald had made straight the way for Mr. Baldwin.

If Mr. Baldwin had been fortunate enough to hold office

during a period of international tranquillity, his premiership would probably have been reckoned among the most
successful. For handling a General Strike or deposing a
recalcitrant monarch, there has been no one like him. His
talent for making mistakes and being inconsistent without
diminishing the esteem in which he is held, is unique. One
day he could assure the House of Commons that the British
Air Force was superior to that of any conceivable hostile
combination of European Powers, and a few days later
explain that he had been misinformed, and that in fact Germany had an overwhelming superiority in the air; announcing a large-scale rearmament programme, he could casually
remark that if he had let it be known at a recent General
Election that he favoured rearming, seats might have been
lost to the Opposition; and still as he stumped down Whitehall, or across the Park for his early morning walk, the
cries of "Good old Baldwin!" were as cordial as ever, and
the cheers at constituency meetings as tumultuous. He has
found less difficulty in jettisoning a colleague than others
experience in giving a housemaid notice, and shown himself
capable of doing effortlessly what the most ingenious and
unscrupulous minds vainly attempt—induce his fellow coun-
trymen to buy, and even read, books on his recommenda-
tion. A word from him in praise of Mary Webb resulted in
a sale of not less than a million copies of her formerly little
read works.[1]

[1] That he alone is capable of this outstanding feat is indicated by the fact
that when Mr. Neville Chamberlain succeeded him as Prime Minister, he
failed to repeat it. The sales-resistance of the public successfully withstood
Mr. Chamberlain's statement, at a Royal Literary Fund Banquet, that his
"favourite romances are those of the elder Dumas and that long superb
series left to us by Joseph Conrad, with his wonderful word painting
and his haunting sense of ever-present mystery."

This remarkable man sprang suddenly from obscurity into prominence in 1922.[1] When Bonar Law died, and Curzon confidently assumed that his moment had at last come, Mr. Baldwin formed his first Government, described contemptuously by Lord Birkenhead as consisting of "second-class brains." Out of this unpromising material he constructed a citadel of mediocrity, a Government of None of the Talents, which has successfully withstood all assaults made upon it, whether from the Left or the Right; which still stands, and in which, incidentally, Lord Birkenhead was glad for a time to find a not very exalted place. Though now in retirement, and an earl, Mr. Baldwin may be regarded as the architect of his country's present leadership, whose personnel he for the most part chose, and whose outcasts he excluded; whose sentiments echo his, and whose

[1] His first important office was Financial Secretary of the Treasury, to which he was appointed in 1917. In 1919 he wrote a letter to the *Times*, signed F.S.T., proposing that the "wealthy classes" should voluntarily contribute a portion of their wealth towards reducing the enormous burden of national debt which had accumulated, and as a gesture signifying awareness of the gravity of the financial situation, and that "love of country is better than love of money." For his own part, he proposed to lay out £120,000 (a fifth of his total wealth) on the purchase of War Loan, which he would present to the Government for cancellation. At the time, no one connected the initials F.S.T. with the little noticed Financial Secretary of the Treasury, though the letter bears unmistakable traces of Mr. Baldwin's style, so characteristic and later so well-known—"I have been considering this matter for nearly two years but my mind moves slowly; I dislike publicity, and I hoped that someone else might lead the way. "When, as Mr. Arthur Bryant puts it in his *Stanley Baldwin*, "under the glaring publicity that floods every past action of a man who has become Prime Minister," Mr. Baldwin's voluntary sacrifice became generally known, the fact that it had been made secretly (Mr. J. C. C. Davidson, later Chairman of the Conservative Party and raised to the peerage, was the only friend to whom Mr. Baldwin confided his intention to relinquish a fifth of his wealth) added to its appeal. According to Mr. Bryant, one person only was induced by Mr. Baldwin's letter to follow his example, though how much the Exchequer gained thereby is not known.

technique follows, though less adroitly, the technique he practised.

His portly figure filled a vacuum, and when the pressure of air trying to rush in became uncomfortable, withdrew. The termination of his career was as well-chosen as its beginning—if, indeed, it has terminated. It would never be surprising to have him back again; to hear once more that mellow, amiable voice explaining how he has torn himself away from Wordsworth's *Excursion*, and pleasant Worcestershire walks, in response to the call of duty; how all must pull along together, masters and men, high and low, and how he is a plain, blunt man, whose mind works slowly, with no cut-and-dried programme to put forward, but anxious only to serve his country, and, as all his listeners will surely know, fit to be trusted. If this ever happens, then let stock-brokers be of good-cheer and buy Government securities; let gas masks be laid aside, armies disbanded, Mr. Churchill reconcile himself to again being out of office, and revolutionaries stick to their Senior Common Rooms; for it will mean that for a while the wicked will cease from troubling and the weary be at rest.

Relations between MacDonald and Mr. Baldwin were harmonious. As they lived next door to one another in Downing Street, with a convenient gate connecting their two gardens, intercourse was easy and informal. With unfailing tact, Mr. Baldwin soothed the Prime Minister's easily ruffled vanity; and MacDonald felt that in his Lord President of the Council he had the helpmeet he needed—like one of those plain, dull wives the temperamental are sometimes fortunate enough to acquire, who fend off creditors, fill hot-water-bottles, make delicious scones, and uncomplainingly efface themselves during meteoric love-affairs. In tranquil times their partnership might have lasted indefinitely, with the possibility of the monotony being varied by their occasionally changing houses and offices.

Alas, this pleasant prospect was spoilt by the times' persistent refusal to be tranquil. The Disarmament Conference had settled down to inertia, Japan was embarking on a "forward policy" (in choosing thus to describe a projected conquest of China, paying faint Nipponese tribute to the gospel of Progress); Dr. Brüning's position as German Chancellor was becoming increasingly insecure, and he was soon to be replaced by Herr von Papen, by General Schleicher, by Hitler; Indian gaols were crowded, even Cyprus was agitated; and a project for a Danubian Federation created all-round apprehension where it was opposed, in case it might be realized; where it was favoured, in case it might be prevented. More, and still more conferences were necessary; and though the Prime Minister had by no means lost his taste for them, his performance, like the sequels to *The Forsyte Saga* which Galsworthy continued to produce until his death in 1933 mercifully put an end to them, showed signs of flagging, and its reception of growing tepid.

Even so, his Conservative colleagues were ready enough to leave his continental tours largely unrestricted provided he did not accompany them to Ottawa, for the Imperial Conference to be held there. Dominion Preferences and other bread-and-butter issues which would come up for discussion, seemed then of vastly greater moment than Danubian Federations or Chancellor Brüning's difficulties; in Geneva or Lausanne the Prime Minister could do no particular harm, but at Ottawa Mr. Thomas was better.

Though Mr. Neville Chamberlain remarked of the Ottawa Conference that "the Empire was there born

afresh," its practical results were meagre, amounting only
to a slight increase in trade within the Empire, which in the
case of the Mother Country was offset by a rather larger
decrease in foreign trade; and though the Prime Minister
continued to express the hope that it would yet prove possible "to remove by negotiation the dangers which will have
to be met in any event," even he was constrained to admit
that at Geneva he had felt "day after day as though I was
looking upon a stage with something moving immediately
behind the footlights, but as if there was something else
there of a different character—an ominous background full
of shadows and uncertainties. Europe is not settled. Europe
is very unsettled. Europe is in a very nervous condition." [1]
With this feeling in his heart, it is not surprising that he
eagerly approved a proposal to summon one more conference, bigger, more comprehensive in its range, with a more
distinguished attendance, than even the Disarmament Conference; a World Economic Conference, over which he
would preside, and which surely could not fail—"The direct
representatives of this Government, that Government, and
the other Government, brought face to face . . . will much
more quickly and much better, as a piece of workmanship,
find the accommodation which will lead to a great world
agreement."

II

In the immutable nature of life, it is necessary that every
hope and every folly, all expense of passion, should be taken
to its extreme. The Euclidian conclusion—"which is absurd,"
must constantly be demonstrated; *reductio ad absurdum*,

[1] Quoted from *Hansard* in *A Strong Hand at the Helm*, a useful collection of utterances by members of the National Government during the
first years of its existence.

more plausibly than dialectical materialism, may be taken as the principle which provides a key to human affairs. There is no stopping short; no moderate hope, or folly, no moderate passion. Lear must go mad, Macbeth await defeat, David when he is old be covered with clothes and get no heat, the Rector of Stiffkey be thrown to menagerie lions, and MacDonald go down in a blaze of conferences, make what is in effect his last bow in the South Kensington Geological Museum to an assembly of representatives of all extant governments, not excepting Liberia.

The World Economic Conference, which was opened by the King on June 12, 1933, began in confusion and pessimism, apart from the Prime Minister, whose hopes would not be dashed, and the Municipality of Amballa in the Punjab, where the tax yield was optimistically estimated on the ground that "the World Economic Conference will bring prosperity to the whole world, and especially to Amballa." A conflict of interests between countries still on the Gold Standard and those with controlled currencies, soon became apparent; and though MacDonald and M. Herriot had both had what were described as satisfactory preliminary conversations with Mr. Roosevelt, the newly elected American President, the policy of the United States was unhelpful. By devaluing the dollar when the Federal Reserve Bank's accumulation of gold was still intact, the President intensified the difficulties of France and the other countries whose inflationary experiences made them cling tenaciously to the Gold Standard when all but they had fled; and his unexpected repudiation of proposals, endorsed by the American delegation at the Conference, for temporary exchange stabilization, removed any possibility of an agree-

ment on monetary policy, and, therefore, of any agreement
whatsoever.

Elated by his election, dangerously full of good intentions, and with the New Deal at its exhilarating beginnings,
Mr. Roosevelt was in a mood to listen to the advice of professors of economics and others, soon to be known as a Brain
Trust, who had gathered round him like authors round
a publisher, and one of whom, Professor Moley, made a
meteoric appearance at the World Economic Conference.
Their advice was varied, and sometimes conflicting,[1] but
with characteristic high-spirits, the President decided to take
the lot. His catholicity was the Brain Trust's undoing. One
after the other its personnel retreated to their classrooms, or,
like Professor Moley, to editorial offices. As has so often
happened, the ignorance of politicians proved tougher than
the wisdom of the learned.

Some embarrassment resulted from the failure of a number of Conference delegates to attend, or even acknowledge
the invitation to a dinner given in their honour by various
liveried companies at Fishmongers' Hall, a name which
seemed to them more suggestive of trade than entertainment,
and of retail trade at that. The Americans especially were
apprehensive that if they went they might find themselves
manœuvred into advertising fresh cod, and perhaps infected

[1] That professors of economics are sometimes in agreement was demonstrated to Mr. Roosevelt by a curious and somewhat embarrassing incident, which took place before he became President. He and Mr. Al Smith,
his rival for the Democratic nomination, made speeches in which the
same passage occurred. It later transpired that each had taken professional
advice in preparing his speech, though it is only fair to point out that the
two professors consulted were friends, a contingency so improbable that
it could scarcely have been foreseen.

other delegations with their caution. At the dinner, when it took place, there were many empty chairs, and members of the Government and other distinguished persons found themselves dining mostly with the representatives of countries so insignificant that they were grateful for the hospitality even of fishmongers.

M. Litvinov employed his time in London in negotiating a series of non-aggression pacts between the U.S.S.R. and neighbouring states. These pacts, though they won him many compliments at the time, have proved no more remunerative than the World Economic Conference itself, whose sessions M. Litvinov was attending while he negotiated them. His presence at a lunch given at 10 Downing Street by the Prime Minister, led the *Morning Post* to complain that a slug had found its way into "our fine English rose."

Germany was represented at the Conference by, among others, Dr. Alfred Hugenberg,[1] an eccentric newspaper proprietor and Krupps director, who had become Economics Minister in Herr Hitler's first Cabinet, a coalition of Nazis and Nationalists which took office some five months before the Conference opened. A memorandum he submitted provided a striking, but scarcely welcome, contrast to the other delegates' platitudinous utterances. It quoted Spengler with gusto, insisted on the importance of racial considerations, claimed the return of Germany's former colonies, and envisaged German expansion eastwards at the

---

[1] He is felicitously described in Mr. R. T. Clark's *The Fall of the German Republic* as combining "the appearance of a hoary, genial, but beardless Santa Claus with ruthless greed for power, unscrupulousness in method, and profound contempt for that large section of the Nationalist leaders whose long tradition still inhibited them from adopting the moral standards of big business."

expense of the U.S.S.R. Such ideas then were regarded as too extravagant to be taken seriously, and aroused more astonishment than concern.

The German Government hurriedly explained that Dr. Hugenberg was expressing only his own personal opinions; his memorandum was withdrawn, and he returned to Berlin, his uneasy partnership with Herr Hitler soon to terminate. "When wood is planed shavings fly," he had remarked in the course of a speech justifying his collaboration with National Socialists, and insisting that the rights and ideals of the Nationalists he claimed to represent would be safeguarded. He was right; shavings did fly, and he was a shaving, fortunate in being allowed to vanish unmolested into obscurity.

On June 15 the Prime Minister said that the World Economic Conference was "one of the most business-like and expeditious conferences I have ever presided over." Considering the number he had presided over, this was high praise. On another occasion he described how, when the subject of adjournment was mentioned at a meeting of the presidents and vice-presidents of the various committees which had been set up, "they all laughed, and we proceeded at once to more serious and practical business." A month later the Conference was adjourned. Like the Disarmament Conference, it stands adjourned still, and with as little expectation of being reassembled. Its single achievement was an agreement, soon broken, to limit exports of wheat; its conclusion was described, not unfairly, by M. Maisky, a Soviet delegate, as a "disorderly rout."

Thus ended the era of conferences. Other conferences there were in plenty, but none which went up and up and up, and on and on and on; rather down and down and down, and back and back and back. The bubble, eagerly blown, had reached an astonishing size, rainbow-coloured, pulsating, and now had burst, leaving no residue. From Versailles onwards, non-stop variety; conference after conference, personnel changing as death intervened, location shifting— Montreux, Lausanne, Stresa, Genoa, Rapallo, many little towns by lakes, by the sea, suddenly crowded, their quiet disturbed by the tapping of typewriters, buzzing conversation; flags flying over their Hotel Bristol, Hotel Beau Rivage, detectives lounging where ordinarily were picture-postcard sellers, guides—"You want to see the sights, mister?" Liberia would nevermore be invited to make its contribution towards solving the world's problems, no Peruvian or Siamese sail over the seas to promote international prosperity and accord.

It was over and done; a faint echo lingering still in a Prime Minister's plaintive cry for personal contacts, in Mr. Lansbury's appeal—"Yet one more conference, yet one more!" Were there among the Philistines before whom Samson made sport, a few who cried out for a barber when they saw their captive bow himself with all his might against the pillars upon which the house stood, saw them begin to rock and sway? It is likely. The house fell upon the lords, and upon all the people that were therein; upon Samson, too. The house fell.

III

When an Anglo-Irish Treaty was concluded in 1921, and the Irish Free State established, with Mr. Cosgrave as the first President of the Executive Council, it seemed as though neither the excessively pro-British Northern Irish nor the excessively anti-British Southern Irish, would give any more trouble. Bygones were to be bygones; Hamar Greenwood's identity was lost in the more genial Lord Greenwood, directing, among other enterprises, innocuous A.B.C. teashops instead of the Black and Tans. Ulster had proved a source of embarrassment to the Conservative Party, much as the Soviet régime had to the Labour Party, through excessive zeal. It was nice to know that imperial bonds were strong and imperial loyalties undiminished, but not nice to be told so too often or too vehemently; Mr. Micawber might have been forgiven if he had occasionally wished that Mrs. Micawber would desert him. From zealous friends and enemies alike, it seemed that the 1931 Treaty had brought deliverance, besides providing the not uncongenial spectacle of former rebels faced with the necessity of putting down rebellion, and using for the purpose the harsh means which, when employed against them, they had found so abhorrent and indefensible.

As long as the opponents of the Treaty, led by Mr. de Valera, were barred from the Dail by their refusal to take the oath of allegiance required of its members, there seemed no reason to doubt the settlement's permanence. The outlook was less promising when Mr. de Valera found a satisfactory formula for overcoming his conscientious objections to swearing allegiance to a constitution which he intended to abolish, and entered the Dail with fifty-seven members of his Fianna Fail Party. After the 1932 election, he was able, with the support of the Labour Party, to command a majority, and succeeded Mr. Cosgrave as President of the Executive Council. Once more, after a ten years' lull, Anglo-Irish relations became strained. The tariff reform controversy had rattled its bones; the cry of "The Pope on the rates!" had again been faintly heard in the land, and now the greatest preoccupation of pre-war politics—the Irish question—was resurrected. Like an expiring conjurer, parliamentary government seemed determined to give a last performance of all its best-known tricks.

Mr. de Valera's abolition of the oath of allegiance and, to all intents and purposes, of the office of Governor-General, and other constitutional irregularities, were not at first taken too seriously. The strength of imperial relationships, it was often said, like the strength of the Church of England, lay in their flexibility and lack of definition. They were so elastic that they could not be broken, so loosely defined that they could not be contravened. A more serious view was taken of Mr. de Valera's refusal to pay the land annuities [1] when they fell due, since this involved the British Government in a financial loss. Imperial relations and Anglican dogma might be all the better for being vague, but where cash was concerned, precision was essential.

The Minister technically responsible for dealing with Mr. de Valera's default on the land annuities, was Mr. J. H. Thomas, the Dominions Secretary; but in the negotiations and conversations which ensued, he was rarely unaccompanied by at least one of his Conservative colleagues. The breezy, colloquial manner which suited friendly, but unimportant, exchanges with Australian or Canadian politicians, was inadequate, it was felt, for handling a situation which involved the obstinate fears of Ulster and the romantic susceptibilities of Southern Ireland, as well as some millions of pounds sterling. What could be better, in inaugurating a telephone service with Australia, than to begin with: "Hullo,

[1] In 1903 it was decided to buy out Irish landlords and transfer their land to the tenants in occupation, who were to repay the purchase price of their holdings in the form of annuities spread over 63 years. The transaction involved the issue of stock guaranteed by the British Government.

Scullin, it's the Old Boy calling!'"? In the case of Lord
Craigavon and Mr. de Valera such an approach was unlikely
to be appreciated; the one preferred resolution to joviality,
and the other, history.

To recover the money due under the land annuities, it was
decided to impose a twenty per cent tariff on imports from
the Irish Free State; and Mr. de Valera retaliated by an
equivalent tariff on imports from Great Britain. Trade between the two countries stagnated; the Irish had no alternative but to eat the large quantity of meat and dairy produce
they were unable to export, and though some British industries, notably coal, were damaged by Mr. de Valera's retalia-
tory tariff, import duties collected on Irish produce coming
into England realized the requisite sum.

There the matter stood for some years, during which Mr.
de Valera earnestly proceeded as far as possible to make the
Free State, later re-named Eire, a self-governing republic,
though without persecuting the Protestant minority, who,
by the standards of most contemporary rulers, might have
expected to suffer at his hands. With his devout Catholicism,
alliance with the Irish Labour Party, enduring popularity
unsustained by terrorism or the curtailment of civil liberties,
approval of General Franco, occasional appearances at
Geneva to rebuke Covenant-breakers, and successful defiance of Great Britain, he has presented ideologues with an
insoluble problem. He fits none of their categories, yet might
be fitted into any. The Soviet Press fell back on labelling
him a kulak, a category which comprises miscellaneous
divergencies from ideological correctitude rather in the same
way that mental cruelty, as a ground for divorce, comprises
miscellaneous divergencies from marital correctitude.

An agreement in 1935, whose effect was to increase Irish

imports of British coal and British imports of Irish cattle, prepared the way for a general settlement in 1938. By the terms of this settlement, negotiated by Mr. Malcolm Mac-Donald, whose interest in bird-watching was reported to have contributed to its successful conclusion, £10,000,000 was paid to the British Government in recompense for the cancelled land annuities, and the control of fortified bases in Free State territory was transferred to the Dublin Government.

Again it seemed that Anglo-Irish relations had been permanently tranquillized, and again there was renewed friction, though this time not with Mr. de Valera's approval. A series of bomb explosions were organized in various parts of England by members of the officially disbanded Irish Republican Army, with the intention of forcing the British Government to abolish the partition of Ireland, and hand over the six counties to Dublin's jurisdiction. Though the I.R.A.'s terrorist activities did not achieve their object, they caused considerable annoyance and some loss of life. It was commonly assumed that they were encouraged, and perhaps financed, from Germany,[1] where, if there was not much

---

[1] It might seem surprising that patriots should thus invoke the aid of Germany, whose way with minorities and subject peoples is notoriously short; but there are many instances which go to show that the promoters of nationalist movements soon become more concerned to damage those who delay the full realization of their hopes than to enjoy the freedom they so urgently demand. Sir Roger Casement can scarcely have supposed that a successful invasion of Ireland under German auspices would result in the realization of Irish independence. In the same way, when Lord Craigavon remarked in 1914 (as quoted in Sir Charles Petrie's biography of Sir Austen Chamberlain): "There is a spirit spreading abroad, which I can testify to from my personal knowledge, that Germany and the German Emperor would be preferred to the rule of John Redmond," he was probably actuated more by hatred of his compatriots in Southern Ireland than by concern for his fellow Ulstermen.

enthusiasm for a united Ireland, there was great enthusiasm for a harassed England.

In all movements which undertake the championship of the oppressed, and demand the rectification of injustices and inequalities, there is, as in Don Quixote, a strong admixture of egotism. Their leaders are usually heroic; but when their heroism is no longer required, they are left disconsolate, and sometimes become embittered. It seems cruel that they should be deprived of the limelight, or at best deserve as veterans only occasional acclamation, for no other reason than that what they agitated for has been wholly, or largely, obtained. In their case, nothing fails like success. The old urge often comes to them to be up and doing for righteousness; to defy the oppressor, and suffer in a good cause. Mrs. Pankhurst finds a platform to appear on; Mr. Tom Mann gets two months for an allegedly seditious speech; and even Mr. John Burns perhaps dreams in the National Liberal Club's afternoon fastness, with a portrait of Sir John Simon [1] looking down sadly upon him, of leading another dockers' strike, addressing another monster meeting in Trafalgar Square.

The unexpected recrudescence of I.R.A. activity was probably due in part to such a feeling of frustrated martyrdom. An aspiring Byron requires a subjugated Greece pining for freedom, and if none exists is inclined to invent one. Irish Republicans had become used to defying an

---

[1] Portraits in the National Liberal Club have had as variegated a career as their originals. Mr. Lloyd George, Sir John Simon and Mr. Churchill have all been up, down, and up again, with a certain amount of manœuvring for position between whiles. They are, perhaps significantly, still up and prominently displayed. Asquith alone has been undisturbed: his reputation has not much fluctuated, and remains undiminished at any rate in the National Liberal Club.

oppressor's heel, and were determined not to allow Mr. de
Valera to deprive them of heel or defiance; if no other heel
was available, his would have to suffice, and as a last resort
he might be defied. They, too, still had a bomb or two up
their sleeve, even if Hitler put them there. "Stand by the
men who have defied the might of Britain" was chalked on
Dublin walls; and it was like the good old days when Britain
was truly mighty and Ireland truly defiant. In the correspondence columns of progressive journals, rather half-
hearted attempts were made to detect in the I.R.A.'s belated
terrorist activities intimations of a subject people rightly
struggling to be free; and when, with Parliament's almost
unanimous approval, the Home Secretary was given arbitrary powers for dealing with I.R.A. suspects, defenders of
civil liberties registered a faint protest. Whether as a result
of the repressive measures taken, or of the German Government's inability to furnish supplies when it required all
available bombs for nearer and more hopeful enterprises,
explosions engineered by the I.R.A. soon ceased with the
coming of war. The Irish Question, like the Indian, the
Egyptian, the Palestinian, the Cypriot, the Maltese, all
questions save one, lapsed, at any rate temporarily, into
obscurity.

IV

The doom of all who invest imaginative hopes in earthly
enterprises and mortal men is for these enterprises and men
to triumph. In fertilizing the Church, the blood of the saints
is ironically used, and prophets who do not reject the kingdoms of the earth when they are offered, must always be
disappointed. Mr. Wyndham Lewis finds a hero in Hitler,
and some years later has pogroms on his hands; Henri Bar-

busse, looking for loving-kindness in a cruel world, glorifies
Stalin, and before long he is glorifying purges; the Children
of Israel are to return to their homeland, wandering no
more, and murderous strife results; W. B. Yeats deserts his
poetic seclusion to become a patriot, and later a senator, and
in Eire is left repining, deprived at last even of senatorial
rights and responsibilities. Celtic Twilight was congenial,
but Mr. de Valera's Celtic Noonday proved a sore disappointment.

Bitterly, if not profoundly, he reflected:

"Money is good and a girl might be better,
But good strong blows are delights to the mind."

Dreams became hopes, and hopes were disappointed, leaving
only anger and love of violence. The dawn he expected did
not break; the half-light he celebrated was of evening, not
morning, and presaged darkness, not daylight. His last
admiration was for General O'Duffy's Blue Shirts, whom
he provided with a marching-song.[1]

If imaginative hopes were abundantly invested in Irish
Nationalism, finding a belated reverberation in London

---

[1] Quoted in *The Poet and Society* by Philip Henderson,

"Down the fanatic, down the clown,
Down, down, hammer them down,
Down to the tune of O'Donnell Abu.
When nations are empty up there at the top,
When order has weakened and faction is strong,
Time for us all, boys, to hit on a tune, boys,
Take to the road and go marching along."

In spite of, or perhaps because of, these later authoritarian sympathies,
Yeats was one of the few pre-War romantic poets who met with the
approval of post-War Marxist poets; he and Gerard Manley Hopkins, a
Jesuit, escaped the contempt lavished upon most of their contemporaries.

railway stations and telephone call-boxes wrecked by German bombs to the greater glory of a United Ireland, even more abundantly were they invested in the Soviet régime. There, in the U.S.S.R., human progress was visibly being made; there a perfect society was in rapid and evident process of coming to pass. Successive Five-Year Plans enchanted, wall-newspapers were counted for righteousness; hospitals, créches, Parks of Culture and Rest, Lenin Corners and anti-God museums, all were pronounced excellent. Even the zoos, Dr. Vevers, Superintendent of the London Zoological Society, reported, astounded visitors by reason of the excellent condition of their animals; while a public schoolboy, when he visited the U.S.S.R., noticed that culture was universal there, and that mere policemen read Dickens and Shakespeare.[1]

It is unlikely that any administrative measures of the Soviet Government, however cruel and tyrannical, would have seriously perturbed its admirers abroad; but when it began to heap obloquy upon, and to exterminate, its own, doubts were implanted and admiration faltered. A series of political trials involving many who had formerly been regarded as revolutionary heroes, spread consternation among the faithful; like eager ordinands suddenly uneasy about the Thirty-Nine Articles, their serenity was disturbed, thought they mostly refrained from giving any public expression to the doubts which had assailed them, and some, like Mr. D. N. Pritt, K.C., and Lord Passfield, con-

[1] See *For Peace and Friendship*, the Report of the Second National Congress of Peace and Friendship with the U.S.S.R., held in London on March 13 and 14, 1937, and addressed, among others, by the Duchess of Atholl, Miss Eleanor Rathbone, the Dean of Canterbury and Mr. G. D. H. Cole. Their pronouncements on this and other like occasions make curious reading in the light of subsequent developments.

tinued manfully to proclaim their unqualified admiration for the impartiality and benevolence of Soviet justice.

The general public, though interested in these political trials, were less perturbed by them, had as few, or as many, tears to shed over the Ogpu's latest victims as over its previous ones. Cannibalism may be disapproved of on humanitarian grounds, but such disapproval is scarcely affected by whether the carcasses consumed are home-bred or imported. When, however, a missionary finds his way into the pot, particular indignation is aroused. It was the arrest by the Ogpu of a number of English engineers, in the employ of the Metropolitan-Vickers Company and resident in the U.S.S.R., on the usual charge of military and political sabotage, which sent special correspondents, among them Mr. A. J. Cummings of the *News-Chronicle*, hurrying to Moscow, and filled newspapers with descriptions and photographs of Soviet judicial procedure.

Great indignation was expressed in most newspapers and in Parliament that the Ogpu should have thus laid hands on British subjects, though occasional voices were raised in justification of the Soviet Government, or at any rate to plead for a suspension of judgment until the case had been tried. The Dean of Canterbury, questioned on the subject, said that he had not had time to study the situation very closely, and so felt unable to comment on it, but added: "Generally speaking, I am certainly opposed to anything in the nature of third degree or torture." Both those who were loudly insistent on the engineers' innocence, and those who assumed or admitted the possibility of their guilt, tended to overlook a more important question—whether the charge which had been preferred against them was one capable of being substantiated or dismissed; whether, indeed, it was a charge as ordinarily understood by Western Europeans, at all.

To Western Europeans a misdemeanour implies laws which may be observed or not observed, whose alleged contravention may be juridically investigated; in the U.S.S.R., and later in Germany, the principle was established that to oppose the existing régime in word or deed, or even in thought, in itself constitutes a misdemeanour; and the same authority responsible for detecting such a misdemeanour was also responsible for charging the culprit, trying and sentencing him, and executing the punishment. As Krylenko, until his disgrace Commissar for Justice, put it: "In the specific nature of their functions there is no difference between the Soviet Court of Justice and the Ogpu. . . . Every Judge must keep himself well informed on questions of State policy, and remember that his judicial decisions in particular cases are intended to promote the prevailing policy of the ruling class and nothing else." [1] The universality of this principle is attested by its subsequent application to Krylenko himself, and even to the Ogpu, whose head, Yagoda, was later arrested and executed. It may be described as a materialist interpretation of the Christian doctrine of Original Sin. All are miserable offenders who have erred and strayed from the Party line like lost sheep, and therefore deserve to be shot; but they may still hope to escape, if they are properly obedient and contrite, by virtue of their Government's infinite mercy.

Such a principle destroys the very basis of Law, though it provides the terrorist with an instrument perfectly suited to his purposes; the whole population is delivered into his

[1] See *Court and Justice in the U.S.R.R.* by N. V. Krylenko. Quoted in an article by the *Times* Riga Correspondent published April 12, 1933.

hands when anyone is liable at any moment to be plausibly
charged with a criminal offence.[1] More effectively than by
any mere display of arbitrary power, all disobedience, actual
and potential, is prevented, and a servile multitude may be
shepherded into polling-booths, given slogans to declaim,
banners to hold up, emotions to register, according to their
ruler's fluctuating wishes. In the U.S.S.R. the total abandonment of Law, and its replacement by terrorism, was obscured by the ostensible application of humanitarian principles to the punishment of non-political offenders. The
fact that many were shot without a public trial for unspeci-
fied reasons of state, did not deter earnest advocates of penal
reform from holding the Soviet Government up to admiration for having abolished capital punishment; and even as
late as 1937 the Rev. Hewlett Johnson could quote with
approval a friend's estimate of a "colony for criminals
adjacent to Moscow" as "more marvellous than Canterbury
Cathedral."

The German Government made no such attempt to com-
bine terrorism with measures pleasing to the Howard
League; and the Gestapo's activities, therefore, tended to be
most deplored by those who were most tolerantly disposed
towards the Ogpu's. They vehemently denounced in the
Third Reich what in the U.S.S.R. aroused no indignation,
righteous or unrighteous, like vegetarians undertaking a
pious pilgrimage to a slaughter-house because it displayed a

---

[1] An early practitioner of this technique was Calvin. The régime he
established in Geneva bears a marked resemblance to the contemporary
Totalitarian State, with secret police and ideological trials—for instance of
Servetus, who was induced before he went to the stake to ask Calvin's for-
giveness. The régime was based on the Word, that is God's will as understood by Calvin; to disagree with Calvin meant repudiating the Word, and
so was a crime punishable with death. See *Calvin and the Reformation* by
James MacKinnon.

notice recommending nut-cutlets; and their confusion was
comical, and sometimes piteous, when the two régimes combined forces, the one's abolition of capital punishment and
criminal colonies more marvellous than Canterbury Cathedral, proving no impediment to collaboration with the other,
as it had proved none to the execution of innumerable death
sentences.

In the case of the arrested engineers, little account was
taken of theoretical considerations; and attention was largely
concentrated on the question of the engineers' guilt, and on
what, assuming they were innocent, could be the motive
behind their arrest. When it was announced that two of
them, Mr. Thornton and Mr. MacDonald, had made confessions, bewilderment increased. That Russians should confess
was scarcely surprising, and in keeping with the Dostoevsky
tradition which, though past its prime, still lived.[1] A
Dostoevsky character, invited to confess, might be expected
to respond readily and voluminously, and in confessing, not
to be bound by probabilities, or by any concern for consistency; but an English engineer was different. If he confessed, it must either mean that he was guilty, or that he had
been drugged or otherwise deprived of the command of his
faculties. Many highly coloured accounts, some purporting
to be first-hand,[2] of Ogpu technique in handling recalcitrant

[1] As has often happened, the crumbs from the highbrows' table provided
material out of which Hollywood concocted a banquet of its own; *Crime
and Punishment* vanished from Bloomsbury bookshelves, to reappear as a
breath-taking drama of "Love . . . Hate . . . Fear battling in a mighty
conflict of emotions."

[2] Some were first-hand—for instance, Professor V. Tchernavin's account
of the treatment he received at the Ogpu's hands. This included what
prisoners called "the conveyor," which involved their being made to run
from storey to storey of the Ogpu Headquarters until they either confessed or dropped exhausted. See also Professor Tchernavin's *I Speak for
the Silent.*

prisoners, appeared; and a Tibetan drug was mentioned
whose effect was to make docile the most resolute heart.

The engineers' trial was lavishly reported, Mr. Cummings
professing himself on the whole satisfied that it was correctly
conducted. Mr. MacDonald, the only one of the engineers
who had been retained in custody, persisted in his confession,
though at one point in the proceedings he retracted it. This
resulted in a short adjournment, after which he resumed
his plea of guilty. The Russians who had been accused of
complicity, and who were tried at the same time, confessed
their guilt with appropriate abandon and contrition, perhaps stimulated by the summary execution, before the trial
began, of thirty-five of their fellow-countrymen. A verdict
of guilty was brought in against all the engineers except one;
Mr. Thornton was sentenced to three years' imprisonment,
Mr. MacDonald to two, and the rest were deported. By way
of protest against this verdict, the British Government imposed an embargo on all Soviet imports; and the Soviet
Government retaliated with an embargo on all British imports. Shortly afterwards, Mr. Thornton and Mr. Mac-
Donald were released; the embargoes were lifted, and a new
Anglo-Soviet Trade Agreement was negotiated.

Round the subsequent succession of political trials, a large
literature grew up, heated accusations and counter-accusa-
tions being made in places most remote from Ogpu prisons
and firing squads. An American committee, under the
chairmanship of Mr. John Dewey, undertook the difficult
task of investigating Trotsky's defence against the many
and varied charges preferred against him, and admitted by
his alleged accomplices, in Moscow, and published its somewhat inconclusive findings;[1] little organizations came into

[1] See *The Case of Leon Trotsky*, verbatim report.

existence in London, Paris and other capitals, calling themselves Trotskyist, or Leninist, or anti-Stalinist, according to
their fancy; strange by-products, with their obscure sheets
and incomprehensible polemical fury, of distant slaughter.
The *Daily Worker* and a few other publications continued
to add their small contribution to Moscow's large volume of
abuse hurled against former idols when they were unmasked,
obediently piping their falsetto "shoot the Reptiles" in
unison with *Pravda*'s deeper note; and a party of Left-Wing
undergraduates staying in the country, diverted themselves
on a rainy day by enacting one of the trials, in their high-
pitched undergraduate voices pouring out Radek's repentance, mouthing Vyshinsky's rage, until a maid brought in
tea and hot buttered scones.

Apart from these specialists, the general attitude was one
of utter bewilderment. Such elaborate crimes confessed to at
such length and with such precision; such sudden falls from
heights so dizzy; a general or admiral sedately marching in
George V's funeral procession, an ambassador, called Excel-
lency and much sought after, dispensing embassy hospitality
to respectful guests who felt they were imbibing proletarian
virtue with their champagne,[1] in a moment degraded, represented as loathsome traitors and criminals—what could it
mean?

A government based on terrorism requires constantly to
demonstrate its might and resolution. Saint George must

[1] Sokolnikov, for some years Soviet Ambassador in London, was recalled
in 1932; and there were rumours that he had been arrested, and even executed. To counter these rumours, intourists were taken to see him in his
Moscow flat, where, though greenish looking, he was indubitably alive.
With a noticeably mirthless laugh, he would draw his visitors' attention to
this fact, and they be suitably impressed. He was disposed of in the 1937
batch of Old Bolsheviks, along with Radek, Piatakoff and others.

continually slay his dragon, the dragon ever growing wearier, Saint George's thrusts ever more mechanical. This continuous performance heartens the mighty in their seats, and awes the humble and meek, besides providing a convenient means of exterminating actual and potential rebels. It is the mysticism of power, in its technique and temper reminiscent of the Book of Revelations, that terrible expression of the human heart's most cruel and destructive appetite, which, being so intense, must be so fantastic in its manifestations. To equate the Book of Revelations with a legal code, to translate its rage into an enlightened judicial procedure, was beyond the ingenuity, if not the credulity, of even most ideologues, though some valiantly tried.

The same tendency to dramatize the conquest and exercise of power soon showed itself in Germany. There, too, Saint George went on slaying his dragon with apocalyptic fervour, only in this case it was chiefly Jews, rather than the class enemy, who received his blows, and whose abasement made the mighty conscious of their might and the humble conscious of their humility. Germans, with their love of action, usually preferred a public orgy of slaughter, whereas it suited the Slav temperament better to fabricate a confused fantasy of plots and stratagems, and look forward to inevitable death sentences while demonstrators obediently clamoured for blood, and the accused vied with one another in proclaiming their guilt and repentance.

The Reichstag Fire Trial provided, for those that had eyes to see, a clear indication of the essential similarity between Soviet and Nazi terrorism. A half-witted Dutchman named Van der Lubbe, and a number of German and foreign Communists, were charged with having set fire to the Reichstag building. As in the Soviet trials, the counsel for the defence

were cowed and futile, the evidence heard was confused and
sometimes contradictory, the atmosphere of the Court suggested rather a tribal blood-sacrifice than a judicial inquiry,
and Van der Lubbe's bearing recalled Mr. Thornton's description of his state of mind when he succumbed to Ogpu
pressure and signed the confession which he afterwards retracted: "I thought it would be better for me to sign the
protocol in which my supposed crimes were set out. But I
am not really guilty of these crimes . . . I felt helpless . . .
apathetic." One of the foreign Communists, Dmitrov,
proved tougher than anyone Soviet judges had been required
to handle, and delighted many with his spirited and vivacious
retorts; while Mr. Pritt, instead of applauding the Nazi version of the judicial procedure he found so admirable in the
U.S.S.R., showed his displeasure by participating in a model
Reichstag Fire Trial which was arranged in London under
Liberal auspices. Van der Lubbe, who provided Mr. Stephen
Spender with the subject for a poem, was executed; the German accused were imprisoned and no more heard of; and the
foreign Communists were deported. Dmitrov, one of the
last political exiles to gain admission to the U.S.S.R., was
given an enthusiastic reception in Moscow, where he soon
became an important influence in the Comintern. As the
memory of his triumph faded, and Soviet policy grew less
sympathetically disposed towards the aspirations of international revolutionaries, his importance diminished, until, like
many another, his whereabouts, and even his continued
existence, became uncertain.[1]

1 While it lasted, Dmitrov was, perhaps, the chief hero among Communists and their sympathizers, at any rate outside the U.S.S.R. He made
a romantic appeal, whereas the Soviet panel of heroes (apart from the
fact that fluctuations were difficult to keep pace with) were somewhat
drab, and from long occupancy of the centre of the revolutionary stage,

V

As imagined thrillers, even as authentic revelations of the Chicago underworld or international drug traffic serialized in a Sunday newspaper, episodes, like the Moscow Trials and the Reichstag Fire Trial might pass; but as part of the everyday lives of ordinary people, they were disconcerting. The policeman on his beat, scrutinizing doorways, bundling along a drunk and incapable; the horseguards, splendid and immobile in Whitehall; Cabinet Ministers assembling in Downing Street, the King driving in his motor-car to Buckingham Palace—these were mild and familiar manifestations of authority, worth a curious stare, sometimes even a cheer, but mostly observed without fear or undue respect. Was it possible that they too might become terrible and strange; in their ways, secret, bloodthirsty? Would Sir Samuel Hoare one day confess that he had plotted murderously, Sir Kingsley Wood mysteriously vanish, taken to a remote cellar and there done to death? Guy Fawkes was still celebrated each fifth of November, urchins with blackened faces collecting pennies, and bonfires lighted, rockets leaping into the sky; but who would suppose the stuffed sack with ribald face and ancient hat, absurdly crumpling as flames reached it, a veritable man?

In Hyde Park on long June evenings a voice might sometimes be heard, one among many and diverse voices, de-

had lost much of their bloom. In *The Novel and the People*, Ralph Fox refers to Dmitrov as providing "an example of moral grandeur and courage worthy to stand beside the greatest in our human history," and projects a novel based on his life, to be called *Man Alive*. If Fox had lived to execute this project (he was killed fighting with the International Brigade in Spain), he might have been embarrassed by Dmitrov's subsequent obscurity, which would have made *Man Perhaps Alive* a more suitable title for a novel about him.

manding bloody revolution, carelessly listened to by casual strollers, but soon deserted; and there were Blackshirts who, until the wearing of political uniforms was banned, held meetings, marched, sometimes with resultant disorder. The revolutionary voice was more curious than impressive; the Blackshirts made but a poor showing, notable rather for their capacity to stir up opposition than for their own numbers or prowess. One existed by virtue of the other. They were complementary, and in some cases, interchangeable.

If Sir Oswald Mosley announced a march to the East End at the head of his followers, it provided an occasion for clenched fists to be raised, mounted police to be called Cossacks, and Spanish Civil War slogans to be repeated: "They shall not pass!" Few there were who tried to pass; a thin black line of villains, reflecting in their strangely mixed attire their leader's fluctuating sympathies with Italian Fascism and German National Socialism.[1] Police escorted them, until hostile or curious spectators made it necessary to disperse them.

Similarly, if Communists assembled, it provided an occasion for arms to be uplifted, and perhaps some aspiring Horst Wessel to get himself rough-handled. Young men with beards sold the *Daily Worker* in the streets; novelists led their heroes by devious ways to solidarity with the toiling masses, and poets sang in *vers libres* the praises of the Soviet Union. The Film Society strenuously applauded the

[1] Latterly, Sir Oswald Mosley has tended to abandon his former advocacy of the Corporative State, and to base his policy and procedure almost exclusively on the Nazi model. The reception which followed his marriage to Mrs. Bryan Guiness was given by Dr. Goebbels, not by Count Ciano; and his uniform, once solely Italian, has, or had on the last occasion he appeared in public wearing it, a strong Storm-Trooper admixture; on the armlet, instead of a Swastika, two marks suggestive of lightning flashes.

storming of the Winter Palace at Petrograd in the many
versions of it presented; and the Unity Theatre was satirical
to the delight of largely unproletarian audiences. Fathers in
clubs complained that their sons had become Communists
at Oxford; and well brought up daughters suddenly announced, sometimes in the presence of servants, that they
proposed henceforth to devote themselves wholly to the
Class War.

It was easy to recognize in Sir Oswald Mosley a Lillipu-
tian Führer, and to distinguish between the October Revolution and the October Club. These were not ominous,
might play their little parts as long as circumstances were
favourable and cash, mostly inherited or allowed, was forthcoming—Blackshirts enjoying a brief spell of larger fame
when Lord Rothermere became their champion, only to
abandon them as suddenly as he had taken them up, and
thenceforth receiving no mention whatsoever in the Press;
Communists, conspiratorial without much necessity, heroically wrestling with Lenin's Collected Works and not less
heroically modelling their speeches on Stalin's, only notori-
ous when some clergyman's son, instead of confining himself
to dialectical materialism, in his simplicity laid himself open
to a charge of attempting to subvert armed forces of the
Crown. The tide of violence and lawlessness which seemed
to be approaching, came from without rather than from
within; strange deeds, in their nature inconceivably remote,
in space near, and ever nearer; strange men, as unlike
Cabinet Ministers as London mounted police were unlike
Cossacks, and whose procedure bore no resemblance at all
to passing Acts of Parliament; not right-honourable, or
honourable, or learned, or gallant, no protracted debate
with occasional processions through Aye and No lobbies,

and reasoned amendments carefully inserted; decisions suddenly, recklessly taken and ruthlessly executed.

Frail by comparison seemed all the apparatus of constituted authority—umbrella against sword, bowler hat against
helmet, words against deeds, paper against steel, money
against passion, mental fight against actual. Was England
truly saved when the Pound was saved? it began to be wondered. Were England and the Pound indeed one and the
same; greatness recovered when the Budget was balanced,
and courage sufficiently displayed in daring to reduce unemployment benefit?

VI

Saved or not saved, England still had its National Government, and was to continue to have it. Its huge majority
operated automatically; and usually the only oratorical
onslaught it need fear was from Mr. Lansbury and his little
band, augmented as, one by one, lost leaders drifted back
when convenient by-elections provided them with constituencies. Virtue had gone out of them, never to return;
their heyday was passed and over, only Mr. Herbert Morrison stemming the tide of defeat by gaining and retaining
control of the London County Council. Though their numbers increased, and the circumstances of their great defeat
were forgotten, their spirits still dropped. Even Mr. Maxton
seemed to have lost his fire, repeating mechanically what
formerly he had said passionately. The cause remained, but
its presentation had become sepulchral. In an earthquake it is
difficult to summon up enthusiasm for town-planning; when
the ground underfoot is shaking and cracking, even stag-
gered holidays with pay lose much of their appeal.

Some dropped away from the National Government,
dead branches; but the main trunk continued green, and

small new shoots occasionally appeared. Snowden, who had
departed with Sir Herbert Samuel, derived what satisfaction
he might from being a viscount (in Mr. Churchill's words,
"Surrender value of his Socialist policy"), and made Mac-
Donald the particular target of his spite. It was "a positive
danger to the country," he said in the House of Lords, "that
its affairs should be in the hands of a man who every time he
speaks exposes his ignorance or incapacity," neglecting to
add that he had himself played a not insignificant part in the
events which resulted in MacDonald being entrusted with
the direction of the country's affairs. His fellow peers listened to the attack with surprise, but without much evident
indignation; that it was deserved, was possible, but that Snowden should make it, surprising. Writing his memoirs, which
appeared in *John Bull,* provided him with an occupation in
his last years, and shortly before his death it was rumoured
that he was meditating a re-entry into public life, presumably as a Liberal, the only party he had never helped to
attain power and denounced as treacherous and incompetent
after it had attained it. Swift's epitaph might have suited him
—"Here he lies, where his furious indignation can no more
lacerate his heart," except that, in Swift's case, the furious
indignation which lacerated his heart was directed against
his enemies in particular and the whole human species in
general, whereas in Snowden's case it was usually directed
against those who had once been his political associates.

MacDonald's disappearance was more gradual. He slowly
faded away, existing at last in a kind of twilight; there and
not there, making an appearance in Parliament and at public
functions, once collapsing at a Lord Mayor's Banquet in the
Guildhall, sometimes speaking, certainly moving, smiling,
shaking hands and otherwise indicating that he was alive

and in possession of what faculties he had, yet difficult to
believe in; in the House of Commons, often seated alone, as
though none cared to take their place beside so ghostly a
figure. His resignation from the Premiership was announced
on June 6, 1935, on grounds of physical incapacity, and once
more, and for the last time, he appeared at Seaham Harbour
to appeal for votes. Inflated German marks were on this
occasion of no avail; pickaxe and shovel were alike unserv-
iceable, and working-class friends distinctly unfriendly.
He often had difficulty in making himself heard, always in
making himself understood, and when he succeeded, was in
scarcely better case. The contest he afterwards described as
"a tremendously keen one and a filthy one as well," and retreated to Hampstead before its result—a majority of more
than 20,000 for his opponent, Mr. Emmanuel Shinwell, was
declared. "All I want," he said piteously, "is sleep, and still
more sleep. My energies are absolutely spent up." To add to
his misery, he heard that his son, Mr. Malcolm MacDonald,
had also been defeated at Bassetlaw.

Any of his colleagues who may have deduced from this
account of his condition that the Office he held was likely
soon to be available, were speedily disillusioned; from being
a "completely done-in old man," he reappeared the next
morning quite brisk and vigorous, still Lord President of
the Council, his son still Colonial Secretary, and still convinced that for the Government to keep its National character their continued membership of it was essential.

Seats had to be found for them, and as none of their
National Labour supporters showed any readiness to vacate
theirs, other possibilities were considered. The convenient
death of the member for Combined Scottish Universities
necessitated a by-election, which, it was thought, might pro-

vide MacDonald with an opportunity to return to the House
of Commons. He was a Scotsman himself, and had shown
himself ever zealous for education in all its branches. What
could be more fitting, then, than that he should represent in
Parliament the learning and the learned of his native land?
At first the proposal was not kindly received. The *Glasgow
Herald* complained that MacDonald was "an unsuitable candidate in every respect," and that "the way in which he has
been practically forced upon the Universities is deplorable,"
going on to remark that "if universities are to be a happy
hunting-ground for politicians who cannot find seats elsewhere," their special parliamentary representation would
soon be without any justification. It was also recalled that
MacDonald had himself in 1931 spoken in favour of abolishing the right to an extra vote of "those who become graduates and have to pay, I think £1 for it"; "If," he had said
then, "you want materialism at its very worst, masquerading
under the most sacred guise, you find it in the universities
for generations"; and here he was four years later appealing
in the name of Scotland, the "auld mither," to this masquerading materialism to support his parliamentary candidature.
Thanks largely to Mr. Baldwin's astute management, his
appeal, despite its unfavourable circumstances, was not made
in vain. Combined Scottish Universities took what Seaham
Harbour had rejected, and returned him with a comfortable
majority. Thenceforth, he languished, talking vaguely of
going through his papers and preparing an account of the
momentous events in which he had been concerned, but
never doing so, and scarcely comforted any longer by the
thought that duchesses would welcome an embrace from
him, if indeed (which was improbable) they still would. He
left for one more journey, one more mind-broadening and

barrier-breaking-down enterprise, remarking that what he sought was "that most elusive of all forms of happiness— rest," the unusual lucidity of this desire suggesting that it was truly experienced. He died at sea, and was brought home on a cruiser with a Union Jack over his remains, a curious and not unfitting end to a curious life.

Mr. Malcolm MacDonald's case proved, if anything, more difficult to handle than his father's. Various constituencies were approached without success, until the bestowal of a peerage left a vacancy at Ross, a scattered Highlands constituency, whose repeatedly independent-minded electorate, like the graduates of Combined Scottish Universities, displayed a certain restlessness at being presented with a candidate defeated elsewhere and with whom they had no evident connection. This restlessness also was somehow soothed into quiescence, and though he was opposed by an Independent Conservative, Mr. MacDonald was soon safe and sound in the House of Commons again, before long almost the sole remainder, and certainly the most eminent specimen, of National Labour there.

Of the three, Snowden, MacDonald and Mr. Thomas, who had earned the gratitude and admiration of their fellow-countrymen by promoting, and then entering, a National Government, Mr. Thomas looked like proving the hardest to dislodge from it. He was not obstinate like Snowden, or subject to ill-health like MacDonald; Free Trade meant little to him, Derby continued to elect him, and, as he remarked when he spoke against the taxation of Co-operative Societies and voted for it, he was accustomed to play for his side. It seemed probable that he would be long at the Dominions Office, and if removed thence, have to be accommodated elsewhere.

In 1936, however, unforeseen circumstances necessitated even his retirement from office and from Parliament. After the presentation of that year's Budget, rumours were prevalent that an exceptionally large amount of insurance had been placed with Lloyd's against a rise of 3d. on the income tax and an increased duty on tea, both of which measures were included in the Budget's provisions. This insurance, it was suggested, pointed to a leakage of budgetary information, for which only a member or members of the Cabinet could be responsible, since they alone were informed of the contents of the Budget before its publication. Rumours became so insistent that a Tribunal was set up to inquire into "whether, and, if so, in what circumstances and by what persons, any unauthorized disclosure was made of information relating to the Budget for the present year or any use made of any such information for the purposes of private gain." In the course of its proceedings the relations between Sir Alfred Butt, M.P., and Mr. Alfred Bates, both of whom had taken out Budget insurance, and Mr. Thomas, were investigated. Mr. Bates had, it appeared, paid over to Mr. Thomas £20,000 for the right to publish his Autobiography in the *Leader*, a periodical mostly devoted to competitions, of which he was the proprietor. Needy authors might regard this payment as exceptionally handsome, especially in view of the fact that the Autobiography was as yet unwritten, but Mr. Bates pronounced himself satisfied with the arrangement.

In giving evidence, Mr. Thomas pointed out that he was always in his office by nine o'clock, and had therefore come to be called "the charwoman's statesman." His natural impulse, he said, had been to resign from the Cabinet when rumours impugning his honour began to circulate, but a friend had advised against it; "For God's sake, Jimmy, don't resign, or all manner of constructions will be put on it," his friend had pleaded, and "I thought on the balance this was sound advice, and I carried on, answering all my questions, and braved up." When the Tribunal's public sittings had ended, but before its Report had been prepared, he did resign, on the ground that, in view of the "way in which my name and private affairs have been handled about, instead of being a source of strength to the Cabinet, I shall merely be a drag on it, and not in a position to pull my full weight." Mr. Baldwin accepted his resignation with deep regret, adding: "You have acted as I should have done in your place"; and the *Times* wished that it "might have had a different setting, as, doubtless, did also Mr. Thomas."

The Tribunal's Report found that "there was an unauthorized disclosure by Mr. Thomas to Sir Alfred Butt of information relating to the Budget, and that use was made, by Sir Alfred Butt, of that information for the purpose of his private gain."

Sir Alfred's and Mr. Thomas's resignation from the House of Commons followed, and then both disappeared from public life. Mr. Thomas made a fugitive reappearance as a director of the Crystal Palace; but when this elaborate edifice was largely destroyed by fire, his directorship presumably lapsed.

VII

Snowden, MacDonald and Mr. Thomas were only the National Government's trimmings, distasteful or ornamental according to personal predilections, but not necessary to its continued existence. They came and went, but it went on for ever; occasionally rearranging itself, but always the same;

like a repertory company whose different plays create a
momentary surprise, until the actors' familiar faces are recognized. Sir John Simon might be at the Foreign Office, at the
Home Office, at the Treasury, but he was always Sir John
Simon; whether Sir Samuel Hoare was handling India, collective security, the Navy, the I.R.A., or civil defence, his
touch did not vary; Sir Thomas Inskip inspired the same
confidence or derision as Attorney-General, Co-ordinator
of Defence, Dominions Secretary or, when he had become
Lord Caldecote, as Lord Chancellor. They bumped along,
encountering occasional obstacles in their way, removing
or circumventing these; His Majesty's Government, and as
far as could be seen, likely to remain so indefinitely. The
replacement of Mr. Lansbury by Mr. Attlee did not appreciably add to their difficulties; the Opposition's on-
slaughts were easily withstood (though Mr Churchill's not
always so easily), and the bestowal on its leader of a stipend
of £2,000 a year made him seem one of themselves.

The approach of another General Election taxed their
ingenuity. A Doctor's Mandate, which had served them
well before, could scarcely be asked for again; in four years
their doctoring might be presumed to be over, and a cure,
if there was ever to be one, achieved. Nor, so brief is public
gratitude, could they expect to attract support because they
had secured savings-bank deposits, when they were endangered. They were still National, certainly, with party differences all laid aside. Attempts had been made to remind
the electorate of this by sending out loud-speaker vans
equipped to display talking-pictures of Mr. Baldwin, Sir
John Simon and MacDonald, as well as other pictorial representations of the National Government's achievements at
home and abroad. The vans toured London and the prov-

inces, stopping occasionally at street corners, where a small crowd, mostly juvenile, would collect round them. What interest they aroused was somewhat languid, their reception scarcely enthusiastic. The esteem in which the National Government was held appeared to have diminished; though it might readily be admitted that its leaders had in all sincerity sunk their political differences, doubts had come to be felt as to whether, in fact, they had any to sink. A pick-me-up was clearly required, and Mr. Baldwin soon devised a suitable one. A good stiff peace and soda, taken last thing before a General Election, got rid of that tired feeling and generally toned up the Government's system.

The specific had been suggested to him by the result of the Peace Ballot, and by the success of the Labour candidate at a by-election in Fulham (a Conservative majority of 14,000 was transformed into a Labour majority of 5,000) fought on the issue of collective security. With these two object lessons before him, Mr. Baldwin came forward as the League's best friend, and promised that he would "never stand for a policy of great armaments." "You want peace," he said to the electorate; "you have shown your anxiety that support of the League of Nations should be the Government's policy. . . . I declare to you that we accept that policy. Trust me to put that policy into effect." The electorate did want peace, and had been encouraged to believe that support of the League of Nations would ensure it; did trust Mr. Baldwin to put that policy into effect. They had voted in their millions for peace in the Peace Ballot, and now were provided with another opportunity to vote for peace in the General Election. They availed themselves of it, and the National Government was returned with only a slightly reduced majority. It had taken office to defend the Gold Standard, and soon had to abandon it; now it had been re-elected to defend peace, and would, before this term was run, have to conduct a war.

Peace was the last deception in a series of deceptions.[1] In 1931 money was saved, in 1935, peace; and when it became apparent that in reality neither money nor peace had been saved, that both were irretrievably lost, what was there left to save? Only, it appeared, souls; and that salvage no one on Front or Opposition or Cross or Back benches, seemed equipped to undertake; not even Mr. Baldwin. With the promise of peace, demagogy for the time being exhausted its ingenuity, reached an impasse. "You want peace," Mr. Baldwin had said; and it was true. They wanted peace, but were not to have it.

[1] In the course of a debate on rearmament in the House of Commons in November 1936, with surprising candour Mr. Baldwin explained his tactics in the 1935 General Election. There was, he said, "probably a stronger pacifist feeling running in this country than at any time since the War. . . . At the election at Fulham, a seat which the National Government held was lost on no other issue but the pacifist." If, in such circumstances, he had used the great majority at his disposal to promote rearmament, "it would have defeated entirely the end I had in view." He could not think of anything "that would have made the loss of the election, from my point of view, more certain." Therefore, he decided for the time being to keep his belief in the necessity for rearmament to himself, even announced that "there has not been, there is not and there will not be any question of huge armaments or materially increased forces," and "we won the election with a large majority." Having won it, and with five years to run before another General Election, the previous objection to rearmament no longer operated, and they could go ahead with it. Such, in Mr. Baldwin's own words, "appalling frankness" was too much even for his devoted followers, and for a little while his prestige waned. By his handling of the Abdication crisis, which followed soon after, however, he recovered, and more than recovered, his old position, and continued to be venerated for his honesty and simplicity and directness; as one whose mind might work slowly, but whose heart was in the right place.

VIII

Peace had been voted for, Mr. Baldwin was again Premier, and the Fulham by-election and the Peace Ballot might safely be forgotten. What was now required was to rearm. For this purpose, money was gladly voted. The Labour Party offered no serious opposition, but contented itself with abstaining from divisions, and the Archbishop of York contributed his blessing—"More clearly to-day than at other times, we see how rightly the forces of the Crown are spoken of as services. . . . They are organized for service . . . for the service of safeguarding those treasures of civilization that we have inherited from the past." England had been weak, but now was to be strong again. Parliament had decreed it, money would ensure it—so many million pounds translated into so many guns, aeroplanes and trained personnel; incidentally, this capital expenditure, unlike capital expenditure on roads, houses and other peaceable enterprises, serving to diminish unemployment and promote prosperity.[1]

So simple a policy proved in practice suprisingly difficult, if not impossible, to execute. Though the money was duly spent, at least vanished from the Treasury, the strength it was to have purchased failed to materialize. Weakness obsti-

[1] At the World Economic Conference Mr. Runciman, then President of the Board of Trade, explained that a careful investigation had been made into the possibilities of reducing unemployment by financing public works. It had been demonstrated, he said, beyond any possibility of doubt, that an expenditure of £1,000,000 led to the employment of only 1,000 men directly, and 2,000 indirectly. This was uneconomic, and would not be countenanced by the British Government. When, some years later, increased expenditure on armaments was followed by a considerable decrease in unemployment (at one point, to 1,300,000), it was assumed that the latter circumstance was a consequence of the former, and that the Government, of which Mr. (by this time Viscount) Runciman was still a member, deserved credit for having thus reduced unemployment.

nately persisted. It was as though Fate had determined to keep Mr. Baldwin to his election pledge however hard he tried to break it. He had said that he would never be a party to substantial rearmament, and now that he wanted substantial rearmament, he could not procure it. As with Midas everything he touched turned to gold, so with Mr. Baldwin everything he touched turned to peace. When Members of Parliament clamoured for a Co-ordinator of Defence, he could only give them Sir Thomas Inskip, spending weeks struggling to produce one who would inspire more confidence, but doomed at last to produce Sir Thomas, to the accompaniment of loud laughter. They asked for guns, and he gave them departmental credits; they asked for national security, and he gave them the collective security they had told their constituents they would ever uphold, but in their hearts believed, not unreasonably, to be most insecure.

Parliament, reflecting the mood of those it represented, gave an impression of waiting—like the elderly inmates of a private hotel waiting for the post, though they have no particular reason for expecting a letter; or waiting for evening to come and the blinds to be drawn, though they have no particular reason for preferring evening to day. A strange apathy was apparent, occasionally broken when some event, exceptionally violent, impelled attention. Then for a little while voices were raised demanding an explanation, prophesying woe, pleading that still it was not too late if only at this eleventh hour. . . . Soon this clamour died away, and the old apathy returned; the waiting, no one knew for what.

Days passed, and months, and the business of life proceeded; money made and lost, newspapers appearing, attention concentrated now here, now there, now on this, now on that; deaths noticed, Horatio Bottomley's, and the fact

that it fell on Derby Day pointed to by a clergyman as a
fitting circumstance in view of the deceased's services on
behalf of that great national event; Prince Yusopoff, in a
witness box, describing to learned judge, counsel and public
how he and others had murdered Rasputin and disposed
of his massive corpse through a hole in the ice-bound Neva,
this done to demonstrate the libellous nature of a film on
the subject, one of many libel actions, lawyers eagerly scrutinizing published matter of all descriptions for what might be
actionable; a Talking Mongoose achieving some small notoriety when an employee of the B.B.C. successfully claimed
that his interest in one resident in the Isle of Man had been
contemptuously referred to, and his reputation and professional prospects thereby damaged; a lieutenant confined in
the Tower on a charge of espionage, also achieving notoriety, revived some years later after he had served a term of
imprisonment, when it was believed that a voice broadcasting nightly from Germany, was his.

The business of life proceeded, as in some form or another
it ever must; but now somewhat dispiritedly, without much
zest, like players performing to a sparse house at the end of
a long run, speaking carelessly the parts they know so well
and had once strained to make impressive, neglectful of
gestures once laboriously rehearsed, anxious only for the
curtain which, falling, will release them for ever from roles
become tedious with constant repetition.

Even good works lost their savour; even progress, though
continuing, palled. Slums should be abolished. They were
shameful, and disgraced a society which had too long tolerated their existence. Belatedly, slums were discovered and
denounced. Let them be pulled down one and all, and better,
happier dwellings erected. Slum-clearance was advocated,

and sometimes undertaken, but ceased with the coming of
war—itself a clearance process, though not only of slums.

Social services gained momentum, but from their own
weight rather than from any new impetus; went rolling onwards, gathering much moss in the shape of salaried personnel, bureaucratic departments which constantly grew,
each new cell added soon beginning itself to multiply. The
nation's teeth, the nation's eyes, the nation's intestines, all
its organs, internal and external, were improving, as published reports and ministerial statements testified. Nor was
the nation's mind neglected. A Committee for Verse and
Prose Recitation arranged readings of "good poetry and
plays" in public houses, drinkers temporarily laying aside
their pints of bitter and games of darts, and suspending their
conversation, to listen to undergraduates, attired with suitable carelessness, declaiming dramatic pieces. "It is probable," the Committee reported, "that not since Shakespeare's
day has there been such an opportunity of gaining a cumulative experience of entertaining people in the inn by good
poetry and drama," and went on to explain that it had
proved unnecessary "to make wholesale concessions in literary and dramatic standards to give real enjoyment" to un-
cultivated audiences. Higher and lower education received
attention; and if new schools were rarely built, it was because, with a declining birth-rate, a shortage of pupils was
to be anticipated—more education than pupils requiring it,
more infant-welfare than infants, more eye and dental treatment than eyes and teeth. Scholarship facilities were extended, until, it was said, even the Universities of Oxford
and Cambridge drew more of their undergraduates from
elementary and secondary schools than from public schools.
To augment its resources, Oxford University appealed for

funds, which came in scantily until Lord Nuffield began to contribute; then showed a mighty increase, the last of his donations, bringing the total up to well over £1,000,000 so overwhelming the assembled University Senate with gratitude when it was announced, that the Vice-Chancellor found himself unable to utter words, but had to content himself with making appreciative gestures. London University acquired a site in Bloomsbury, where a massive building soon began to rise. By the time it was completed the University had scattered, and the building was used to house a Ministry of Information; still the same line of business—informing, but a different branch from the one originally intended.

With one small token setback, taxation, like the social services, went on effortlessly increasing; the inevitability of its increase detracting from the Budget's majesty. Formerly its presentation had been perhaps the most solemn of all parliamentary occasions—Chancellor arriving, top-hatted, with his leather satchel, his face inscrutable, and crowded benches and public gatherings waiting in hushed silence for the dramatic moment when he divulged the closely guarded secret of what new impositions be proposed and what existing ones were to be rescinded. Now, though Members still assembled in strength, their attention was liable to wander, and once in the debate which followed the Chancellor's speech, the House was actually counted out.

The nation's accounts had lost their fascination; like a melodrama, in its day breathlessly followed, and later becoming tedious or laughable because too little related to contemporary circumstances. In the Chancellor himself—Mr. Chamberlain, and later Sir John Simon, there was no lack of solemnity; he felt the deep seriousness of the business in

hand, reverently announced expenditure and estimated re-
ceipts, and virtuously balanced them. He could no other.
For him, the process was still valid—one good Budget at
least shining in a largely budgetless world.

For him valid, and for some others; but for most, not. Up
and up and up the Budget went if nothing else did, until its
increases became fanciful, and Members of Parliament, when
the income tax reached seven-and-six in the pound, merely
laughed. How distant then seemed the time when to save
eleven million pounds by reducing unemployment benefit
was heroic! What anguish then for the Friends of Economy! Their friendship had to be bestowed on other causes,
and Economy left friendless—unless, mostly aged, they were
content to bestow it on none, Friends of Themselves only
during their last days.

Mr. A. P. Herbert, Independent Member for Oxford
University and long-standing contributor to *Punch*, energetically espoused the cause of divorce law reform. Newspapers had been deprived of the right to report divorce court
proceedings, and were forced to content themselves with
going through each session's long list of cases in search of
high-born or wealthy or otherwise distinguished adultery.
This was, for them, the only yield. Undistinguished adultery was born to blush unseen, only appearing in minute
type in the *Times* Law Reports, bringing profit to lawyers,
tedium to judges; productive of hotel bills, and evidence
by chambermaids and lodging housekeepers, mechanically
spoken after holding up a Bible, seldom, if ever, read, but
worn from being often grasped and sometimes kissed. Adultery was the essential ingredient in these proceedings—one
part of adultery to so many parts of non-adulterous ecstasy,

anguish, pleasurable or tedious or indifferent companionship; sometimes only adultery, neat.

Thus the Law paid its small tribute to an ancient conception of marriage, contracted for better or for worse, till death us do part, and valid until swept aside with other such foolishness in favour of a more up-to-date attitude. Marriage had long since become the Marriage Question (He has me, he has me not . . .), towards the elucidation of which many had contributed from many different standpoints; among others, M. Blum, whose contribution, forty years old, was resurrected and admired when he became French Prime Minister, by that time more grandfatherly than husbandly himself. What M. Blum had seen clearly long before any possibility of a *Front Populaire* existed to find its chosen leader in him, the Law persisted in ignoring, and continued to demand its pound of adultery, duly measured and cut away nearest the heart.

This Mr. Herbert determinedly set himself to change, and partially succeeded in changing. The legislation he sponsored allowed divorce on grounds of desertion, cruelty and lunacy, though to make it palatable to ecclesiastical opinion he was forced to admit a provision whereby a couple joined in holy matrimony could not contract out, even with adultery, until a stated period of time had elapsed—for better or for worse, until five years us do part. Mr. Herbert's pertinacity in getting through all its stages a Private Member's Bill dealing with so delicate and controversial a subject, was much admired; and though his Bill was criticized by less patient reformers for not going far enough, it was considered as marking an important stage in the realization of the Life Beautiful.

Another important effort in the same direction was con-

cerned with the Abortion Laws. A distinguished surgeon
out of public-spiritedness informed the police that he had
performed an abortion on a young girl whose pregnancy
was the result of her having been raped. Legal proceedings
were instituted, and the surgeon was acquitted, thereby making it easier for abortions to be performed in such cases in
the future. This, too, seemed only a small step forward to
abortion enthusiasts; but it was a step in the right direction,
and they were grateful. One of them, female, wrote that
when at last suitable legislation on the subject was introduced, it would have to "satisfy the eugenic conscience of
the community."

Sad it was for these reformers that just when their labours
were bearing fruit, when the bigotry which had for so long
frustrated their efforts was showing signs of total collapse,
outside circumstances over which they had no control should
arise to deprive them of the victory they deserved. Year by
year resistance to the provision of birth-control information
was diminishing, adultery losing its sting and abortion its
odium, marriage broadening down from precedent to precedent and divorce being brought within the reach of the
poorest household; and then the process was violently interrupted. In the black-out, expecting sirens to sound, husband
and wife were glad of one another's company even though
their mating was eugenically unsuitable; children, spaced or
unspaced, seemed precious, and abortions, with death and
destruction threatening, unnecessary. The community's
eugenic conscience was for the time being quite dormant.

IX

Not social services, or the Budget, or one another's eloquence, or the need for reforming laws relating to divorce and abortion, held the attention of Members of Parliament for long. Internal dissensions there might be, but they were soon forgotten. Groups formed only to unform again; opposition to the Government among its supporters died almost before it was spoken.[1] Mr. Lloyd George's Council of Action was mostly inactive, and when active, ineffectual, "We Can Conquer Unemployment" gave place to "We Can Conquer Germany," and that, surprisingly, to "We Can Make Peace With Germany," without much evident result. Nor were Sir Stafford Cripps's efforts to promote a United Front any more productive than Mr. Lloyd George's to acquire followers who were not also relatives. He went on and off the Labour Party Executive, and at last was subjected to disciplinary action. At a Labour Party Conference, he attempted to justify his policy of inviting the collaboration of Liberals, Communists, Pacifists, federal-unionists, all progressive forces of whatever character, to defeat the Government, and the methods he had adopted to attract support for it; but his speech was unsympathetically received. Much of it dealt with attacks which had been made on him for being wealthy—a condition he admitted to, but held justifiable in the circumstances. To gain re-admission to the Labour Party, a promise never again to engage in subversive activities and an expression of regret for past misdemeanours,

[1] A Conservative Member, Sir Stanley Reed, prefaced some mild criticism of the Government by remarking that "if he thought that a single word of what he was going to say in the remotest degree showed the slightest lack of confidence in the Prime Minister, he would cut out his tongue." This drastic operation proved unnecessary.

were required of him, and the latter he resolutely refused to
furnish. Thus was he left isolated, a one-man United Front,
in himself a compendium of progressive views, Stafford
Egalité, with a weekly publication, the *Tribune,* in which to
publish his views and his photograph, and a lucrative practice at the Bar to provide funds for the same.

What alone truly aroused the interest of Members of
Parliament, and brought them hurrying to their places,
and filled the Order Paper with questions which, when
answered, gave rise to many others, were events outside
their precincts, a distant spectacle. They hung on words
spoken elsewhere; watched, enthralled, a play in which they
had so far been allotted no parts, and yet in whose denoue-
ment they felt they were involved. The Rhine, they had
been told, was their frontier, and thither their gaze turned;
Minister of Agriculture, or of Home Affairs—let him be
brief, and soon make way for the Foreign Secretary or his
substitute.

In such circumstances, a new leader was required. Mr.
Baldwin was a home product, a rough-hewn slab of Splendid Isolation. When he visted Aix-les-Bains, it was for a
cure, not to establish personal contacts with foreign statesmen. Elections he could win; but with battles threatening,
it was time for him to go. One was needed who would venture forth, an umbrella in his hand, and parley with the
enemy.

When a business finds itself in difficulties, and a new
managing-director is required, it is customary either to make
a break with the past and appoint an outsider in the hope
that new methods and new vigour may revive a declining
enterprise, or to promote the senior ledger-clerk, who has
faithfully kept the firm's books for forty years, knows all its

affairs, and may be relied on to look after the interests of those from whom he has for so long been accustomed to take his orders. In choosing Mr. Baldwin's successor, the latter alternative was favoured; after Mr. High Mind came Mr. Slow Mind, and now Mr. Lowly Mind. MacDonald had proclaimed peace, Mr. Baldwin had promised it, and Mr. Chamberlain would bring it, palpable—a paper triumphantly waved in the air and uproariously welcomed. Appeasement was henceforth the word, an umbrella henceforth the symbol, *sauter pour mieux reculer* henceforth the procedure.

CHAPTER VI

News from Somewhere

CIRCUMSTANCES crystallize in a man as thoughts crystallize in an idea. Mental stress and bewilderment is momentarily relieved; "Eureka! Eureka!" "Lo, I have it!" the
troubled cry, and for a little while are no more troubled.
Political stress and bewilderment evokes the same cry—
"Eurekamen! Eurekamen!" "Lo, we have him!" The eyes
of all rest, enthralled, on one who lightens their darkness,
makes coherent their incoherence, speaks when they are
dumb. In his Autobiography,[1] Kipling describes how when
he was in South Africa, Rhodes, sighing, restlessly turning
from side to side on a sofa, would say to him: "What am I
trying to say? What am I trying to say?" The same question is constantly being put—sighing, turning restlessly from
side to side: "What are we trying to say? What are we
trying to say?"

Rhodes looked to Kipling to give him vocality; others
have looked to God, with perhaps happier results. When
there is no God, nothing in the wide universe more than
Man, no wisdom greater than his, no being more lasting
than his being or patience exceeding his patience, then the
Word is Flesh indeed, and desperate becomes the need for
imperfection to signify perfection, finitude to signify infini-
tude. Blessed are the pure in heart, for they shall see God;
cursed are the impure in heart, for they shall see Man.

[1] *Something About Myself.*

Among Germans especially, defeated and full of a sense of humiliation and inferiority, there was a craving to be told what they were trying to say; and many who came forward to tell them. Charlatans of all descriptions flourished;[1] brotherhoods and sisterhoods and brother-sisterhoods, high thought and low thought, free love and bought love, *Wandervögel*, *Nacktkultur* and hey nonny nonny. Happy days were there; strange things floated to the surface, stayed a little while exposed, and then were re-submerged, until out of the chaos came no new visage, but old familiar lineaments—an aged Field-Marshal, Hindenburg, with cropped hair, heavy moustache and deep raucous voice. The mountains laboured and brought forth a mountain.

Within Germany, Hindenburg's election as President of the Reich in succession to a shoemaker Socialist, provided a lull; without, it occasioned surprise and some anxiety, but also relief, on the general principle that a visible iceberg is less menacing than unseen mines and torpedoes. The relief was short-lived. With all his seeming solidity, Hindenburg was a shadowy figure, starting up out of the past and temporarily conveying the illusion that nothing had really happened since, as a young lieutenant, he mounted guard outside Versailles, with Bismarck within. He did not meet the requirements, it was not for him to reveal what Germany was trying to say. What connection had he, ancient, raucous Field-Marshal, with wandering Messiahs in blue capes, and the many voices crying "Heil!"; the many to whom the blue

---

1 See *The Dear Monster* by G. R. Halkett. Herr Halkett gives a detailed account of the career of a certain Muck Lamberty, who in 1921, wearing a blue cape, with great success preached his gospel of *Glut ist Geist*— Ardour is the Spirit—in Thuringia. He was frequently hailed as a Messiah, and only came to grief when, as a result of the free exercise of his own *Glut-Geist*, he laid himself open to charges of sexual promiscuity.

horizon beckoned—*Wir wollen wieder in's Blau?* What were *Wandervögel* to him, or he to *Wandervögel?* His part was to make straight the way for another.

The other, Hitler, whose moment had at last come, was a product of forces outside Hindenburg's range. Poverty and frustration had fired his spirit, weakness made him strong, torments known only to the meek and lowly driven him along. He on honey dew had fed and drunk the milk of paradise; and many closed their eyes in holy dread, and longed to weave a circle round him thrice. Materialism's insanity found its culmination in him; he focused the obscure longings of all who lived by bread alone and found it bitter. The glitter of Imperial Vienna had passed away, and he who had envied it, remained; the War was lost and over, and he who had fallen on his knees in a paroxysm of thankfulness when it began, found his opportunity in the confusion left when it ended; the new Social Democratic Germany, beloved of all the enlightened, with its guitar-playing innocence, and browned sea-bathers, and fraternal delegates, hearty in hand-shaking, and voters voting merrily—this new Germany, to which he belonged, he would bring to completion in a way surprising to its admirers. His roots were in the shifting present, thin soil productive of quick growth. Before he was much known, when his ambitions were still so circumscribed that he could write to a friend: "I do not require much from life. It would be sufficient for me for the movement to last, and for me to earn my living as editor of the *Völkische Beobachter*," [1] comrades in the Volunteer corps, *Wandervögel* enthusiasts, singing, folk-dancing, discussing, were delighted when one among them drew in charcoal a swastika on his helmet, and all gaily followed his

[1] Quoted in *The School for Dictators* by Ignazio Silone.

example. This was the first appearance of a swastika on a German helmet. Thus was it launched, to go on its way, death beckoning.[1]

Perhaps Hitler's greatest asset, abroad as well as at home, was the incredulity which his intentions aroused. They were so confused, seemed so fantastic, that it was difficult to believe they were seriously entertained even by those who supported him. At first he was laughable; and the fact that Lord Rothermere was one of his early admirers only confirmed this impression. Even when the Nazi vote increased enormously, still few envisaged the possibility of his becoming Chancellor; even when he had become Chancellor, it was confidently assumed that he was no more than a puppet figure, easily manipulated by forces behind the scenes, variously described as Prussian militarists, big industrialists, and the owners of large estates reluctant to have their lands sequestered. His alliance with the Nationalists, it was felt, would inevitably lead to his becoming their prisoner; armament manufacturers had financed him, and now he must execute their orders. Conservatives, perhaps remembering MacDonald, drew comfort from the thought that one who had been so poor and neglected would surely be awed by the company of the great, and overwhelmed when he found himself with all that money could buy at his disposal; Liberals built their hopes on the fifteen years of representative government, proportional representation, civil liberty, and other benefits which Germany had enjoyed under the

[1] See *The Dear Monster* by G. R. Halkett. The swastika's range in Germany, between folk-dance and goose-step, is apparent in one of its few public appearances in England on the cover of Kipling's works. There, too, the range is between *Rewards and Fairies* and *Captains Courageous*. When Hitler adopted the swastika, Kipling abandoned it, complaining that in any case the Nazis used it the wrong way round.

Weimar Republic, whose loss, they assured themselves, would not for long be tolerated; Socialists and Communists kept up their spirits by insisting that Fascism, of which the Nazi régime was one of several manifestations, represented capitalism's last desperate attempt to prevent the proletariat's inevitable seizure of power,[1] and those of indeterminate political convictions, or none at all, over pints of beer and in railway carriages looked knowing, and remarked that no one survived who put the Jews against him, and that in any case Germany had no money.

To the general amazement, none of these comforting hypotheses was substantiated by events. The Nationalists whose prisoner Hitler was to have been, soon ceased to count, only the irrepressible von Papen somehow continuing to exercise shadowy authority, mostly on foreign missions, a German Boneless Wonder; the big industrialists who were to have manipulated their puppet figure, were themselves manipulated, sometimes out of existence; high-born associates seemed to awe Hitler little, and the availability of luxurious living to leave him unexcited. The old Field-Marshal who, whatever else he might do, would never break the oath he had sworn to uphold the Weimar Constitution, broke it for Hitler's sake, and having broken it, soon died, bequeathing Germany to its Führer, his last month, it was said, not very coherent, murmurs breaking sometimes from his aged lips which suggested he thought Briand and Strese-

---

[1] For instance, Mr. John Strachey—"Fascism is the organized expression of the determination of the landlords to stick at nothing in order to stay in power. How can one ever reason with men who do not grasp this most basic fact in the world situation to-day?" (Quoted in *Who Is for Liberty* by Hugh Ross-Williamson.) "This most basic fact," while it may seem irrefutable to Mr. Strachey, would puzzle German landlords, who might readily admit that they had stuck at nothing, but would require a lot of convincing that they had stayed in power.

mann still among the living, and expected, perhaps, to receive
them again, hopeful of peace. Votes were taken, all voting,
and none, or almost none, dissenting. The Sovereign People
spoke with one voice, Hitler's; exercised their sovereignty
through him, were triumphant at last in his triumph. What
Rousseau had envisaged, Robespierre tried to realize, parliamentary government fumbled after, now at last had come
to pass.

Sovereignty resides in the People—that is, in a street mob,
in a Nation, *une et indivisible*, in a State, in a Party, in a
Leader. *Ein Reich, ein Volk, ein Führer.* The Sovereign
People owe allegiance only to themselves; their enthronement must, therefore, result in their utter subjection to an
abstraction—their own corporate existence, as embodied in
the State, and, finally, in a demagogue who identifies his
and the State's will. Becoming Sovereign, the People had
to become slaves; and the Totalitarian State, whether in its
classless, socialist society or Third Reich version, is the full
realization of their slavery.[1] When in 1939 the French President, and M. Daladier, M. Bonnet and other members of the
Government appeared in top hats to celebrate the 150th
anniversary of the Revolution, delivering orations in praise
of Liberty, Equality and Fraternity to a not very enthusiastic gathering of Parisians, without knowing it they were
celebrating the birth of the Totalitarian State. It was not

[1] See *Dictatorship, Its History and Theory* by Alfred Cobban. Marat,
Mr. Cobban points out, was perhaps the first to see clearly that if the
People were sovereign, with the Paris mob as their executive agent, their
action needed to be directed by a "military tribune, a supreme dictator."
But for Charlotte Corday, Marat might have played this part himself; as it
was, it was left to Robespierre, and after him Napoleon. In Hitler it finds
its apogee. The Totalitarian State's line of descent from the French Revolution and through nineteenth-century political theory, is also traced in
Beyond Politics by Christopher Dawson.

they, top-hatted, who were the legatees of the Revolution, but their regimented enemies across the Rhine. In the storming of the Bastille, which they now, clutching umbrellas, their check-books in their pockets, recalled, was implicit the burning of the Reichstag. *Le jour de gloire est arrivé* —but not for them.

As the wonder of Hitler's achievement of power became accustomed, he became an obsession. His voice was often heard, families gathering round radio sets to listen, fascinated and appalled, to its shrill frenzy, an alien sound to fill their quiet sitting-rooms, remarkably contrasting with the modulated, genteel accents which their loud-speakers ordinarily discharged. Newspapers were full of his doings and his photograph; his book, *Mein Kampf*, was often quoted, summarized, published in expurgated and then in unexpurgated editions, one publisher requesting readers to remember that the author was self-taught, and the book, like *The Pilgrim's Progress*, written in prison; another proudly announcing that his edition "paid no royalties to Adolf Hitler." A publican advertised his beer as having "put the hit in Hitler"; plays were recommended as likely to induce forgetfulness of Hitler, and a book, according to its blurb, was so entertaining that it would "put Hitler's nose out of joint." Conversations, whatever their beginnings, had a way of ending in Hitler; many were the books about him, newspaper interviews with him, recollections of him.

His features, his little moustache, his drooping hair, became most familiar. Stock Exchanges fluctuated with his moods; if he went three times to hear *The Merry Widow* troops were disbanded and frontiers left unguarded; a partiality for an American actress aroused sudden hope that she might receive some of his passion, and Germany correspondingly less. Clergymen referred to him in their pulpits; novelists brought him into their novels and poets into their poems; politicians whom he had derided found consolation in being able to advertise themselves as having been attacked by Hitler, in the expectation of thereby attracting larger audiences to their meetings, and Sir Thomas Inskip told his constituents that Herr von Ribbentrop had been kind enough to inform him that a speech of his had given Hitler "great satisfaction."

If Hitler was indisposed, he was mortally ill,[1] while many believed that he had died already, and that one of several doubles was impersonating him, presumably not reflecting that in such a case the outlook was blacker than before his supposed demise, since it meant that his aims might still be achieved even though his leadership was not available. This theme was worked out in detail by an ingenious American in *The Man Who Killed Hitler*, which was serialized in the *Sunday Express*, where it was described as "the most amazing book of modern times." Its publisher, it was explained, had been threatened with death and kidnapped, but had refused to be intimidated; though admittedly fiction, "all of it could happen. At the end you will wonder—'Did it really happen?'" *Hitler's Last Year of Power* was another book whose title understandably recommended it to a large public.

It is doubtful if any human being in his lifetime has ever before so focused the attention of his fellows, so stirred up in them hatred or admiration, or, more often, a mixture of both. His appearance in power was signalized by a burning

---

1 The illness most commonly attributed to formidable foreigners (for instance, to Napoleon, Lenin and Mussolini) is syphilis. Hitler's reputation for chastity has prevented this attribution. Cancer is the second favourite, and with that he has often been credited—of the throat, that being, in his case, the organ most needing to be put out of action.

Parliament, and followed by a bonfire of books—Thomas
Mann, Ernst Toller, Remarque, Stefan Zweig, Jack London
even, all consigned to the flames; institutes for sexual research all gutted, apparatus thrown out of the windows,
diagrams and charts torn down and destroyed. Such acts
of vandalism and obscurantist fury aroused the anger of
those to whom Parliament signified freedom, and books
wisdom. Professor Einstein, when he refused to return to
Germany, was offered academic posts in the United States
and in England, and Commander Locker-Lampson's hospitality; Oxford and Cambridge indicated their disapproval
of the Third Reich by refusing to participate in celebrations
at Heidelberg University, and when Dr. Rosenberg, a Balt
who had been largely responsible for formulating Nazi
foreign policy before Hitler became Chancellor, visited
London, he was given a chilly reception.

Yet if the main current of opinion was hostile, some there
were whose hearts responded to Hitler's acts and ideas. To
them it seemed fitting, if not desirable, that Parliament and
books should burn. They recognized a vague kinship with
this violent gesture of impatience with the spoken and
written word's supremacy. Even when their lips spoke
against it, their blood was for it. The Nazi who said: "When
I hear the word 'culture' I cock my pistol," was easily presented as a destroyer of civilization; but how if civilization
deserved to be destroyed? How if there was no civilization
left to destroy, only débris, rubbish, easily inflammable?
Then the flames which consumed the Reichstag, and *All
Quiet on the Western Front*, and sexual research institutes,
were purificatory, necessary perhaps.

As many adhering to the Left journeyed to the U.S.S.R.,
there to offer thanks and admire all that they were shown,

so did their corresponding type of the Right make Hitler their hero and the Third Reich their paradise. If the Rev. Hewlett Johnson detected in the Soviet régime the highest extant realization of Christian principles, Major Yeats-Brown, after searching for and finding a *guru* whose guidance he could accept, made the more guarded statement that it was his "honest conviction that there is more real Christianity in Germany to-day than there ever was under the Weimar Republic." [1] A debate between the Dean and the Major on what constituted "real Christianity" would have been illuminating, but was not arranged. Corresponding to the ladies who had met Russians whose eyes glowed proudly when Stalin's name was mentioned, were other ladies who had met Germans whose eyes similarly glowed when Hitler's name was mentioned. "I don't exaggerate," Miss Enid Bagnold wrote, "when I say I have seen business men blink with something like tears when they speak of the Führer." Against Lord Passfield reverent in Moscow, might be set Lord Rothermere reverent in Munich; Lord for Lord, they cancelled out. Whether the thought of Hitler made Lord Rothermere blink with something like tears, he has not divulged, but even in 1939 he considered him "a very great gentleman." [2] Later, Hitler fell in his esteem to become "the Mystic of Berchtesgaden," and even lower. Stalin suffered a similar eclipse in the estimation of many of his foreign admirers, though not even Mr. Shaw, who continued to venerate him, ventured to describe him as the Mystic of the Kremlin.

Round Hitler a spiritual as well as a physical combat raged. Whatever he did, however often he shifted his ground and broke his promises, he held the world's attention. The spell was not broken—like a lover, constantly unfaith-

---

[1] See *European Jungle.*
[2] See *Warnings and Predictions.*

ful, yet ever taken back, in one passionate caress unity re-established and separation forgotten. He was the very *zeitgeist*, its light shining in his eyes, its words on his lips— the little man dreaming of greatness, romantic heart belied by shabby face, china-blue eyes and small moustache claim-ing their part in the majestic scheme of things; magic case-ment cloth, and new, unhappy, present things and battles soon to be.

Every road led to him, and ended in him. He was the Shape of Things to Come, now come. Progress he brought, and votes, all imaginable blessings. Each unrealized self could find realization in him, none frustrated, self-expression available for all, instead of only in co-educational schools, University Extension classes, and other places which special-ized in facilitating it. "I am by nature an artist, not a poli-tician," he said to Sir Nevile Henderson, British Ambassador in Berlin;[1] and, on another occasion; "I am the first of a race of supermen who will come to rule the earth," thus ful-filling what many prophets, from George Sand to Bernard Shaw, had foretold—how a genius or superman would arise and teach future generations how to live. Creative evolu-tion had created him; in a Godless world, he was God.

Being such, how could he be resisted? The co-educated might rage against him, but he was the self-expression they had been promised; democrats might complain, but he was Democracy's apogee; pacifists hurl abuse, but who had praised peace more rapturously than he? Opposition col-lapsed, faltering when it recognized itself in him. Can sparks oppose a flame, or breath oppose a whirlwind? His enemies' weapons were pointed against their own breasts;

[1] See *Documents Concerning German-Polish Relations and the Outbreak of Hostilities Between Great Britain and Germany on September 3, 1939.* H.M.'s Stationery Office.

and if they fired them, they must destroy themselves. Jericho's walls fell flat when Joshua's trumpets blew, not because the trumpets were strong, but because the walls were weak, tottering already, and in the trumpets' blast heard their own decomposition. In the early days of National Socialism, Hitler was known as the Drummer; when he beat his drum, walls fell, first within Germany and then without.

The course of his triumphant career was followed with wonder and fear. From being laughable, he became dangerous; from being dangerous, incredible. The ideas he propounded were dismissed as unsound and mutually contradictory, their falsity easily demonstrated; yet they appeared to be irresistible. *Hitler, the Pawn* brought solace, but this pawn continued to dominate the board, until it began to be wondered whether such a pawn might not be preferable to pieces with ostensibly greater possibilities. His racial theory—how absurd it was! Scientists and others clearly showed that there was no Aryan race, and that, if there were, Germany had no particular claim to belong to it. On the theory, he lost; on its application, won. In Germany, racial origins were anxiously investigated, and those who could not demonstrate unpolluted Aryan extraction submitted to severe penalties, some taking their lives, and those who could, fleeing.

Refugees became a familiar sight in London, many to be seen in and around the British Museum, congregating there, some in the Reading Room itself, forgetful of their woe as their eyes absorbed printed words and the smell of the volumes stacked around them assailed their nostrils, publishers and newspaper offices and universities besieged by them, Herr Doktors desirous of an occupation. Their guttural talk was often heard, their unfamiliar overcoats and hats frequently noticed. In successive waves they came, from Germany, from Austria, from Czechoslovakia; each of Hitler's advances registered by their arrival, distant ripple of a large disturbance, swallows which made a winter. Money was raised to help them, and indignation expressed at the treatment they had received; the League set up a Bureau, and later a Commission, to give them assistance, Lord Winterton grappled with the problems they raised, and a proposal was made to settle some of them in British Guiana, where, it appeared, there was an upland plain whose climatic excellence and economic possibilities had not hitherto been adequately appreciated. Of the measures taken on their behalf, perhaps the most widely known and enjoyed was the Mayor of New York's action in appointing to guard the German Consulate a police officer named Finkelstein, whose highly semitic but jovial countenance was reproduced in most newspapers.

Other refugees than Jews came, ceaselessly arriving and pleading to be admitted, some threatening suicide if they were made to return whence they had come; a shipload left at large, unable to find a port where they might disembark. Each new upheaval sent its quota; all languages were heard, all varieties of complexion seen. When a hayfield is mown, rabbits collect in the last little patch of standing grass; so did refugees collect in the corner of Western Europe which the scythe had still not reached, where letters-of-credit were still valid, Parliament and books still unburnt, stock-prices still quoted, restaurants still buzzed with unrestrained conversation, butter was still more evident than guns. Authors and journalists came bearing typewriters, often with revelations to dispose of; professors and scientists and exiled monarchs and prime ministers came; Dr. Freud came, settling in

Hampstead and there devoting himself to proving that Moses was an Egyptian, there dying; distraught women and children and aged Rabbis came—a forlorn company, hopeful that they had found a refuge where they would be troubled no more, and likely in that to be disappointed.

II

One man's love can permeate the world, and so can one man's hate. The tears which Christ shed as he looked down on Jerusalem, filled innumerable other eyes; the pity he felt for men coming and going, passing in and out of doorways and up and down streets, was reproduced in innumerable other breasts. The resentment and self-pity which possessed Hitler when he felt himself scorned and rejected, was similarly reproduced. As he fawned on those unlike himself, large and blond and brutish, so did others; as he was filled with loathing of the opposite type, his own, dark and furtive and subtle, so were others. His hatred, passionately stated, proved infectious. It swelled into a mighty roar of hate, echoing and re-echoing through the world.

He dramatized his hate as a conflict between Jew and Aryan, darkness and light, horror unspeakable and virtue irreproachable. Weakness Through Misery and Strength Through Joy; and this dramatization proved acceptable. Many who had found thinking with their minds unprofitable, were ready to follow him in thinking with their blood. Minds worked slowly and laboriously, but blood warmed easily and effortlessly; more convenient than accepting guilt, was transferring it to another; not Man's corrupt nature, but certain corrupt men, were to blame for individual and corporate inadequacy.

The hate Hitler generated formed a magnetic field, which

reached far, particles of hatred stirred, like iron filings by
a magnet, to fall into its pattern. Even as far as England
the field reached, though here, distant from the centre, the
force was only faintly felt, the pattern only faintly traced.
Sir John Simon found it necessary to issue a statement that,
despite a Biblical name, he was of Welsh extraction; Lord
Camrose, proprietor of the *Daily Telegraph*, brought a successful libel action against an organ of the British Union of
Fascists for having falsely implied that he was a Jew; in one
of his articles. Dean Inge suggested that Jews were using
"their not inconsiderable influence in the Press and in Parliament to embroil us with Germany." This suggestion was
indignantly challenged by, among others, Sir William
Crawford, President of the Institute of Incorporated Practitioners in Advertising, who wrote that, though he had
acted for a number of Jewish firms, never had he received
from them "any suggestion or instruction that advertising
policy should in any way be influenced by, or attempt to
influence, the editorial policy of the papers selected to carry
the advertising campaign"; and when Dean Inge was asked
to substantiate the charge he had made, he admitted that it
had no other foundation than information given him by a
journalist to the effect that when his newspaper adopted a
policy sympathetic to Germany, Jewish business firms which
advertised in the paper stated that, unless the policy was
dropped, they would cancel their advertising contracts.

Anti-semitic slogans were chalked on walls and in the
roadway, coldly or indifferently eyed by most passers-by,
but remaining, until rain washed them away; windows of
shops belonging to Jews were broken, and in the darkness
offensive epithets shouted. In less unedifying forms, the
same tendency was apparent; Mr. Douglas Reed in *Insanity*

Fair denounced the Nazi régime to the satisfaction of its
most determined adversaries, but in *Disgrace Abounding*,
handled Jews unkindly. Anti-semitism was in the air, an
unmistakable tang. The exploits of Julius Streicher, epi-
leptic schoolmaster and Governor of Franconia, were read
of; his *Der Stürmer* envisaged, with its lurid accounts of
ritual murder, its sexual abnormality and sadistic hysteria.
Could such things be? it was wondered. Did these dark
recesses still exist in human nature, the shadows lurking
there unexorcised by all that had been gained in knowledge
and amenities? Were matriculants, and even bachelors of
arts and science, as susceptible as savages to cruel supersti-
tions and morbid impulses? If the light that was in them
were darkness, how great was that darkness!

Hitler beat his drum, and walls fell. To withstand him,
a contrary principle to his hate and the destruction it brought
in its train, was required, but was not forthcoming. If minor
devils cannot be cast out in the name of Beelzebub, prince of
devils, how much less can Beelzebub be cast out in the name
of minor devils. Only some Roman Catholics and Protestants were truly defiant—they and Ludendorff, aged lunatic
and once Hitler's ally. Those who acknowledged a God,
were able to challenge the pretensions of a man because they
knew more than Man, whereas those whose hopes were confined within human dimensions—how were they to cry
"Hold!" to human vainglory? Where progressive forces,
seemingly strong, vocal and able to command votes, some
their thousands, some their tens of thousands and some their
millions, all faltered, submerged by the Progress which
Hitler ordained, Pastor Niemöller,[1] blind former U-boat

---

[1] Because of this resistance, Pastor Niemöller was admired by many who
would have found him, in his character and attitude of mind, as anti-

commander and National Socialist sympathizer, would not submit.

Ludendorff's opposition to the Nazi régime was of a different order; lunacy's privilege rather than faith's responsibility. In his fortnightly magazine, *At the Fount of German Power*, mixed up with anti-semitic fury, astrological predictions and other occult matter, appeared criticism of the Third Reich when everywhere else it had been suppressed. Later, the magazine, suddenly popular as the single remaining opposition organ, was also subjected to the *Gleichschaltung* process, and lapsed back into its original obscurity; and Hitler and Ludendorff, ceremonially but not very cordially, met and conversed together.[1] After this ceremonial meeting, Ludendorff continued undisturbed with his pagan rites, occasionally to be seen wearing horned headpiece and other Wagnerian accoutrements. When he died, he was given a State funeral, though at subsequent private obsequies his remains were consigned to Valhalla to the accompaniment of ancient German chants and ritual, strange

pathetic as he would have found them. He is, for instance, the hero of a play, *Pastor Hall*, which Ernst Toller wrote shortly before he committed suicide in New York. It is certain that Pastor Niemöller would have suffered the same persecution, and for the same reasons, at the hands of the short-lived Communist Government in Bavaria, of which Toller was a member, as he has at the hands of the Nazi Government. One of Hitler's minor achievements has been to promote strange admirations. Under the stimulus of dislike of him, democrats have thought gratefully of King Carol, atheists of the Pope, and Left-Wing Socialists of Mr. Churchill, while the ex-Kaiser became, by comparison with his successor as All-Highest, a benign figure, Doorn Santa Claus, fond of hewing trees, and distributing gifts to the poor and aged, and conducting family prayers.
[1] Whatever else they may have discussed, they are unlikely to have recalled their past collaboration at Munich in 1923, when a revolt was arranged, but at the crucial moment Nazi participants failed to appear, and Ludendorff was left to advance, solitary, in top hat and frock coat, against the assembled police.

figures, presumably friends and retainers, appearing in suitable costumes, and making strange moan.

The ease with which Hitler triumphed spread consternation—books and Parliament gone, without a blow struck in their defence, though Parliament was later resurrected, each member in identical uniform, with identical mind, and stirred to identical emotions, a dream parliament accommodated in the Kroll Opera House (World Economic Conference in Geological Museum, Parliament in Opera House); culture abolished, labelled decadent, and the cultured mostly dispersed; even the Oberammergau Passion Play presented with Nordic Christ and Apostles, except Judas, whose Jewish appearance was permitted. Such devastation was fearful to contemplate. In quiet universities hearts were troubled;[1] and the peace and security of cathedral closes seemed less certain than before. Bank accounts, though amply replenished, were haunted by a phantom overdraft, which threatened at any moment to become a real one.

To abolish this phantom overdraft, and establish a credit balance, was the burning desire of many. They shouted their indignation, wrote it,[2] made films and plays of it, resolved it, conferred on it, longed for an opportunity to prove it with deeds, in some cases with their life-blood. Yet when they thought to grapple with their enemy, they found them-

[1] Mr. F. L. Lucas, for instance, entitled his Journal for the year 1938, which he spent mainly in Cambridge, *Journal Under the Terror.*

[2] In *Journey Through Life* M. Amedée Ozenfant gives a selection of protests by French writers and artists. His own contribution to the Symposium was: "Artists, writers, scientists, see what is happening in Germany, think of it. Can you remain neutral? Close your ranks. Act. Every thought that leads to war is a cancer-thought. A single, united front against the old cancer-thoughts!" This statement may be taken as typical of countless resolutions, manifestoes, speeches, and other public utterances, whereby intellectuals of all descriptions relieved their feelings and tried, without much success, to demonstrate their resolution.

selves grappling with one another. They girded on their
armour, took up their weapons, and with their battle cry on
their lips—"For Saint Democracy and Civilization!" went
forth to combat, only to discover that they were charging
furiously against their own ranks.

Looking round the field anxiously, they saw, as they
thought, one resolute enemy at least. Against outstretched
arms, clenched fists were raised defiantly. Let them, then,
raise a clenched fist in defence of freedom and culture, peace
and happiness; making what reservations they thought fit
in the light of past qualms over trials and obedient confessions, but resolutely raising their clenched fists. Stalin became their antidote to Hitler; Marxist hate should abolish
Nazi hate, and Marxist falsifications correct Nazi ones. Had
not the Webbs proclaimed a New Civilization, based on perfect democracy, justice and equality between man and man,
and Sir Bernard Pares revised his former unfavourable
opinion of Soviet judicial procedure? [1]

Even the Duchess of Atholl had come to treat sympathetically what once had been anathema to her; even Mr.
Garvin, faithful admirer of Mussolini, had reached the conclusion that "there is, in fact, no firmer ally than Russia in
the defence of freedom." [2]

[1] In the *Times* of April 25, 1933, he wrote, of the Metropolitan-Vickers
Trial, that the "confessions of the accused Russians are not worth the
paper that they are written on," that owing to the subservience of Soviet
courts to Communist policy, there is no point in bringing the accused to
trial at all, and that the determination of the Bolsheviks to "reduce human
beings to pulp, and implant everywhere fear, suspicion and servility, produce moral casualties which far more than outweigh the possible realization of any theory"; in the *Observer* of March 7, 1934, he wrote, of the
Radek-Sokolnikov Trial, that its verbatim report "calls for serious study,"
that wrecking activities were "proved up to the hilt," and that "convincing evidence" was adduced.
[2] See editorial paragraph in the *Observer* of March 19, 1939.

At the Paris Exhibition, Soviet and Nazi pavilions faced one another, each feverishly aiming at being taller than the other, in front of each figures symbolic of what seemed most sublime—heroic German and heroic worker, of plaster made, and soon the worse for wear. Were these pretentiously frail pavilions straining to be huge, truly defiant? Or the same, one a reflection of the other, and inside the same strident emptiness, graphs and statistics demonstrating prosperity's advance, photographs displaying happiness and the lineaments of leaders by all beloved? Too happy, happy mortals to be thus prosperous, thus to smile, and to be thus blessed in their leaders.

Two twin plaster giants confronted each other in pretended defiance, and huddled round them small edifices, failed or aspiring giants, in one of these a representation of Mr. Neville Chamberlain in waders, fishing; the whole constructed and arranged under the direction of M. Blum, its completion constantly delayed by labour and other difficulties; indeed, completed never, closed and demolished when still incomplete.

III

A conflict which would not crystallize, was thought to have crystallized in the Spanish Civil War. Here, it seemed, was a clear issue—between the defenders and destroyers of Democracy, between constitutional and arbitrary authority, between freedom and servitude. The cause of the Spanish Republican Government was warmly espoused by enlightened opinion; the cause of the Insurgents,[1] by unenlightened.

[1] As in the case of the Abyssinian conflict, the nomenclature used indicated the sympathies felt. The Republican side was commonly designated "the Reds" by sympathizers with General Franco, and "the Loyalists" by

General Franco sent his Moors into battle to fight for Christianity, Mussolini sent his legionaries to save Spain from Communism; the International Brigade, composed largely of Communists and Communist sympathizers, fought to make Spain safe for Democracy, and Spaniards fought, it may be assumed, for the most part because they had to. Disinclined to fight for or against Christianity, Democracy, Communism, or, indeed, anything at all, the British Government adopted a policy of non-intervention, to which twenty-seven other Governments were invited, and consented, to adhere, though mostly intervening—"Let there be no war!" and now: "Let there be non-intervention!" Between them all, much blood was shed and much suffering endured, without any of the causes invoked receiving any appreciable benefit.[1]

Spain became, for the time being, the centre of interest. Journalists who had been together in Addis Ababa, met again in Madrid, Barcelona, Bilbao, and on the banks of the Ebro; military commentators elucidated pioneer and other movements, and referred knowingly to Spanish winter con-

---

its own sympathizers; the Insurgent side was "the Rebels" or "the Fascists" to those who hoped for its defeat, and "the Nationalists" to those who hoped for its victory. Neutral opinion used "Republicans" and "Insurgents." "Junta" for General Franco's side, probably indicated a slight bias in its favour.

[1] Occasional voices, not infected with the prevailing confusion; for instance, a statement addressed by the Bishop of Barcelona to his flock, and quoted in *The Martyrdom of Spain* by Professor Alfred Mendizabal— "You are the ministers of a King who cannot abdicate . . . who cannot be dethroned, because He is not enthroned by the votes of men. Men did not place the crown on His head, men will not take it off. Everything falls after a time . . . thrones collapse and royal crowns roll in the mud. Alone the Kingdom of Christ remains standing . . . because it is guaranteed by the Word of God."

ditions which made operations impossible, as they had previously to Abyssinian rains, and would later to Polish mud. Friends of the Soviet Union became for the duration Friends of Republican Spain; clergymen attested that churches in Barcelona and Madrid were freely operating, and other clergymen that they had been destroyed or were being used for sectarian purposes; parties of Members of Parliament visited one or other side, and reported on what they saw enthusiastically or critically according to their predilections. Round Guernica a battle raged long after fighting there had ended, some insisting that it had been ruthlessly destroyed by German bombing-planes, others that local Communists had set fire to it before removing themselves. Until other horrors invalidated it, Guernica was the current symbol of ruthless aggression, and was made the subject of a picture by Picasso.

Mr. Stephen Spender announced his departure for Insurgent territory, where he would serve the Loyalist cause;[1] Mr. Auden contributed a poem in blank verse on the conflict's dialectical implications; Professor J. B. S. Haldane's spirit was uplifted in Madrid, Major Yeats-Brown's in Burgos, and Mr. Attlee met with an enthusiastic reception when he paid a fraternal visit to the Republican Government. In honour of the occasion, one of the International Brigade's companies was named after him, the other British contingent having been named after Saklatvala. Americans who had volunteered for service in Spain preferred older heroes—Lincoln and Washington rather than Sacco and Vanzetti—for their patrons. Mr. Attlee, Saklatvala, Lincoln, Washingon—under these confused auspices the Brigade fought valiantly, attract-

1 In the course of a poem, he remarks that in Spain there was a bullet addressed to him. If so, it was not delivered.

ing to itself the adventurous, the idealistic, and sometimes the despairing, from all parts of the world. These at any rate had managed, to their own satisfaction, to make explicit a conflict they felt was implicit in the circumstances of their lives. Fortunate, perhaps, those who died; not living on to doubt again, and wonder if blood shed in Spain had truly served the cause they had at heart.

Such doubts came, if at all, later. While the Civil War was in progress, it seemed certain that in Spain Good and Evil were at last joined in bloody combat. The immense Pasionaria was often photographed, vehemently spouting righteousness; novelists were able to dispose of their heroes, when their 80,000-word course was run, by sending them off to fight in Spain; and Anarchism, prevalent in Catalonia, made a small comeback. Mr. Herbert Read, for instance, explained how, after a long, troubled pilgrimage, which took in on its way, as well as M. Benda, Dialectical Materialism and *The Wasteland*, he found himself a convinced, though not a practising, anarchist;[1] and others pointed out that, though Anarchism was ordinarily believed to aim at the total destruction of all authority,[2] as worked out by Catalonian Anarchists it was productive of something scarcely distinguishable from Welwyn Garden City.

The campaign's course was followed with deep interest, maps of Spain frequently published. Fashionable parties were organized to visit the Franco-Spanish Frontier and

[1] See his *Poetry and Anarchism.*
[2] For instance, Bakunin, the founder of the Anarchist Movement in Spain, was once driving through Germany, and saw some men setting fire to a house. He at once jumped out of his carriage, and enthusiastically helped them, without asking whose the house was or why they were setting fire to it. That the house stood was sufficient justification in his eyes for demolishing it. See *Bakunin* by E. H. Carr.

watch hostilities when they took place in that area; and
men-of-letters, or of politics, or of both, weary of reviewing
books, turning over thoughts often turned over; of dining
in restaurants where the cooking was excellent and the
charges moderate, and of meeting one another in rooms soon
crowded and stuffy, sherry steadily consumed and conversation incessant—were exhilarated and spiritually refreshed by
a stay in Barcelona. It was real, it was earnest, it was lively,
as they explained in many a subsequent thousand words for
many a subsequent guinea.

Meanwhile, the Non-Intervention Committee proceeded
with its labours, like the Disarmament Conference mainly
concerned to keep itself in existence. This not inconsiderable
feat, it performed, in the teeth of intervention before which
a feebler Committee would have faltered, and probably col-
lapsed. Though it cannot be said to have appreciably diminished the number of foreigners who participated in the Civil
War, or the amount of war material sent into Spain, it
devised, got unanimously approved, and provided personnel
for, an ingenious system of coastal and frontier supervision,
and obtained at various times from all the Governments
concerned assurances that they would prohibit the departure
of any of their nationals who intended to serve with General Franco or the International Brigade. Though the war
was long, the Non-Intervention Committee was longer;
when it met for the last time, Madrid had fallen to General
Franco, Pasionaria vanished, International Brigade been
disbanded, and even Mr. Hemingway and Mr. Ralph
Bates departed to seek elsewhere material for stories and
films of life in the raw. At its last meeting, the twenty-seven
non-intervening Governments were solemnly released from
the various undertakings they had given, but mostly not

observed;[1] the question of unpaid monetary contributions was considered, and a share-out of remaining cash planned. Despite so innocuous an agenda, even on this occasion its proceedings were not quite unruffled. The fact that Albania's arrears had been written off as irrecoverable, on the reasonable ground that its Government, having been put to flight by Italian troops, no longer existed, evoked a strong protest from the Italian delegate, who indignantly insisted both on the continued existence of the Albanian Government, and on its readiness to pay its way as a non-intervener.

Was it a rehearsal, the Spanish Civil War, with the first-night coming on shortly; players not yet word-perfect, costumes and make-up still requiring attention, scene-shifters clumsy at their duties, spot-light not always finding the required face? Non-Intervention, a comedy, to be followed by Intervention, with markedly similar cast and action, but scarcely a comedy.

IV

As though to make good what Nazi bonfires had consumed, many were writing books; many books were being published and circulated. For each book destroyed, ten should be produced, as, in Gandhi's *Satyagraha* campaign, for each volunteer knocked senseless, ten more came for-

[1] Ceremonial welcomes were arranged in Rome and Berlin for the Italian and German troops who fought in Spain, and both Mussolini and Hitler, in the speeches they made on these occasions, ridiculed the Non-Intervention Committee and boasted of how they had ignored its agreements. Perhaps the German attitude to the Civil War was best expressed by a German who remarked to Miss Nora Waln (see *Reaching for the Stars*) that it was "better than manoeuvres." According to Mr. G. T. Garratt, the German Government, while sending troops to fight for General Franco, aimed at protracting the conflict by also providing the Republican side with a certain amount of war material.

ward to offer meek pates. At night typewriters tapped, pencils and pens moved across paper. Rare was it to find anyone who had never envisaged writing a book, never thought that he or she might put down words, to be set up in type and seen by other eyes. Vast quantities of manuscript shifted through the post, to and from publishers, literary agents, newspapers, periodicals. Much ink flowed, and much paper was consumed. At conferences of librarians it was mentioned as an encouraging circumstance that readers were ever increasing, and desirous of non-fiction as well as fiction. The *Sunday Times* and the *Observer* grew bulky with publishers' advertisements, which loudly announced books for all tastes, with reviewers' opinions appended—what Mr. Howard Spring could not lay down, and had chosen for his Book of the Month; what had kept Mr. Ralph Strauss awake into the small hours of the mornings, and Mr. Swinnerton found delectable. Mr. Wells impatiently clamoured for an encyclopaedia,[1] larger and more comprehensive than any hitherto published, a tome containing all knowledge, and which would make available the data necessary for a World Brain to plan a World State; and Maxim Gorki, shortly before his death, announced his intention of writing a book in which a day in the life of the world would be exhaustively described, a general invitation being issued to send him suitable material relating to the day chosen.

Book Clubs were founded, Left, Right and Centre, National and International, Religious and Irreligious, which provided their members with congenial literature at reduced prices, and which were described by a well-known bookseller as "the greatest innovation in the history of bookselling

1 See *World Brain* and *The Fate of Homo Sapiens*.

which this decade can show." The most successful of these was unquestionably the Left Book Club, whose originator was Mr. Victor Gollancz, and which soon had a membership of over 50,000. Professor Laski, Mr. John Strachey and Mr. Gollancz chose the books; local branches were founded to discuss them and enrol new members, and meetings were held at the more important of which one or other of the Triumvirate appeared in person. To hear Mr. Gollancz explaining to a responsive audience what the Left Book Club stood for, what it had already achieved and might achieve, the decisive influence it might expect to have in public affairs when its membership reached 100,000, was a memorable experience. His oratory, if not lively, was forceful and earnest; the acclamation which greeted his appearance and punctuated his discourse, suggested rather a Führer than a publisher; willing helpers advanced the cause he had at heart, among them his chauffeur, who, Mr. Gollancz recorded with understandable satisfaction in the *Left Book Club News*, had personally been responsible for enrolling no fewer than six new members.

To the Left Book Club's standard flocked Friends of the Soviet Union, Popular Front advocates, near and actual Communists, all the restlessly progressive who have nothing to lose but their hopes. Providing ideological fare acceptable to all of these was no easy task. There were occasional awkward incidents, as when, in the course of an address by Mr. Lloyd George, it was found necessary forcibly to remove an interrupter who persisted in shouting, "What about the Black and Tans!", and occasional awkward moments, as when the German-Soviet Pact was announced. Sadly then, forward-looking bookseller, bearded, sandalled, surveyed his stock, gloomily envisaging possessing forever many copies of Litvinov's speeches on the indivisibility of peace, many copies of works commending Stalin's implacable determination to oppose Nazi designs. Such difficulties, notwithstanding, on the whole Mr. Gollancz's flock held together, and were satisfied with the books they added monthly to their libraries, a row of the yellow volumes they received soon coming to signify a truly progressive household.

Other Book Clubs were less energetically led, and produced a smaller yield both of converts and royalties, though the old-established and non-political Book Society proceeded quietly along its respectable way, it, too, making a small gesture of obeisance to Leftward tendencies by the appointment of Mr. Day Lewis to its Selection Committee.

Travel books, biographies, autobiographies, novels, all varieties of written matter which could be enclosed between cloth boards or leather, and plausibly called a book, found their way to the shelves, already heavy-laden, of literary editors, by them to be distributed to reviewers with instructions to produce their two columns, their one column, their short notice, or, least of all categories, short notice if worth it; some not achieving even that poor distinction, but left quite unnoticed, never chosen, in due course vanishing none knew where, presumably to be pulped down—from pulp to pulp; oh, written word, where is thy sting!

Barricades of knowledge were erected, piled ever higher; Maginot Line,[1] impregnable let us hope, composed of small and large masterpieces, pocket, crown octavo and other editions, lucid accounts of this and that, surveys historical, sociological, psychological, calculated to increase understanding. Ye are instructed, they are ignorant; the pen is

[1] cf. Lord Horder—"Books are a Maginot Line against hysteria and lies."

mightier than the sword, and to demonstrate its might, must be active. When Dr. Négrin, Spanish Prime Minister, visited France it was counted to him for virtue that he found time to visit the bookstalls by the Seine. Would Goering have so employed his time? Or Julius Streicher? Would Hitler have been seen, between visits to the Quai d'Orsay, bearing away an armful of books to add to his library?

The illiteracy of the rulers of the Third Reich was frequently and hopefully noticed. It was doubtful if they would have been able to pass the School Leaving Examination. Goebbels, it was true, had somehow acquired a doctorate, but in Germany that meant little; and in any case it might almost be said that a revolution was necessary for him to get into print. As for *Mein Kampf*—its first reception was tepid, and sometimes derisory, and its sale unspectacular until German rearmament began. New battalions brought new editions of it in their train; Hitler's royalties and Germany increased together.

Mussolini's literary pretensions were less dubious. In the pre-Axis days, his play, *The Hundred Days*, dealing with Napoleon's return from Elba, was produced at the Old Vic, and kindly received; and a novel he had written long ago to be published as a newspaper serial, appeared in an English translation. His duchesses were plumper than Disraeli's, the pearls they wore larger; but otherwise the Jew who made the English upper classes feel they were useful, and the anarchist who made the Italians feel they were formidable, as novelists were not dissimilar.

The most dangerous men of action are artists *manqués*. Their imagination, finding no adequate outlet, sizzles and boils within them, their rage knows no bounds. If Disraeli's royalties had been smaller, and his creditors more pressing,

a Trotsky instead of Lord Beaconsfield might have resulted;
if Hitler had been more successful as a water-colourist, he
would have visited Nuremberg, if at all, only to erect an
easel there, and with thermos flask beside him, patiently
await the sunset's glow on ancient walls. Napoleon began as
a poet, and overran Europe to forget his bad verses; Count
Ciano's début was a play called *Hamlet's Happiness*, which
scarcely equalled the other not so happy version; Sir John
Simon made an early and fugitive appearance on the staff
of the *Manchester Guardian*, and Stalin requires the Soviet
Press to hail each of his speeches as an epoch-making
enlargement of human understanding, a "priceless contribution to the treasure-house of Marxist-Leninism." Plato saw
that, to secure the stability of his Republic, it was necessary
to ban poetry, but neglected the more important precaution
of banning from authority those who had tried without success to be poets. He should have required aspiring rulers of
the Republic to prove that they had never even considered
the possibility of engaging in any imaginative pursuit;
scribbled verses, a water-colour sunset, any evidence of
traffic with abstractions, should have quite disqualified them.

Napoleon at least gave up writing verses when he took to
winning battles, and Count Ciano, when Hamlet's happiness
disappointed him, threw himself into promoting his own by
marrying Mussolini's daughter; but parliamentarians often
try to double the role of man-of-action and man-of-letters
by the simple expedient of publishing their speeches. Mr.
Baldwin, with his never-failing flair, entitled a volume of
his speeches *On England*, this waste-product of his oratory
competing successfully with many a laboriously prepared
book. Mr. Eden and Mr. Neville Chamberlain were less
successful in the same field, though neither had any diffi-

culty in filling a sizeable volume with speeches they had
made about that most saleable of all topics—peace; and M.
Daladier chose the title *The Defence of France* for a collection of some of his finer oratorical efforts in the Chamber of
Deputies, Corsica and elsewhere. Mr. Churchill has written
as well as spoken, producing among other works, a life of
his famous ancestor, Marlborough; though whether his literary output was the consequence or the cause of his long
deprivation of office, it is difficult to say.

Each disturbance, however remote and inaccessible its
location, produced its book or books. Expiring countries
left behind a trail of best-sellers, and remote places yielded
unexpected royalties. When Abyssinia was invaded, the
letter "A" in the British Museum Reading Room catalogue
became greatly in demand, the pages of Abyssinian references much thumbed. More adventurous spirits, not content
with the quiet pursuit of second-hand information, undertook difficult journeys to the very scene of strife. Some,
speculative, gave their attention to potential danger spots—
in Spain even when Spain was quiet, in the expectation that
trouble was brewing there, and that Spanish experts would
consequently later be required.

As the pace quickened, and interest shifted from place to
place with increasing rapidity, the scope was greater, but
the work more urgent and the harvest of shorter duration.
A week might exhaust China; Persia appear in the headlines
only to vanish thence; India be forgotten, and the reward of
months of patient labour bestowed upon Cyprus get compressed into a single early edition. There was always, of
course, Colonel Fawcett, who, being almost certainly dead,
was unlikely to be found, and Tibet, never-failing resource
of travellers; trustee-stock in which they might invest their

energies in the confidence that, though the dividends earned
might be small, they would always be punctually paid. Who
shall say but that a non-political traveller like Mr. Peter
Fleming chose wisely when he preferred Brazil to Czechoslovakia, Tartary to Jerusalem?

To every corner of the habitable globe went investigators,
economists, sociologists, anthropologists, travellers carefree
or purposive. They collected data, they observed, they
interviewed, got arrested, and fell into casual conversation;
they endured hardships, were droll or earnest or denuncia-
tory or appreciative according to their temper, and sometimes according to the auspices under which their labours
were undertaken. With the informative grain was mixed
often some propagandist chaff. Such a scrutinizing there was
of all places and peoples, whether savages whose sexual
habits might elucidate the fixations of the sophisticated, or
Asiatics eagerly emerging from servitude, or fellow Europeans with parliaments, unemployment, stock-exchanges,
corps diplomatique, and other appurtenances of civilization.

Nor was the home-front neglected. Mr. Priestley weighed
in with his *English Journey*, Mr. Beverley Nichols with his
News of England. Facts were wanted about everyone and
everything—cross-sections of society, symptomatic opinions
and observations, detailed investigations and statistics. The
B.B.C. spouted facts, newspapers were full of them, a
monthly publication was started, and survived for a while,
called just *Fact*. Let us at all costs be factual, photographic,
was the watchword; let us be documentary, armed with
facts against the dreamer and the visionary, wary of escap-
ism's pitfalls. There were documentary films, documentary
novels, documentary articles in newspapers and periodicals.
What was aimed at was to portray life as it is, and without

attempting to reveal its imagined significance. Thus *Macbeth* would be documentary if the number of Thanes on Macbeth's and on Malcolm's side were accurately given, and the political forces brought into play by Macbeth's attempt to found a dynasty, subjected to a careful analysis. The most documentary part of the play as it stands is, perhaps, the drunken porter's speech, since he provides a list of occupational types. The weird sisters may be ruled out as totally undocumentary, and "To-morrow and to-morrow and to-morrow" would only be admissible if dates were specified.[1]

A camera or recording apparatus, it was argued, had no possibility of falsifying the objects or sounds they reproduced; therefore, by emulating them, truthfulness was assured. Such an attitude of mind presupposes that life's outward appearance exhausts its whole nature; if outward appearance is only one among many images of reality, and

[1] An example of documentary technique is provided by Mr. Priestley's account, in *Rain Upon Godshill*, of the making of the film *We Live in Two Worlds*, in which he acted as commentator. He was approached, he writes, by Mr. John Grierson, who suggested that some use might be made of material left over after doing a short film for the Swiss Post Office—"lovely shots of the Swiss peasants in the fields, and so on." On a basis of these lovely shots, Mr. Priestley "concocted a little talk about nationalism and the new internationalism of transport and communications," and the result was "an excellent little documentary film." In the same way, if Dickens had concocted, instead of a novel, a little talk about, say, urban and rural life, on a basis of the drawings round which he was to write *The Pickwick Papers*, that novel would have been documentary. Mr. Priestley is appreciative of the "enthusiasm of these rather solemn young men in high-necked sweaters" who were responsible for the production of successful documentary films like *Drifters* and *Voice of Britain*, who pronounced the word "film" with hushed solemnity, and who seemed to him "figures representative of a new world," but sensibly points out that their claim to portray "real life" cannot be substantiated. "Nearly all documentary films," he writes, "seem to be a very romantic heightening of ordinary life, comparable not to the work of a realistic novelist or dramatist, but to the picturesque and highly coloured fictions of the romancer."

perhaps not the most significant, then a drawing of Blake's might be more documentary than a photograph of the same subject, and his "great Atlantic mountains," though unknown to explorers, and unmarked on any map, as significant as the Himalayas.

To keep to the facts is ever the despairing hope of those who feel their lives disintegrating, whose feet are in shifting sand. They hold on to facts like a drowning man on to a floating spar; facts surely will not fail them, though all else fails. Prostrating themselves before facts, appealing to facts for guidance in time of trouble, they credit them with a validity they do not possess, and lay themselves open to deceptions greater than any the imagination can practise. The camera cannot lie, they assure themselves, and when it does lie quite succumb to its falsehoods. An imaginative symbol like the Cross may delude; but because it is imaginative—that is, a product of an understanding of life's totality, and because it is a symbol, with no pretensions to be more than reality seen through a glass darkly, its power to delude is less than that of a photograph, which bears no relations to life's totality, and which purports to be definitive. Propagandists and advertisers find the camera their most useful instrument, and are more beholden to mathematics than to mysticism.

Mr. Micawber, when he had made a careful calculation of his debts, experienced the agreeable sensation of having honourably paid them; by adumbrating his liabilities, he seemed to have liquidated them. Similarly, to count, to measure, to weigh, to classify, being orderly processes, gave the illusion of reducing to order that to which they were applied. A graph showing the incidence of unemployment momentarily abolished unemployment; to demonstrate statistically that many were hungry was to fill them with good things. The ingenuity, labour and enterprise necessary to state a problem accurately, were in themselves so satisfying, and often so remunerative, that no further action seemed called for. Town-planning flourished without abating ribbon-development; traffic was counted and classified, and road deaths increased; social surveys abounded, and what they had surveyed, continued. Intelligent and plain men's guides to world chaos were common as blackberries, and still there was chaos.

Not a Sign, but a yardstick was wanted. From the London School of Economics and other places went annually many earnest persons, male and female, to plant their tents in depressed areas, housing-estates, malnutrition belts. Juvenile crime claimed their attention, prostitution was not neglected by them, birth-control clinics and after-care committees and vocational centres all were within their range. Members of Parliament disguised themselves as tramps in order to inform themselves of the circumstances in which other forms of Public Assistance than their own £600 a year, were administered; journalists settled temporarily in the slums,[1] and the Council of the British Medical Association set up a committee to determine the minimum weekly expenditure on foodstuffs which must be incurred by families of varying size if health and working capacity are to be maintained, and to construct specimen diets. Some consternation was caused when this committee, basing its calculations on a "normal adult male requiring a daily food intake productive of 3,400 calories," arrived at a minimum

[1] See, for instance, *I Took Off My Tie* by Hugh Massingham. Mr. Massingham found that he was only accepted as a man and a brother by slum-dwellers when he removed his, to them, offensive neck-wear. When they saw his stud, they opened their hearts.

weekly expenditure on foodstuffs which considerably
exceeded what would be practicable for a family subsisting
on unemployment benefit, and for many families whose
bread-winner was in full-time employment.[1] A more moderate estimate was hurriedly prepared by the National
Advisory Commission on Nutrition, which reached the
satisfying conclusion that "all except a relatively small section of the population are obtaining the full amount of
calories they require." Quite a battle raged between protagonists of these rival estimates, though without, as far as
could be seen, the daily food intake of anyone being appreciably affected, unless of those concerned in the controversy, who may have become heated in argument, and
therefore have required some extra nourishment to make
good the calories expended.

If the undernourished soon got forgotten in the excitement of deciding what was the measure of their under-
nourishment, Nutrition continued to receive attention. The
League of Nations discussed it, a committee reporting that
certain specified "protective foods" are required, "particularly in countries with Western civilization, if there is to
be the necessary physical strength and health"; the Gas
Light and Coke Company made it the subject of a film; and
sevenpenny, and even fivepenny, lunches were produced
with oatmeal and herrings for their chief ingredients, and
pronounced both palatable and satisfying by Lord Horder

---

1 For instance, a man, wife and three children whose ages ranged between
one and ten years, needed to spend 20s. 0½ d. per week to charge themselves
with the requisite number of calories. See also *Food, Health and Income*, a
survey by Sir John Orr "of adequacy of diet in relation to income,"
according to which the average diet of 4½ millions of the population is
"deficient in every respect," and of 18 millions shows vitamin and mineral
deficiency.

and others who partook of them. If it had been possible to make a meal of Nutrition, many who went hungry would have been fed; but, alas, Nutrition allayed no hunger, except for self-importance and self-righteousness.

"*Il faut mobiliser nos crédits*," French Cabinet Ministers used often to say in the days when reparations seemed payable, and before it became necessary to *mobiliser nos soldats*; in the same way—*Il faut documenter notre chaos*. Some put in a thumb and pulled out a plum; others attacked the whole dish, hoping to deduce from its total constituents the recipe according to which it had been compounded. This was the procedure of *Mass Observation*, described by one of its originators, Mr. Tom Harrisson, as "the science of ourselves." Teams of observers, on field-work bent, were entrusted with the task of collecting data regarding the habits, opinions, attitude of mind, and other characteristics of different sections of the population. They penetrated into saloon bars, lounged at street corners, rode in public vehicles, attended religious services and political and other meetings, questioning and observing; and the results of their researches were classified and arranged, conclusions being drawn therefrom. All-in wrestling, for instance, was submitted to intensive Mass Observation [1] ("Observer asks his neighbour how he enjoyed it. 'I can't tell you proper—I can't believe my own bloody eyes.' "). "Sample questioning" indicated that "every class of trade was represented, including a police-sergeant, a coroner's officer and a priest," and Observer failed to detect "anything specially cruel or rough in the faces of the audience." To check this impression of normality, Observer circulated a request to arrange ten given items

[1] See *Britain* by Mass Observation (arranged and written by Charles Madge and Tom Harrisson).

in order of preference as conducive of human happiness, and
was gratified to learn from the result that "the wrestling-
fans don't differ in any way from a wide sample of other
males" who had been subjected to a similar experiment. The
fact that they also put Knowledge first, Politics last, and
Beauty next to last as happiness promoters, convinced him
that they were men like unto other men. Having established
the normality of all-in wrestling display patrons, Observer
proceeded to ask 150 of them: "Why do you like Free Style
Wrestling?," and by carefully tabulating the answers he
received, along with any derogatory comments made, was
led to the interesting, but scarcely surprising, conclusion
that "Free Style Wrestling is so successful because it meets
certain needs of the people. . . . It is thrilling, allows
dream-wish fulfilment, and gives the feeling of being a member of a group by talking about it."

A similar technique was employed to detect changes in
public opinion, and to predict by-election results; politicians,
Nature's Mass Observers, derived comfort from approving
letters addressed to them by, they were always careful to
explain, persons representative of all sections of the community.[1] Other collectors of data neglecting outward things
—all-in wrestling, football pools, Lambeth Walk, applied
themselves to the inner-man, hoping thereby to diagnose and
prescribe a cure for spiritual ills. Miss Laura Riding, for

[1] Mr. Chamberlain, at the time of the Munich Agreement, was particularly
insistent on the representative character, and warmly approving tone, of
the large number of letters he received daily. Mass Observation's conclusion, also based on the representative character of the human "samples"
taken, was that pro-Chamberlain sentiment "even at its top-point never
scored more than 54%," and that most people soon "came to feel that we
had let down the whole tradition of England's pledges for honesty, fair-
play and resistance to threats." Probably Mr. Chamberlain and Mass
Observation hit on different cross-sections.

instance, sent a letter to 400 selected persons, ranging between Mrs. Naomi Mitchison and Lord Gorell, and taking in the B.B.C., in which she asked: "What is wrong, and what shall we do about it—we, the women, and the men of inside sensibilities, and the inside selves in many outside persons which lean away from the outer realities towards the inner ones?" [1] The answers she received to this momentous question, she classified under the heads—"Maleness and Femaleness," "The Realistic Approach," and "Beginning from the Inside," and added to each her own commentary on it. From the large quantity of information thus accumulated, arranged and elucidated, she deduced a series of resolutions (among them: "Not to allow our sense of humour to soften what is irritating just because it is also foolish"), whose adoption she recommended.

V

With this craving for facts and abundant provision of them, went, ironically, or it may be inevitably, a craving for fantasy and abundant provision of it. Statistics and horoscopes increased in popularity together; Five-, Four- and Three-Year Plans, New Deals and other collective enterprises, were accompanied by ballyhoo which would have made Madame Blavatsky feel like Swift. Never before, it may be assumed, have statistics been so greatly in demand, never before so extravagantly falsified. The attempts of witch doctors and magicians to delude with burning cauldron and crystal ball, are pitiable by comparison with what has been achieved in the same line with graphs and photography. The desire for what seemed most like life was matched by a desire for what seemed most unlike; and both

[1] See *The World and Ourselves* by Laura Riding.

desires, like the two roads branching to right and to left at the foot of the Hill Difficulty, led astray. Realism and Surrealism, the two roads might have been named, and each, after a broad, macadamized beginning, was soon lost in swampy incoherence. Dialectical materialists floundered helplessly in their verbiage ("When, and so far as, by degrees, primitive men learned, in practice, to discriminate two different and opposed categories in their surroundings the way was opened for a development of the counter-concepts of Nature and Super-Nature. And as they reached this figuration of phenomena by means of production-practice, it was inevitable that this practice itself should be discriminated . . .");[1] dialectical immaterialists in theirs—like Mr. James Joyce,[2] who devoted sixteen years to producing a large work, totally incomprehensible, and entitled, for no apparent reason, *Finnegans Wake*. It was most readers' sleep. Reviewers handled it gingerly, fearful of betraying a lack of appreciation of what the publisher had described as, in view of the fact that it had been "more talked about and written about during the period of its composition than any previous work of English literature," inevitably "the most important event of any season in which it appeared." Mr. W. G. Stonier was one of the few who came out in the open as an admirer, awed by the grandeur of "BABABADALGHAR-AGHTAKAMMINARRONN-KONNBRONNTONN-ERRONNTVONNTHUNNTROV-ARRHOUNAW-

[1] *Communism, Religion and Morals* by T. A. Jackson.
[2] Marx, towards the end of his life, went on voraciously accumulating facts when whatever capacity he had for digesting them had atrophied; undigested facts were his portion. Mr. Joyce represents the opposite process—repudiation of facts, pursuit of incoherence. Both processes end in dumbness—tongue agitating and lips moving, but no comprehensible sound emerging. The glutton who eats and eats and the ascetic who will not eat, fall at last into the same insensibility.

NSKAWNTOOHOOHOORDENENTHURNUK!'',
moved and exhilarated by: "The logos of somewome to that
base anything, when most characteristically mantissa minus,
comes to nullum in the endth: orso, here is nowet bladder
than the sin of Aha with his cosin Lil . . ."; Mr. Harold
Nicolson, more moderate, mentioned that gramophone
records of Mr. Joyce's prose recited by Mr. Joyce, had
pleased Mr. Eliot, and might please him, and announced his
intention of keeping *Finnegans Wake* by his bedside for
occasional reading.

Documentary films portrayed what was, Walt Disney
what was not, equally fanciful and equally admired—real
life told to the children, fairy tales for adults only; Mr.
Hemingway red in tooth and claw, Miss Dodie Smith red in
lipstick and sunset glow; in new Magnitogorsk and in old
Vienna, Karl Marx and Groucho Marx, his the benediction
—"I'd horsewhip you if I had a horse."

Even to the stars the appetite for facts extended, Sir James
Jeans here the provider; while Professor Hogben, with his
Mathematics for the Million, made thousands feel that they
were equipped at any rate mathematically for citizenship
and progress. Einstein's Relativity Theory was explained in
terms that the meanest intelligence could grasp; yearly the
British Association lightened its own and mankind's darkness by explaining why wars happened, populations declined, and education was necessary. Inferiority, Oedipus
and other complexes, were made available for all, and even
typists knew that they were not fond of apples for nothing.
Various sciences, separately pursued, became an entity—
Science. More and better Science, it was felt, would build
Jerusalem in England's green and pleasant land. What was

fallacious was unscientific; Science is truth, truth Science—
that is all ye know on earth, and all ye need to know.

Plans were in the air. As chaos deepened, the planning
industry, both wholesale and retail, boomed, even Mr.
Clarence Hatry, after some years of quiet meditation in
prison, coming forward with his plan, *Light out of Darkness*,
for a drastic redistribution of population throughout the
world. Organizations had plans, individuals had plans, some
only adumbrated in railway carriages and saloon bars, some
publicly launched in books or in leaflets, the products of
old-established firms—Keynes, Josiah Stamp, accommodated
in the right-hand column of the *Times* leader-page. Teams
of planners were formed; summer schools assembled to plan,
and Members of Parliament planned furiously. It was another South Sea Bubble; the public were invited to invest
hope in a variety of enterprises, sometimes in enterprises
whose details were later to be disclosed.

There were many seekers after knowledge, many who
looked for knowledge with the same passionate eagerness
that a spinster surprised in her bath looks for a towel to
cover her nakedness. In their bewilderment they cried aloud
for knowledge, hoping that the anguish of distant stars
might be assuaged by understanding their arrangement in
the sky; that the decay of institutions whose shelter they
required, might be prevented if their origins were known,
and the fears which beset them lessened by becoming comprehensible. As a child frightened in the dark longs to be
assured that a threatening shape is no more than a familiar
wardrobe, so did they long to be assured that what threatened their security and habitual ways was unremarkable.
Surely, instructed by Sir James Jeans about the universe, by
Professor Hogben fed with mathematics, economics no

mystery, the unconscious mind their oyster, taboos not taboo to them—surely, thus informed, they need fear no evil.

Particularly was there a yearning to be informed about the tumultuous events taking place in the world. An understanding of stars and Relativity Theory, though serviceable, might wait; but an understanding of the dangers which beset Prague, Bucharest's intentions and how the Quai d'Orsay's mind was working, brooked no delay. He or she who could elucidate these mysteries, was a saviour indeed. In lifts herded, dropped from upper to nether regions, a glimpse was caught on a poster of Mr. Vernon Bartlett, telephone before him, map outspread behind him, calm and sagacious. He knew; and in the *News-Chronicle*, costing only a penny, his knowledge was available. Madame Tabouis, another light shining in darkness, had her say daily, what she said recorded, quoted from, made the subject of editorial comment—Madame Tabouis writes . . . French opinion takes the view that . . . France is resolute in its determination to . . . Tabouis *une et indivisible.*

Inside stories were in great demand; news behind the news was received with relish. The American Magazine *Time*, which specialized in intimate details of persons and happenings, soon produced a London progeny; private sheets and news-letters multiplied, some cyclostyled and some printed. What Fleet Street knew and was prevented from disclosing, the *Week* disclosed; Commander King-Hall had sources of information not available to others, and fruitfully tapped them. Journalists, once famous for writing more than they knew, now acquired a reputation for knowing more than they wrote. Their dark secrets became their chief stock-in-trade, a nod and a wink more profitable than an editorial flourish. By getting inside Mr.

John Gunther, it was possible to get inside Europe. "All Central Europe is in that man," a publisher's advertisement ran.

In cinemas, even the uninitiated might see with their own eyes and hear with their own ears what Madame Tabouis wrote about and Commander King-Hall understood. News films were popular: *The March of Time* series showed the world on a sheet of cloth; films like *I Was a Nazi Spy* made the Third Reich live in many a picture palace. Nothing was hidden, nothing secret under the sun. Time marched visibly and audibly; all circles, upper, lower and parterre, were informed, all vouchsafed a view of the stage on which their own destiny was being enacted.

For providing information about events, none were better placed than newspaper correspondents. Wherever was excitement, there were they. They raced about the world in search of what was most urgent, most timely; interviewed the great, and witnessed the stuff of headlines. Inside information was at their disposal, and on their typewriters they played each day's tumult. Like bloodhounds following a scent, they followed news, a ravening pack. Trains, aeroplanes, motor-cars, carried them to the scene of all disasters; wars and rumours of wars set them in motion. Censorships might impede, but could not prevent, their activities. They were themselves as sudden and as ruthless as the happenings they described.

Let a régime collapse, they were soon attached to what came after it. Though they might mourn the passing of a Benĕs or a Haile Selassie, their interest in the fallen was soon exhausted. They belonged in the wake of power; where news was, there was their heart also. The present claimed their whole attention; those whom they served—the many eyes so curious, surveying printed sheets, required variety, and scorned yesterday's doings and great ones. They were able to reveal; in hotel lounges and crowded streets, they detected currents of opinion, eager hopes and tremulous fears. Clutching their typed messages, they besieged censorship offices, clamouring for attention; hung lovingly over telephones, little black mouthpiece receiving their eager words; gathered, notebook in hand, round whoever aroused curiosity, vultures whose ruthless beaks would tear out the heart's deepest secrets. Hungry sheep looked up, and were fed by them. Into the Kremlin they had penetrated, met Hitler face to face, waited in Addis Ababa for the rains or Mussolini's army, speeded to distant Manchuria; nor neglected Gandhi's abstemious court, Balkan complexities, King Carol's amours. They had a song to sing, oh, and sang it rowdily and heartily.

First in the field were the American correspondents. They were less trammelled than their English colleagues, more mobile and more energetic. Their own adventurous lives enlivened the information they had to impart and the morals they pointed. Love affairs and *coups d'états* mingled together; gossip made facts more palatable, facts made gossip more impressive. In the messages they sent to their newspapers, they could be unrestrained; seen across the Atlantic Ocean, the affairs of Europe presented an unedifying spectacle which called for righteous indignation and stern judgments. Where on questions of domestic policy, the editorial policy they served was cautious and equivocal, on questions of British foreign policy, it was reckless and straightforward. Correspondents might, and did, complain to their hearts' content of Abyssinia's and Czechoslovakia's and India's wrongs, when their livelihood might have been endangered if they had allowed their sympathy with the victims of oppression to extend to American Negroes; they might, and did, fulminate against League Members' betrayal of their Covenant, when a campaign to induce the United States to accept, and righteously fulfil, its obligations, would have been highly distasteful to their employers. The side of the angels has everything to recommend it as long as operations are conducted far enough away and their outcome is a matter of indifference.

On the side of the angels these American correspondents indubitably were. They did not spare the feelings of the many English readers who meekly accepted their instruction. Fervidly, they condemned British policy, and were scandalized to see such perfidy, and lack of resolution, where in the past had been uprightness and strength. Perhaps it was fitting that the English should be thus dosed with the medicine they had formerly been lavish in dispensing. In the days when waves alone mattered and they ruled them, it had been their part to hold aloof and pronounce moral judgments on unruly and unprincipled Continentals; now, having the same sky, they were involved in the same disasters as the rest of Europe, and put to the same shifts to escape or postpone their consequences. The voice of reason and of principle came from across the Atlantic instead of from across the Channel.

Mr. John Gunther got, successively, inside Europe and Asia, leaving three more continents for him still to penetrate; Mr. Negley Farson, Mr. Vincent Sheean, Mr. Knickerbocker, Mr. Duranty and others provided each his spirited European survey. As invalids soon accumulate a collection of powders, pills, bottles of medicine, once hopefully received and hopefully taken, then, when no cure resulted, left to litter a medicine chest, so did contemporary ills leave their litter of books, their immense documentation.

VI

If happenings were of absorbing interest, so were the persons concerned in them. Men marched as well as Time, and to get inside the eminent was as needful as to get inside Europe. Illustrated periodicals like *Picture Post* specialized in revealing their way of life; biographers produced intimate, and usually authorized, studies of them, and revealing anecdotes were often told, gaining accretions and polish by their repetition, until a standard version was obtained and used for all occasions. Wives, friends, relatives and acquaintances partook of this glory; Goering's brother, Hitler's half-sister, a clergyman who had known Mr. Neville Chamberlain in his sisal-growing days, Stalin's ancient and belatedly discovered mother, who had once suckled him, and while murmuring his pet-name, So-so—these, too, were interesting.

It used to be confidently assumed that as society became more theoretically equalitarian, so it would inevitably become less snobbish. The reverse has been the case. Social position and wealth have come to have an almost mystical significance; to be observed with the same superstitious reverence as religious relics, and to focus the same curiosity as haunted houses or murderers. To catch a glimpse of a Society wedding, crowds wait patiently, undeterred by rain or blustering wind, their short reward coming when they see the bride and bridegroom pass by, red carpet underfoot. That is their ecstasy, vision ineffable—how beautiful they are, the lovely ones!

Newspapers have abundantly catered for the demand thus set up for information about the high-born and the wealthy; the profession of gossip-writer has become a lucrative and honourable one, which even peers have not disdained to embrace. Day by day, and particularly on Sundays, intimate accounts of the doings, habits and apparel of the great, have been provided. Nor have the great been backward in voluntarily furnishing information about themselves. Not bashful, they; evincing little desire to hide their light under a bushel, but rather, as Lord Castlerosse has explained, sometimes embarrassingly eager to prove themselves worth a paragraph.

Thackeray, in *The Book of Snobs,* defined snobbishness as mean admiration for mean things, though admitting that he himself was not above feeling gratified when, arm in arm with a duke, he met a fellow-commoner. The attributes of those who have power are admired and imitated because it is hoped that if the attributes are cultivated, the power will follow; a squirrel, if it could, would sport a mane and cultivate a roar in the hope of thereby becoming lionly. After a proletarian revolution, the endeavour is to speak like a bricklayer rather than like an Etonian, and ancestral origins are eagerly scrutinized for evidence of humble stock. If the B.B.C. ever begins to drop h's, prepare for trouble. Even the more zealous Fabians were occasionally ungrammatical in anticipation of better days; and Balliol's products have indicated by corduroy trousers and bast shoes their sense of the way the wind was blowing. Similar instances of snobbishness reversed are frequent in contemporary novels; the well meaning bourgeois, after some hesitation and spiritual travail, is accepted by true-blue proletarians as one of themselves,[1] rather as, in Victorian novels, the weedy, low-born boy of scholarly tastes becomes acceptable to radiantly athletic aristocrats.

To invest materially in revolutionary hopes is a hazardous proceeding; few are prepared to buy ideological futures, though many to advertise them. Upper-class revolutionaries have usually preferred to equip their children with the old-school tie they denounced, or at most have availed themselves of establishments like Dartington Hall, which inculcate equalitarian theory without jeopardizing manners and accent by its practice; while a sentimental escape from their dilemma has been provided by the conviction, widely held among them, that aristocrats and proletarians have a natural

[1] For instance, *One Life, One Kopek* by Walter Duranty. The hero, Ivan, after being sent to Siberia on a false charge, and there getting hold of a copy of *Das Kapital*, becomes a Bolshevik. He is of mixed aristocratic and peasant extraction, tough and handsome, and manages always to be well provided with money. Women of all classes fall for him at once, and he is not behindhand in responding to their advances. While staying in an aristocratic country house, he makes the acquaintance of Perkins, an English butler. Perkins considers Ivan a very fine young gentleman, and treats him with particular deference. In the course of a respectful conversation, he gives him an account of English social life, the gist of his remarks being that a Bolshevik in Russia is, roughly, the equivalent of a gentleman in England, and that Socialism is built on the playing-fields of Eton. Take, again, the following conversation (in *The Big Firm* by Amabel Williams-Ellis) between a number of true-blue proletarians. They are discussing an upper-class comrade named Wynne, who has lately come among them—

" 'That Owen Wynne's more like a foreigner in a way, you know, Stan.'

" 'I think he's ever so good-looking,' said one of the girls, with a side glance at Harold.

" 'Doesn't he have a lovely pullover, too!' said the other.

" 'D'you know I had to tell him who Ernie Bevan is?' There was a general laugh at this.

" 'Ye shouldn't make a mock of the young man! Ye should be able to take account of the fact, when ye find a specimen of the workers-by-brain eager to co-operate with the workers-by-hand . . .' "

bond of sympathy, and a common enemy in the middle and
lower middle classes. Thus, by demonstrating their willing-
ness to throw in their lot with the proletariat, they demonstrated their artistocracy; and even if they were not technically blue-blooded, might regard themselves as one of the
"unconscious, anonymous artistocrats" to whom, among
many others, Mr. Wells has looked to make the world fit for
Mr. Wells to live in.

To such nuances of snobbishness, only a sophisticated few
were susceptible; most were content simply to venerate
power's obvious manifestations. Titles, money and good
looks sufficed for them, and on these, as purveyed by gossip-
writers, they feasted. Peers and baronets, even of recent
creation, they were glad to know of, and knights had a place
in their esteem; for details of clothing worn by the eminent,
parties given, marriages arranged and executed among
them, they were avid; politicians, authors, church digni-
taries even, a practised hand could make interesting by
subtly disclosing their earnings, personal appearance, matrimonial or amorous circumstances and drolleries.

When power is an absolute, with no transcendental origin,
requiring no sanction other than a human one, those who
exercise it must be miraculous. They hold their power by
virtue of their own qualities alone; how extraordinary, then,
must be those qualities! How extraordinary must they be!
To reveal their extraordinariness, was the function of the
publicity which, in all its varied forms, ceaselessly played
round them. Atticus, in the *Sunday Times*, one fount
among many, told his readers that it would not surprise him
to discover Lord Nuffield dancing in the moonlight on the
grass, and when M. Blum came to London to persuade the
Labour Party not to oppose conscription, mentioned that

his step was as light and eager as he imagined Romeo's to have been. Strange moonlight dancer, and strange Romeo —elderly French politician, formerly preoccupied with marriage, and now with conscription.

If Atticus's imagination thus played with philanthropic millionaires and sprightly French politicians, to what heights might it not be expected to reach when Royalty was its object? In the nineteenth century, there were zealous republicans (for instance, in his youthful days, Joseph Chamberlain), and it was thought that their number would certainly increase as the franchise was extended; on the contrary, manhood, and still more womanhood, suffrage has almost extinguished Republicanism, and carried the Monarchy to a popularity before undreamed of. As an antidote to the Stuarts, the Hanoverians were perfect; they imposed insuperable obstacles to being admired, and since they could not speak English, and disliked England, it was reasonable to assume that their part in the nation's life and government would be small. Yet, though in succeeding years the Crown's constitutional powers dwindled, its prestige increased, until the reigning Sovereign was considered beyond criticism, and made the object of a veneration which the civilized accord only to sacred, and savages to magical, symbols. Queen Victoria was respected, King Edward VII was admired, and King George V was adulated.

This adulation was, if anything, more prevalent among the lower than the upper classes; the *Times* has, for Royalty, its particular organ note ("At Christmas and at other times he has talked to his people, a father to his children, till his voice is as well known as his face . . ."), but the *Daily Herald* and the *Daily Mirror*, if less unctuous, are not less wholehearted.[1] It is the difference between Evensong at St. Paul's and a revivalist meeting. Only the *Daily Worker*, all its adulatory resources expended on Stalin, has taken an habitually critical attitude; while Mr. Maxton has occasionally made a republican speech in the House of Commons, and led the two or three still faithful to his leadership into the Lobby in support of it.

No other voice of criticism has been heard. Rarely have European monarchs been the recipient of such frequent, unanimous and unqualified professions of loyalty. Nor can it be said that this loyalty is the creation of the Press, radio and other instruments whereby it often finds expression; they are the hot-plate, but the dish was warm already. Newspapers can fan enthusiasm, but seldom create it. No one waited all night in inhospitable streets to see Lord Beaverbrook pass by, when all his organs were strenuously proclaiming the gospel of Empire Free Trade, and he its prophet; nor did Friends of Economy find themselves surrounded by a press of eager admirers when the *Times* warmly espoused their cause.

Enthusiasm for the Monarchy and the reigning monarch might be compared to enthusiasm for a smartly turned out four-in-hand in a street crowded with Austin Sevens, chara-bancs, motor-bicycles and other mechanically driven

---

[1] The following conversation, alleged to have taken place between a small girl and a Chelsea pensioner, was recorded, with the comment that its "beauty and simplicity were such as few novelists would ever invent":

"The old man, leaning down to the girl, said in a quiet, rather husky voice: 'Have you ever seen the dear King?'

" 'I think he's very sweet,' said the girl, looking up, and then added seriously: 'I think the old King was very kind—and very sweet.'

" 'They are all sweet—the royal personages,' replied the pensioner with a wonderful dignity.

" 'I *love* the Royal Family!' said the little girl with a fervent earnestness."

vehicles, hooting and emitting exhaust. It is because everyone has a vote that the Monarchy, not dependent on votes, makes so great an appeal. Politicians must come at intervals and humbly protest their benevolence and public spiritedness, but the Monarch is under no such necessity; politicians wear black, carry umbrellas, need money, bulge their pockets with papers and crumple their collars with energetic oratory but the Monarch rides resplendent in a golden carriage, and never will sit on any Board of Directors, or have to endure being questioned by Miss Ellen Wilkinson; politicians, in relation to the People, are in the position of a husband, easily intimidated, heard munching toast each morning at breakfast and each evening letting out the cat and bolting the front-door, but the Monarch is a lover, whose visits are gratefully received, and whose absences need not be accounted for. When, in his Christmas broadcast, King George V said to his listeners: "God bless you all," they were moved in a way that MacDonald's "My Frrriends" did not move them. The King's blessing, delivered in his deep, harsh voice, brought him no evident advantage, but MacDonald's friendship required recurrent General Elections to stimulate it.

Popular esteem for the Monarchy, and the affection in which King George V personally was held by his subjects, were indicated by the enormous, and often spontaneous, enthusiasm evinced when his Silver Jubilee was celebrated in August 1935. The King and Queen made a series of visits to various parts of London, and wherever they went they were acclaimed; greeted more often with "For He's a Jolly Good Fellow" than with the National Anthem. Traffic was suspended in streets leading to Trafalgar Square, Piccadilly Circus, the Bank and Buckingham Palace, and an enormous

crowd circulated, gazing up at flood-lit buildings, cheering
whenever an occasion to cheer presented itself, and moving
ceaselessly; as though in movement, without any direction,
governed only by the ebb and flow of others moving, their
spirits found release—orderly in their restlessness, restless in
their orderliness, and paying their tribute to what Dr.
Dearmer has called "the miracle of Royal Democracy," in
themselves constituting it.

Other members of the Royal Family were not less popular. The Prince of Wales, as the Archbishop of Canterbury
put it, brought "into every part of our public life his vivid
and stimulating interest"; the marriage of Prince George,
later Duke of Kent, to Princess Marina, was attended, again
to quote Dr. Lang, by "a vast company of witnesses who
had already, with warmth so swift and spontaneous, taken
the Duchess to their hearts." The B.B.C. played its part with
gusto and efficiency; descriptive writers went to it with a
will, and a scene was presented, both to those present and to
those absent, which had about it, as a B.B.C. commentator
inevitably remarked, a "quality of faëry——" "A few minutes later came the Princess Marina. A vision of loveliness in
white and silver, smiling and bowing, she drove slowly by,
in a swirl of scarlet jackets, dancing white plumes, flashing
swords, and accompanied by an entrancing combination of
sounds—the plop, plop of cantering horses, the jingle of
harness, the pealing of joybells, and the huzzas of the happy
crowds."

It was a continuous, and much appreciated, pageant,
whose zest never flagged though its temper varied—solemn,
joyful, intimate, or mournful, according to the occasion's
exigencies. When it was known that King George V was
ill, little groups of people were constantly to be seen by

Buckingham Palace, waiting for bulletins to be posted; and newspaper placards, neglectful of all other topics, bore the simple announcement: "The King." Households gathered round their radio sets to hear the latest account of the King's condition, and shops procured stocks of mourning; morning, evening and Sunday newspapers were ready with their special editions, framed in black, illustrated with photographs of George V's career and of the notable events of his reign, and gossip-writers prudently laid in a store of royal anecdotes, needful when grief at a beloved Sovereign's decease made their usual topics unpalatable. Broadcasting for the first time enabled practically the whole nation to follow from hour to hour the course of the King's illness, almost to be present at his bedside. They gathered round him, waiting for him to expire, their King; in some mysterious way, themselves.

"The King's life," they heard, "is moving peacefully towards its close"; waited to hear it again—"moving peacefully towards its close"; heard at last that he was dead. Though expected, his death was still a shock; brought a dim sense that much else was moving to its close, though, alas, not peacefully. Some were constrained to make their way through silent streets, and stare up at shuttered windows behind which he lay, nevermore to be seen, bearded and genial, smiling from passing motor-car or carriage, hat in hand; nevermore to pronounce a conference open, or lay a foundation stone, or attend football-match, trooping of colours, race-meeting; nevermore to receive outgoing and incoming Cabinet Ministers for hand-kissing purposes, ambassadors and visiting monarchs, both Oriental and Occidental. He represented the principle of continuity, sorely needed, and once lost difficult to re-establish. "Firm amid the riot of change," Professor G. M. Trevelyan had written on the occasion of the Silver Jubilee, "our Monarchy and the free Parliamentary Constitution of which it is the head still stand erect, and the British Empire still remains amid the crash of other Empires and the destruction of other liberties." Now that the King whose 25 years on the Throne was then celebrated, had gone, firmness amid the riot of change and erectness of Monarchy and free Parliamentary Constitution were less confidently assumed.

VII

King George V's obsequies were accompanied by demonstrations of popular affection even more marked than at his Silver Jubilee celebrations. A continuous procession filed past his coffin when it lay in state in Westminster Abbey, and dense crowds waited from daybreak, sometimes all night, to see his funeral, and the many foreign notabilities who had come to London to attend it. He was mourned long and ardently, newspapers protracting their grief, as though reluctant to forego a subject so easy to be sincere about, and lending itself to such eloquent composition, and anxious to take full advantage of a situation they felt might not recur—monarch universally regretted, universally praised.[1]

[1] Previous Hanoverians had often been universally execrated, and, until Queen Victoria, none of them much mourned. "There never was an individual less regretted by his fellow creatures than this deceased king," the *Times* wrote of George IV. "What eye has wept for him? What heart has heaved one sob of unmercenary sorrow?"; and the *Spectator* of William IV: "He had little information and strong prejudices. Though sufficiently conceited and self-willed, he was easily imposed upon and led by the designing. . . . Notwithstanding his feebleness of mind, his ignorance and his prejudices, William IV was to the last a popular sovereign, but his very popularity was acquired at the price of something like public contempt." (Quoted in *The Magic of Monarchy* by Kingsley Martin.)

The new King, Edward VIII, was greeted with the same unanimous approval as had been accorded his father. When he was Prince of Wales, he had been made the object of ceaseless adulation; and though, after his abdication, some claimed to have had grave doubts of his fitness to succeed to the Throne, and unfavourable signs and portents were remembered,[1] at the time no such doubts were given public expression, or other than favourable portents noticed. A discerning eye might have seen an ill-omen for his reign, more than in any horoscope, in the fact that his companion, when he watched the heralds proclaiming his accession, was an American lady, Mrs. Ernest Simpson, who had divorced one husband, and was in process of divorcing another. Such discerning eyes were few, if only because the photograph taken on this occasion was, at the time, withheld from publication.

Mrs. Simpson's first newspaper appearance after King Edward came to the throne, was in what is ordinarily the last place journalists or their readers look for sensational matter—the Court Circular. She appeared there as having dined with the King, along with her husband, Mr. and Mrs. Baldwin, Colonel and Mrs. Lindbergh, and others. Some eyebrows were raised, but not many. The Court Circular is not widely read, and most, carelessly scanning it, would find nothing outrageous in unknown and apparently innocuous, names appearing there as well as known ones.

Gradually, however, though all newspapers, even the *Daily Worker*, scrupulously observed their self-denying

[1] At King George V's funeral, "as the gun-carriage bearing the coffin crossed the tramlines at the corner of Theobald's Road, the ball of diamonds, topped by a sapphire cross, fell from the Imperial Crown and rolled from the coffin to the roadway——" *His Was the Kingdom* by Frank Owen and R. J. Thompson.

ordinance to avoid mention of Mrs. Simpson, the number of those who knew of the King's intimacy with her increased. Rumours spread easily, particularly such rumours, and when there is no published or broadcast information, speculation is unimpeded. In any case, the American Press soon threw itself with characteristic energy and thoroughness into the task of publicizing Mrs. Simpson and her royal friendship, finding the theme one after its heart. Wires buzzed, ink flowed, correspondents were active, and impressive bricks were made without much straw. Never, it was contended, had there been such a human-interest story since Mark Antony sacrificed an Empire for Cleopatra, and then there were no sob-sisters to do it justice. On this occasion, American journalists were determined that no leavings should remain to be used by some subsequent Shakespeare. They would do the work themselves, and do it well; did it so well that, despite attempts to prevent them from reaching an English audience,[1] they were heard across the Atlantic. Newspaper cuttings circulated, arousing sometimes indignation, but always interest; and talk became incessant.

After King George V, that such commentaries on the King's private life should be conceivable, let alone credible, represented a sudden and drastic change. The Court in his time might have been dull, but it was impregnably respectable and provided no sob-sister pabulum. Above all, it was solid; and solidity was the most necessary quality of all in a sovereign and his way of life. So much thought solid had proved unsubstantial; and now was the Monarchy itself to partake of the same unsubstantiality? Was the gold of the Imperial Crown to suffer the same fate as the Gold Standard?

[1] The English distributors of *Time* on several occasions took the precaution of removing pages which dealt with the King and Mrs. Simpson.

To be Prince Charming suited a prince, but a King Charming would never do; firmly and properly had Prince Hal put away Falstaff, along with other princely things, when he became King Henry. Let King Edward do likewise.

He showed little inclination so to do, in that sharing the fate of many of his generation, who, youthful, were required to be mature, and in maturity persisted in being youthful. His position demanded of him that he should suffer pomposity gladly, and bear the dull burden of authority without the delight of exercising it; whereas his inclination was to dispense with ceremonial respect and make his own will felt; be both less and more than the King who ruled before him. The same conflicts run throughout Society, taking different forms at different levels; bricklayers, clergymen and kings betray the same restlessness in restless times, crave similarly to free themselves from the past's dead weight and let their egos thrive, and, having freed themselves, are similarly forlorn. What befell King Edward makes the same pattern as what has befallen many of his subjects.

Sunshine cruises were popular, and the King took one. They combined travel and carefree companionship, besides providing an opportunity to get brown and wear little clothing; they, too, went *wieder in's Blau*—all aboard for the good ship Swastika. To the sun, the tired looked for vigour; outward and visible symbol of energy and warmth, it must be capable, if anything was, of reviving hearts which have lost their zest, desire grown cold. On the sea-shore, on ship's decks, by swimming-pools and rivers, on roofs and in gardens, bodies lay motionless and inert, like batteries on a garage shelf patiently being charged; if no sun was available, a substitute luminary found in electrical apparatus, crackling forth energy when a switch was turned on.

The King chartered for his sunshine-cruise a luxury yacht, *Nahlin*, reputed to have cost £250,000. He and his friends gaily sailed about the Eastern Mediterranean, putting in occasionally at ports; entertained at Istanbul by Kemal Ataturk, whom, it was reported, the King on the spur of the moment invited to visit him in London. Reports in the English Press of their movements were scanty, and Mrs. Simpson was deleted from the photographs taken in their published version. It was a *wandervogel* holiday, a *Constant Nymph* holiday, a *Glut ist Geist*, Over the Hills and Far Away, There's Wind on the Heath and Booze in Bottle, Brother, holiday.

Still no open reference was made to the King's friendship with Mrs. Simpson and the comments it had occasioned, though the *Times*, as was afterwards apparent, dropped occasional veiled hints, using, for instance, remarks ostensibly dealing with the appointment of Mr. Duncan to be Governor-General of South Africa, to point out that a sovereign "should be invested with a certain detachment and dignity . . . which are not so easily put on as a change of clothes." While staying at Balmoral, the King gave an impetus to gossip by leaving the Duke of York to deputize for him at an Aberdeen hospital-opening ceremony, while he waited outside a near-by station to meet Mrs. Simpson. Lairds, gillies, aged retainers, all were surprised and bewildered by the suddenness with which accustomed formality became informality; curtsies scarcely required, and ceremonial door-openings and announcements of meals served and respectful conversations, all superseded, or hurriedly and carelessly executed.

The case of *Simpson* v. *Simpson,* heard at Ipswich Assizes, though in its procedure, brevity and circumstances, indistinguishable from innumerable other such cases, languidly conducted and little noticed, attracted much attention. American correspondents and photographers assembled in large numbers, but various stratagems were adopted to prevent them from effectually operating. They went sadly away, none the less able to provide photographic and other material sufficient to fill pages of the newspapers they served. In England, there was no more than an announcement, separately given, to the effect that Mrs. Simpson had secured a decree nisi, costs being given against her husband, and evidence of misconduct furnished by employees of the Hotel de Paris, Bray.

After the *Nahlin* cruise, came the King's visit to South Wales, whose distressed areas had been surveyed, fulminated against, recommended upon, and otherwise received bureaucratic and demagogic attention, but continued to exist. The King was deeply moved by the welcome he received from the distressed inhabitants of these distressed areas, and by the melancholy circumstances of their lives. His sympathetic smile was appreciated, as was his reluctance to keep to the itinerary which had been arranged; and it was noted with satisfaction that he refused to put himself wholly in the keeping of his Ministers in attendance, Sir Kingsley Wood and Mr. Ernest Brown. Several times the police cordon was broken; hymns were passionately sung, and miners' lamps joyously waved in the darkness. "I am going to help you," the King said, and in the message of thanks for the welcome he had received, repeated it—"Something will be done for you."

He had said it, their Prince, and now King, Charming—

that something would be done for them, and they were comforted. If he, a King, wanted to do something for them, surely he could do it, when the efforts of Chief Commissioners, Secretaries of State, Members of Parliament, even Labour ones, however well intentioned and informed, had all proved fruitless. Let him give the word, and at last the stagnation of twenty years would be ended. A King could work the miracle; not promoting a parliamentary Bill, or requiring votes, or preparing a report; just ordering—"Let this desolation be desolate no longer, and these outcasts no more outcast!"

Enthusiastic accounts of the King's tour appeared in most newspapers. A new age seemed to have dawned; the King would deliver his people as of old, instead of leaving deliverance to querulous politicians, who either wanted to help the poor by taking from the rich, or help the rich by preventing the poor from improving their conditions. This dilemma, only a King could resolve—disperse South Wales's misery without adding to Lord Rothermere's, increase its prosperity without reducing his. Lord Rothermere, no less than South Wales, rejoiced at the prospect of its being resolved.

The *Times* did not share in the prevailing jubilation, and ventured to point out that, in accordance with constitutional practice, the Sovereign could only act through his Ministers. South Wales miners might rapturously cheer the King, and pointedly ignore the more prosaic Sir Kingsley Wood and Mr. Brown, but it was on them, not on him, that responsibility rested to execute any undertakings carelessly given in an emotional moment. The King was a symbol, they were responsible administrators; and these separate functions must not be confused.

Now was clearly audible the first rumble of an approaching storm, which, despite appearances to the contrary, would dislodge the King, and leave Sir Kingsley and Mr. Brown unharmed. Dr. Blunt, Bishop of Bradford, unknowingly started it—like an elderly visitor at a Swiss mountain resort who, wandering amiably along in knickerbockers, carelessly kicks aside a stone and releases an avalanche. In the course of an address to the Bradford Diocesan Conference, on the necessity of preserving the Communion Office as part of the Coronation Service, Dr. Blunt remarked that the benefit of the King's Coronation depended, among other things, on "the faith, prayer and self-dedication of the King himself"; that he commended him to God's grace, "which he will so abundantly need . . . if he is to do his duty properly"; that he hoped he was aware of his need of divine grace, but wished "he gave more positive signs of his awareness." The Bradford Diocesan Conference dispersed, each clergyman to his vicarage or rectory, each dean to his deanery, the Bishop to his Episcopal residence, as they had after many another such conference, probably few, or none, of them realizing that their blameless and earnest proceedings would have repercussions far beyond the parish and diocesan magazines in which they ordinarily appeared, the innocuous and rarely animated discussions which ordinarily resulted from them.

The next day, a number of provincial newspapers, notably the *Yorkshire Post*, had leading-articles commenting on Dr. Blunt's address. These were the advance guard, and soon heavy artillery, cavalry, tanks, pursuit planes, and even poison gas, were brought into action. All other news was discarded, all restraint laid aside. The photographs from which Mrs. Simpson had been deleted, reappeared with her in them; American newspapers were full of good things which now might be used; Mr. Simpson, and his predecessor, Commander Spencer, were brought into the light of day. Like a pack long held on leash, then suddenly released; newspapers leapt after their quarry, making good, and more than making good, in a few days the distance lost during months of tantalizing frustration.

If, for Mr. Baldwin, the resultant situation was awkward, it was one with which he was well equipped to deal. After the Hoare-Laval Pact, he had fallen ill, and been ordered some months of rest; but when he reappeared in Parliament, his step was still faltering and his appearance still jaded. It seemed almost as though, like his predecessor MacDonald, he would not so much resign the Premiership as let it fall listlessly from his hands. The difficulties which Dr. Blunt had unwittingly brought to a head had the immediate effect of reviving him. Like a soldier, after tedious months of unfamiliar ease in the South of France, called into action again, his lassitude vanished. Here was something he understood, something he could handle as no one else could. It was Dr. Blunt who was going to require recuperation, not he. Long interviews with the King, late appearances in the House of Commons with members all impatiently awaiting what he had to say, were invigorating rather than exhausting; speeches based on "scrappy notes," and apologized for in advance, but perfectly fulfilling their function, took less out of him than answering supplementary questions on the progress of rearmament. No sealed lips this time—perfect frankness.

The King, Mr. Baldwin explained, had expressed his intention of marrying Mrs. Simpson, and Mr. Baldwin had told him in the friendliest manner that he did not think such a marriage would meet with the approval of his subjects, since

it would involve the lady becoming Queen. No cons
tional issue had arisen, nor was any pressure being bro
to bear on the King, either to make up his mind at once, or
to renounce Mrs. Simpson. When Mr. Churchill asked, not
unreasonably, for an "assurance that no irrevocable step
would be taken before a formal statement had been made
to Parliament," Mr. Baldwin was non-committal; the next
time Mr. Churchill asked for such an assurance, he was
irritable, as though to complain that surely he had enough
to bear without that being brought up again; and the third
time it was only necessary for him to look pained, for indignant voices to be raised calling on Mr. Churchill to resume
his seat, which he did in some confusion. Thus silencing
Mr. Churchill was perhaps the most difficult part of Mr.
Baldwin's task. The King was constitutionally silent; Parliament's silence he was skilled in procuring, and Mrs. Simpson
soon withdrew to Cannes, where she issued a statement to
the effect that she was willing, "if such action would solve
the problem, to withdraw forthwith from a situation that
has been rendered both unhappy and untenable."

Still insistent that no constitutional issue had arisen, Mr.
Baldwin next dealt with the possibility of a morganatic
marriage. This proposal, he said, he had, as in duty bound,
laid before the Cabinet, but was not surprised when it was
unanimously rejected. There the matter stood—morganatic
marriage ruled out, Mrs. Simpson as Queen ruled out, no
pressure brought to bear on the King, and above all no constitutional issue. Could anything be more straightforward?

Straightforward it might seem to Mr. Baldwin and to
Members of Parliament, but to others, not so straightforward. The King, it appeared, was making up his mind, but
about what? Not whether or no he should marry Mrs.

Simpson, morganatically or royally, because Mr. Baldwin
had said that was impossible; not whether or no he should
abdicate, because Mr. Baldwin had said no pressure was
being brought to bear on him; not whether or no he should
dispense with his present Ministers, and appoint others, or
rule without Parliament, because Mr. Baldwin said no
constitutional issue had arisen. What, then, was he being
called on to decide?

No one quite knew. Comment was endless and confused;
rumours circulated, and each individual had his point of
view, rarely expressed with lucidity. The topic became an
obsession, precluding all other interests. Once more there
was the feeling, experienced so often in recent years, to be
experienced again, that some vital issue was being decided,
but without any clear awareness of what that issue was,
or how forces were aligned, who was friend and who enemy,
who for righteousness and who for unrighteousness. Noisiest
supporters of the King were Sir Oswald Mosley, Mr. Pollitt,
Lady Houston, Lords Rothermere and Beaverbrook, the
Catholic Times and *Social Credit*, which saw "a conflict, enacted before us at the moment as on a stage," between the
King and a Banker Cabinet, "between the philosophy of
Social Credit and that of International Finance Credit";[1]
while opposition was most marked among those who formerly had been exceptionally lavish and unctuous in praise
of him—for instance, the *Times*, which belatedly discovered
that his father's last days were clouded on his account, and,
later, that "His Majesty's circle was too largely composed
of men and women . . . who cared less for his welfare than
for their amusements."

Between these two extremes, there was a great diversity

1 Quoted in *The Magic of Monarchy* by Kingsley Martin.

of opinion—the romantically inclined who saw in the King one who must choose between love and a kingdom, and chose love; Socialists who saw in him an incipient Fascist leader, and other Socialists who held that he was being victimized for his proletarian sympathies; persons themselves in matrimonial difficulties whose hearts went out to a fellow-sufferer, and persons fearful of matrimonial difficulties whose hearts hardened against one who might by his example encourage a more lenient attitude towards divorce; the snobbish who, even though they might never have occasion to, could not bring themselves to envisage curtseying to Mrs. Simpson, and anti-snobs, fond of reciting Burns, who would welcome a Queen without rank's guinea stamp, and whose mother had once, it was said, taken in lodgers in Baltimore.

Out of this confusion rose Mr. Baldwin's voice, reassuring and confident, recounting all his dealings with the King, sometimes repeating the very words used:

"I am going to tell you something I have long wanted to tell you. I am going to marry Mrs. Simpson, and I am prepared to go."

"Sir, that is most grievous news."

Perfect harmony had existed between them; then friendship, far from being impaired, had been strengthened, was, indeed, a friendship of affection. Throughout, the King had behaved as a great gentleman, showing every consideration, and refusing to leave Fort Belvedere and come to Buckingham Palace, because of the cheering crowds he knew would greet him. Now the King had taken his decision to abdicate; freely taken it, without any constitutional issue arising. Let them all leave it at that. Let them not judge, or imagine vain things, but accept, as indeed they must, the King's renunciation of the Throne, and fall in with his wishes by according their fullest loyalty to his successor.

This masterly oration met with the almost unanimous approval of Parliament, only Colonel Josiah Wedgwood mentioned the possibility of a toast again being drunk to a King Over the Water, and Mr. Buchanan, an I.L.P. Member, sensibly observing that if Mr. Baldwin's and others' lavish praises of Edward VIII were sincere, there would have been no reason for them to get rid of him. These were solitary and unappreciated voices; it was Mr. Baldwin's day, the greatest triumph of his career. An historian looking back on it hereafter, recalling the adroitness with which he confused the issue, while at the same time giving an impression of clarifying it, the skill with which he arranged his case and the eloquence with which he presented it, may well reflect that, had he but devoted a quarter of the ingenuity required to unseat his King to unseating Hitler, the decade he largely dominated might have ended less precariously.

VIII

After making a farewell broadcast, Edward VIII, become Prince Edward again, and later to become Duke of Windsor, left England to Mr. Baldwin, and went abroad. In the ten days between his departure and Dr. Blunt's address to the Bradford Diocesan Conference, an astonishing reversal of popular sentiment took place. A mighty engine of publicity, moving at a great speed in one direction, was suddenly stopped, brakes jammed on with loud groaning and grinding, and the engine laboriously put into reverse gear. In totalitarian countries, where a single driver controls steering wheel, gear lever and brakes, such an operation is easy; a word suffices to bring it about—one day Bolsheviks sub-human scum, and the next valued allies; one day the Third Reich a menace to peace, and the next best guarantor of its continuance; a Röhm or a Yagoda transformed overnight from heroes into villains. When instead of one large orchestra with one omnipotent conductor, there are many little bands, string, wood, brass, professional and amateur, all producing their own versions of a selected composition, to change that composition is a difficult undertaking. Some conductors will take longer than others to master the new harmony; some, out of obstinacy or obtuseness, will continue with the old one, or take the opportunity to apply for a rise in salary; separate instruments, even, may prove obdurate, trumpet or 'cello blithely continuing to disregard the changed score, thereby producing discord.

A King credited with all virtues, whose charm and sincerity had been constantly praised, whose fitness for his high calling had never before been questioned, had suddenly to be put down from his eminence, scorned and rejected, and in his place another King exalted. It took time, it could not be done in the twinkling of an eye. The Archbishop of Canterbury, prone to misjudge prevailing sentiment,[1] weighed in too soon with what seemed a malignant attack on a fallen adversary—"Even more strange it is that he should have sought his happiness in a manner inconsistent with the Christian principles of marriage, and within a circle whose standards and ways of life are alien to all the best instincts and traditions of his people," and was, in con-

[1] At the beginning of the last war, he came in for much obloquy by recalling in a public address how, when Queen Victoria died, he had seen the Kaiser and King Edward VII kneeling together by her mortal remains.

sequence, for a time highly unpopular. Subtler and better-timed denigratory efforts were more efficacious; and it soon became apparent that an idol had indeed fallen, that whereas King Edward VIII had been admired as few individuals have, the Duke of Windsor would easily be forgotten.

Interest in him soon subsided; his marriage to Mrs. Simpson, celebrated in Paris, received less attention than the Duke of Norfolk's, and when, on the outbreak of war, he returned to England for a few days, his presence was scarcely noticed. Even in the United States, where the romantic circumstances of his abdication had been so strenuously publicized, his fame dwindled; a projected visit there, under the unpopular auspices of Mr. Bedoux, originator of a scheme for speeding up factory production, was abandoned in consequence of unfavourable newspaper comments upon it; and the American lecture-tour of the clergyman who officiated at his marriage, discontinued for lack of support.

An episode which, it was often said, would never lose its fascination, became uninteresting even before it was ended. Like a glutton who eats the early courses of a dinner so voraciously that he has no appetite left for the savoury, public curiosity was sated by the time the Duke's reward for the sacrifice of a kingdom became available; that he should choose to abdicate rather than renounce the woman he loved, was enthralling, but when, having abdicated, he came to marry her, the event was little noticed. Even in South Wales, he was no more beloved; he had said that something would be done, and nothing had been done; and the Cap d'Antibes, where he took up his residence, was too unlike the Rhondda Valley, too undepressed an area, for much sympathy to flow between the two in either direction. Whatever of his popularity remained, finding expression, for instance, in the purchase of Edward VIII Coronation mugs, and other mementoes of his short reign, perished in the icy blast of hatred which continued to blow from Printing House Square, Church House and other high places even after its purpose had been served—that frigid, calculated hatred which the English upper classes reserve for those they have unremuneratively adulated.

Having destroyed one King's popularity, it was necessary to establish another's; and by the time King George VI's Coronation took place, to judge by the enthusiasm of the crowds which assembled to watch it, the status quo ante had been restored. George V might have been again on the Throne; indeed, the resemblance between the new King and his father, in character, appearance, and even in voice, was frequently drawn attention to. The visits he made, accompanied by the Queen, to France, Canada and Washington, were a great success; his reign gradually came to seem contiguous with George V's, with no intervening Abdication, and the Monarchy gave every appearance of having passed into smooth waters once more.

CHAPTER VII

Sick Men of Europe

H ITLER provided an age with its image—"I proceed like a somnambulist." Eyes glazed and unseeing, mind blank and unthinking, arms reaching forward to touch but never touching, step confident but directed nowhere—such was his and Time's march, observed by all with helpless absorption.

Scene by scene, the play unfolded, actors hissed or acclaimed, comic relief and tense moments succeeding one another; intervals occurring, with buffet visits, stroll in the street outside or casual conversation, but soon the lights again lowered, and eyes again focused on the stage. From one part of the world to another, the scene inconsequentially shifted; time was similarly inconstant, but the theme never varied. Theme inescapable, its working out not to be prevented; each incident, large and small, each character, major and minor, contributing to its development, until the final curtain came, the applause or derision, and lights were put out, performance done. Theme inescapable—graven image lifted and loudly adored, graven image shattered and hearts made humble again; bread alone sufficient and eagerly gorged, hunger remaining and bread sufficing not; unto Caesar all rendered, and Caesar clamouring still for more.

Germany's growing power was the chief preoccupation. As it grew, fear grew. Each fresh realization of its growth, created more fear than the one before—bursts of fear, crises, with uneasy lulls in between. Something should be done, it was felt; but nothing was done. Perhaps the Nazi régime would collapse, but it did not collapse. The League still might gather together its shattered structure and act, but it could not, even though, to compensate for Germany's withdrawal, the U.S.S.R. became a member. Plebiscites and elections conducted in Germany were clearly absurd; in the Saarland, with a plebiscite conducted under the League's auspices, surely the result would be different, but it was not. There, too, ninety per cent obediently voted in favour of incorporation in the Reich.

Though it was known that Germany was rearming, by the terms of the Treaty of Versailles conscription could not be introduced, but it was, and soon afterwards an Anglo-German Naval Agreement concluded, whereby a thirty-five per cent ratio in all categories of ships except submarines was fixed; this agreement, too, like the one whose renunciation it celebrated, in due course renounced. If now, the Treaty of Versailles must be regarded as no more operative, Hitler himself had solemnly announced that he regarded the Locarno Treaty as still binding. Ends of cigars smoked by Briand, Sir Austen Chamberlain and Stresemann when it was negotiated, were still piously preserved; the pen with which it was signed, still extant, and the garter presented to Sir Austen to mark the occasion, sometimes apparent on his calf, until calf and garter both vanished from sight. That instrument surely might be relied on, but could not. Hitler announced to the Reichstag that even while he was speaking, German troops were marching into the demilitarized Rhineland, and would at once begin the construction of fortifications there.

Each stage in this process was marked by solemn protests, diplomatic notes, conferences, appeals to the League, statements of policy, editorial fulmination, heated parliamentary debates and questions, agitated coming and going of politicians, discussion both private and public, both spoken and written. Like frightened householders who hear a burglar below, the British and French Governments discussed what preventative measures they should take, picked up a poker and then put it down again, shouted downstairs that if the burglar did not make off, they would fall upon him, or at least call the police; even considered parleying with him, perhaps proposing that if he left the fish knives, they saw no objection to his taking other cutlery in reason; at last, fell back on deriving what comfort they might from the thought that at any rate he did not know the formula for opening the safe.

Mr. Eden, like Henderson before him and Mr. Lansbury after him, visited various European capitals for the purpose of engaging in frank discussion with those in authority, and thereby clearing the air. Discussion, presumably frank, was duly engaged in, but the air not cleared. With the same end in view, he addressed an ingenious questionnaire to the German Government in the hope of elucidating its intentions; but his questionnaire was never answered, and the German Government's intentions, therefore, unelucidated. M. Laval, similarly bent, also visited European capitals; and M. Herriot went to the U.S.S.R., where he was cordially received, pronounced the catering excellent, the countryside delectable, the population bonny and the Government benevolent, and prepared the way for the conclusion of a Franco-Soviet Pact.

There were ominous rumblings in a number of places, later to achieve notoriety—Danzig, Memel, Sudetenland. In Austria an attempted Nazi coup failed, though it resulted in the brutal murder of the Chancellor, Dollfuss, who, despite his former slaughter of Social Democrats and establishment of a Corporative State, became momentarily a much honoured martyr in the democratic cause. The failure of this coup was reassuring. A union of Germany and Austria, considered by many a righteous endeavour before Hitler became Chancellor, now was unthinkable; and in any case Mussolini would never allow it. He might contravene the League Covenant to conquer Abyssinia, but would never contravene it where a neighbouring State was concerned.

Alas, one contravention of the Covenant led to another; after sanctions Mussolini cared little for the League, and was never again likely to be in the running for a Nobel Peace Prize. The Rome-Berlin Axis was already in process of being forged; Mussolini's admiring gaze was already turned towards the Third Reich, and soon the goose-step, called *Passo Romano*, would be seen in Rome—little, dark Italians spiritedly kicking their legs into the air, like a flute playing Wagner. When Hitler did give the order for his troops to march into Austria, the other end of the Axis remained quiescent, rewarded by a telegram—"Mussolini, I shall never forget this."

Through the jungle of international affairs, Mr. Eden continued to push his earnest, but somewhat indecisive, way. Since his advocacy of the abandonment of sanctions and acceptance of the policy of non-intervention in Spain, his popularity had declined; as Mr. Baldwin sagely remarked, it had been roses, roses all the way for him, but the brickbats had to come, as any old parliamentary hand well knew. Those who had looked to him to lead them to collective security, did not conceal their disappointment; still the wicked triumphed and the weak were downtrodden, as when Sir John Simon was Foreign Secretary, and, what

was even more distressing, the danger of the strong having
to choose between also being downtrodden and offering
resistance, grew ever more imminent. That Abyssinia should
have been abandoned, was disgraceful, but that England
might be similarly threatened, appalling. Love of peace was,
it seemed, like patriotism, not enough; and to implement it,
rearmament had become necessary, and was actively, though
not very effectually, undertaken.

When a law-abiding citizen, returning home with money
in his pocket, meets with robbers, it is natural that he
should try and ingratiate himself with the least villainous
looking among them, in the hope of thereby making resistance unnecessary.[1] Mussolini seemed more recognizably a
human being than Hitler; towards him, therefore, appeasing activities were first directed, and a gentleman's agreement concluded guaranteeing the status quo in the Mediterranean. It soon became apparent that the gentlemanly
contracting parties had different ideas as to what the status
quo signified, Mussolini seeing no disturbance of it when
Italian troops participated in the Spanish Civil War, or when
Italian submarines sank British ships carrying supplies to
the Republican Government. It was difficult, indeed, to
imagine what, short of draining the Mediterranean and

[1] An alternative tactic is to persuade himself that the robbers have other
victims in view, and will never bother about him; whistling the while to
keep up his spirits. This is Splendid Isolation, for long the policy of Lord
Beaverbrook's organs, which persistently put forward the view that
Europe's difficulties were no concern of the British Government's, and
that there would be no war. Let everyone, they urged their readers,
quietly proceed with his own affairs, and sleep quietly at nights, because
(often in capitals) THERE WILL BE NO WAR. Like the French king
who would not have it that he must die, and who tried, by avoiding
funerals, to avoid death, Lord Beaverbrook would not have it that there
must be a war, and tried, by assuming it would not come, to prevent its
occurrence.

settling Hottentots on the land thus made available, would, in Mussolini's view, constitute an alteration of existing conditions there.

An ungentlemanly agreement concluded at Nyon, resulted in no more British ships being sunk outside Spanish territorial waters; but Italian intervention in Spain proceeded vigorously, though at Guadalajara in the wrong direction—away from, instead of towards, the enemy. As Lord Halifax later admitted in the House of Lords, Mussolini made it clear from the beginning that, gentleman's agreement or no gentleman's agreement, he would not tolerate General Franco's defeat, and would continue to intervene in the Spanish Civil War until his victory was assured.

To continue to appease him in such circumstances, was an undertaking which required exceptional faith, if not gullibility; and Mr. Eden's good will, as far as Mussolini was concerned, was exhausted. He, too, must join the little company of discarded Foreign Secretaries; like them, later find his way back into the Cabinet in another capacity. As far as appeasement was concerned, he had reached the limit of his capacity; but another was waiting, whose ardour for appeasement was unquenchable, and faith in its efficacy, unshakable. Lord Halifax succeeded Mr. Eden; Mr. Chamberlain wrote Mussolini a letter intended to facilitate an Anglo-Italian Agreement. This agreement, when it was concluded, again laid down that the Mediterranean status quo should be preserved, and specified that Italian troops should be withdrawn from Spain, the Italian garrison in Libya reduced, and anti-British propaganda emanating from Italian sources discontinued. It survived Italy's annexation of Albania, the participation of Italian troops in all General Franco's campaigns, and in his several times postponed

victory celebrations in Madrid, and the continuous vitupera-
tion of Signor Gayda and others, and may be regarded, as
far as any agreement concluded among mortals may be so
regarded, as indestructible.

Having tasted appeasement, Mr. Chamberlain developed
a voracious appetite for it. He had hitherto, apart from his
pronouncement that sanctions were the "very midsummer
of madness," shown little interest in foreign affairs; now he
took to them with a beginner's passion and recklessness,
though not luck. As, in his business days, he had been accustomed to go after a contract in person when less enterprising rivals contended themselves with submitting a written tender, so now he was determined to go after peace in
person. A chat with Mussolini or with Hitler, even a
friendly nod to Stalin, would make all the difference.
Chamber of Commerce Quixote, Knight of the Woeful
Countenance, bearing umbrella instead of lance, his chivalry
Rotarian, his accoutrements funereal, he set forth hopefully to save the world from an impending catastrophe.

His setting forth, with Lord Halifax, his Sancho Panza,
trotting faithfully beside him, was signalized by one of
Hitler's vitriolic speeches, soon followed by the German
occupation of Austria. The explosion momentarily delayed their progress; but when its fury was spent—protests
all made, statements of resolute fidelity to existing engagements duly registered, and impossibility of tolerating further acts of aggression duly adumbrated in unmistakable
terms—they picked themselves up and proceeded on their
way. If the Italian Government's contemptuous disregard
of obligations solemnly undertaken, was no impediment to
concluding a gentleman's and later actual, agreement with
it, why should the German Government's short way with

treaties impede the conclusion of an Anglo-German Agreement? It was announced that Lord Halifax, in his private capacity of huntsman, would visit Germany for the purpose of seeing a hunting exhibition which had been arranged there.

The proposed visit was made the subject of much angry comment and suspicious speculation. In it was seen the hand of the Cliveden Set, a mysterious entity whose reputed chief figures were Lords Astor, Lothian and Londonderry, and whose activities, directed towards promoting an Anglo-German understanding, and perhaps towards emulating Nazi methods in England, needed to be, and were often, exposed. For some months the Cliveden Set bobbed about on the surface of political gossip, and then vanished. Herr von Ribbentrop, its alleged mainstay, returned to Germany to become Foreign Minister there, his assiduous cultivation of, and by, high-born and influential persons, unfruitful,[1]

---

[1] Ribbentrop's particular hatred of England, and the loathing he came to arouse in, particularly, those whose esteem he had sought, and perhaps to a certain extent gained, may be attributed to the fact that the Nazi régime as expounded by, and embodied in, him, seemed presentable. Subsequent disillusionment on this score equally enraged him and the disillusioned. Goering and Goebbels have the merit of looking their parts; but for a Nazi even approximately to convey the impression of an upper-class Englishman, and then outdo his less presentable associates in virulence and malignancy, was indefensible. Ribbentrop's position was a difficult one. He wanted to be a social success in London, and at the same time ambition necessitated that he should be considered an ardent Nazi in Berlin; the former aim led him, for instance, to enter his son at an English public school rather than at one of the establishments in Germany which inculcate National Socialist views and behaviour, the latter, to give the Nazi salute when he was received by the King. Between the two aims he floundered uncomfortably, generating chagrin which later found vehement expression. The Bolsheviks have wisely refrained from sending abroad envoys likely to meet with the same difficulty; the danger of anyone, however well disposed towards the Bolshevik régime, detecting an approximate Etonian in, for instance, Litvinov or M. Maisky, is infinitesimal.

and Kremlin Set soon replacing Cliveden one in his esteem.

Lord Halifax went to Berlin, and paid a visit to Goering, but after so inauspicious a send-off, any hopes which may have been entertained that he would engage in remunerative political conversations, were disappointed. Towards yet another explosion, events were moving; and appeasement had for the time being to be held in suspense.

II

After Austria, it was Czechoslovakia's turn to receive the propagandist barrage which preceded a Nazi attack. This composite State, set up by the Treaty of Versailles, had long been regarded as a model of sound administration and correct international behaviour. It was democratic, faithful to the League, chose professors for President, and had a close alliance with France; like a slum-settlement, stood out amid ramshackle surroundings as a little oasis of order and enlightenment. For strategic reasons, the Sudetenland and its German-speaking inhabitants had been included in Czechoslovakia; and it was with these Germans that Hitler was for the moment concerned.

As the storm blew up, it was realized that, though England technically was under no obligation to go to Czechoslovakia's assistance, if France were involved, England would also be involved. The British Government was not in a position to disinterest itself in the situation which had arisen, and as a sympathetic and helpful gesture, decided to dispatch Lord Runciman to Prague. He was to consider himself, it was carefully explained, an unofficial "investigator and mediator," and not in any sense an arbitrator.

As an investigator and mediator, he went; in his own

words, like one "set adrift in a small boat in mid-Atlantic," [1] investigating much and mediating little, heard of here and there, reported to have brought about a more hopeful outlook, reported not to have made much progress, reported to be on his way home, disconsolate. Various plans were devised for meeting the Sudeten Germans' grievances—Plan Number One, Two, Three, Four, all agreed to with reluctance by the Czechoslovak Government, and all obsolete before they were published. More than Lord Runciman or a plan was necessary if the mounting fury of the Nazi Press and wireless, the German troops concentrated on the Czechoslovak Frontier, were not to achieve their intended purpose. Investigating a charge of wild elephants is a thankless enterprise; to mediation they are insensible, and to plans impervious.

How strange is the human will in its operation; whether it be directed towards subduing a piece of earth and those scraping its surface with implements or feet, or whether towards subduing a single carcass, making that a kingdom to be subdued—always, how strange. For Czechoslovakia Hitler howled, and others in unison with him; [2] and as his howls became more insistent and frenzied, attempts to pacify him became more tremulously eager. Mediation and investigation did not abate his clamour, nor the four plans, devised in rapid succession, another begun before the previous one was finished. Supposing, then, he were actually given the Sudetenland he demanded. Who would dare to propose it, lurking in the background, many minds, unspoken? "If," the *Times* wrote, "the Sudetens are not

[1] See *Munich and the Dictators* by K. W. Seton-Watson.
[2] "Surge of voices, as in a menagerie where all the animals have gone mad, but by some trick can still be made to bay and howl in unison." (Mr. Fish Armstrong in *Foreign Affairs*. Quoted in *Munich and the Dictators*.)

satisfied with the last Czech offer, it can only be that they do not find themselves at ease within the Republic. In that case it might be well for the Czechoslovak Government to consider whether a solution should not be sought on some totally different lines, which would make Czechoslovakia an entirely homogeneous State by the secession of that fringe of alien populations who are contiguous to the nations with which they are united by race."

There, it was out, it had been spoken. Let Czechoslovakia enjoy the blessings of entire homogeneity by shedding fringe of alien and now discontented populations, thereby purified, and perhaps strengthened; yield. Echo answered: "Never, never!" Other newspapers raged, and from the Government came an indignant repudiation of what had been suggested. Such a solution would never be countenanced; wicked to make it, laughable that it should ever have been seriously entertained. There would be a plan—Plan Number Five, Six, Seven, Eight; but a plan. That was certain.

Concessions proposed and envisaged were fuel thrown on to a fire, whose flames leapt up each time it was replenished; Hitler's demands, like Othello's jealousy, grew by what they fed on, until the appalling possibility arose that what the *Times* had proposed, what would never, never be conceded—even that might not satisfy him. A partial French mobilization was announced, and war seemed imminent. Each successive crisis approached nearer it—like a seducer whose advances are repulsed with dwindling resolution; each time they are attempted, greater liberties allowed before restraint is imposed. From being infinitely remote, war had become conceivable, possible, probable, and now almost certain.

To prevent it, Mr. Chamberlain decided that, like Chancellor Schuschnigg before him, and many another after him, he would go to Berchtesgaden, flying there because of the urgency of the situation. When his intention was announced, a great sigh of relief was heard; since the National Government was formed, no such heartfelt thankfulness had been felt and expressed. Thank God for him, too; like MacDonald, he had greatly dared, not only taking his political life in his hands, but, to the extent that air travel was dangerous, and to him unfamiliar, his physical life as well. A bomber carried him to Germany, depositing him there, first of a number of such innocuous cargoes, both human and paper, thus to be deposited. Journalists expatiated upon the imaginativeness and heroism of his enterprise; politicians voiced the pride they felt that England in her hour of need should not lack another Chatham, or at any rate a Pitt; and in a club a voice, not wholly sober, was heard recalling Trafalgar as the nearest historical parallel to the present occasion.

At Berchtesgaden warm handclasps were exchanged, long conversations conducted; strange meeting, likely ever to be remembered—Good-Day To All This and Good-Bye To All That momentarily brought together; Mars and Mammon in earnest conference; expiring and upsurging force, meeting, like two well-buckets, one on its way down to be filled and the other on its way up to be emptied.

Back Mr. Chamberlain came, bearing with him proposals thought to be acceptable to Hitler, probably acceptable to the British Government, though, as the *Times* mildly remarked, unlikely "to make a strong prima facie appeal" to the Czechoslovak Government. These proposals, on examination, proved to amount to what, when previously sug-

gested, had been indignantly dismissed as quite impossible—
the cession to Germany of the Sudetenland. Now they were
possible; Czechoslovak Government, after prima facie disappointment, urged, pressed, given no alternative but to
accept them; Second Trafalgar resulting in Never, never!
becoming Please, please!

The Cabinet having decided to accept the proposals the
Prime Minister had brought back from Berchtesgaden, another flight was necessary to put them in final shape, this time
to Godesberg. Mr. Chamberlain's second departure was
less rapturously acclaimed, and it soon became apparent
that things were not going well at Godesberg. Conversations were interrupted, recourse had to written communication; and when he was asked if the situation might be regarded as hopeless, Mr. Chamberlain's reply was scarcely
reassuring—"I would not like to say that. It's up to the
Czechs now." As there seemed nothing more the Czechs
could be asked, or even forced, to concede, no more plans
conceivable, this was taken as indicating a deadlock whose
only outcome could be war.

In the expectation of hearing a virtual declaration of war,
and with the knowledge that the British Navy had been mo-
bilized, Parliament assembled. The Prime Minister gave an
account of his dealings with Hitler; how at Berchtesgaden
proposals had been drawn up, but at Godesberg more drastic
ones submitted, in their final draft with a time limit added;
how he had "bitterly reproached the Chancellor for his failure to respond in any way," and pointed out that everything
he wanted might be obtained by peaceable means; how
Hitler had told him that the Sudetenland represented "the
last of his territorial ambitions in Europe," and that in any
case he had no wish to include non-Germans in the Reich.

Members of Parliament listened intently to this narrative of events, to which there seemed only one possible conclusion—that France, in accordance with treaty obligations would go to Czechoslovakia's assistance, and England, for the same reason, to France's. The conclusion, ever more inevitable, was awaited with mounting excitement. When would he say them—the words expected and dreaded? As in Budget speeches, often delivered by him there, he had droned on and on, postponing the moment when he told them what they all longed to hear—money which must be paid, so now he postponed coming to the heart of the matter —blood which must be shed. They waited and waited, and while they were waiting Sir John Simon passed a note to the Prime Minister. He paused to read it, smiled. It was their reprieve. A conference had been arranged at Munich; Mussolini was going, Daladier was going, he was going. Out of their places they leapt, waved order papers, some weeping, some making incoherent noises; some too overcome with emotion even to rise or cheer or wave a paper, perhaps offering silent prayers of thankfulness.[1] Clubman that night, again not quite sober, only mumbled his admiration; Trafalgar, or any other historical parallel, inadequate to express his sense of the greatness of the occasion. "Not Gladstone in his most compelling hour had ever won a triumph like that," the *Daily Telegraph* wrote of the reception accorded to Mr. Chamberlain's speech.

Mr. Chamberlain returned from the Munich Conference not only with news that the conflict between Germany and Czechoslovakia had been peaceably settled, though on terms

---

[1] Mr. Harold Nicolson came in for some criticism because he described the behaviour of his fellow Members of Parliament on this occasion, as a case of "mass hysteria."

less than ever likely to make a strong prima facie appeal to the Czechoslovak Government; not only to announce Peace with Honour to the crowds which enthusiastically welcomed him. More even than these great blessings he had brought them—Peace itself; a paper, signed by Hitler, to the effect that their two countries would never resort to war—yet one more solemn undertaking to that effect, the last. He showed it to them, the very document, pointed to the signature upon it; then told them to go home and sleep quietly in their beds, confident that they were secure against molestation, not just for that night and to-morrow night, but for many nights, perhaps for ever. Peace in our time; peace in his time—not even that.

This first ecstasy soon passed. The Munich Agreement turned out to be scarcely distinguishable from the Godesberg ultimatum, and, as executed, to involve still further concessions to Germany. As Mr. Churchill well put it: "The German Dictator, instead of snatching his victuals from the table, has been content to have them served to him course by course. £1 was demanded at the pistol's point. When it was given, £2 was demanded at the pistol's point. Finally, the Dictator consented to take £1 17s. 6d." Even in that, Mr. Churchill was over-sanguine; before he had finished, the Dictator took his £2, and much more. If others experienced such doubts, or, like M. Blum, admitted that their relief was cowardly, the prevailing feeling was one of deep thankfulness. War had approached so near, and now had receded; in Westminster Abbey continuous prayers had been offered for peace, and now were answered; from London many had fled in panic, and now might return; supplies of food had been laid in, and now might be eaten; money had been sent abroad, and now might be recalled; wills had been hurriedly made, and now might be forgotten; trenches had been dug in public parks and private gardens, and now might be filled in; gas masks had been distributed and tried on, and now might be discarded; fear been prevalent, and now was quite banished.

The bestower of these benefits, Mr. Chamberlain, was held up to admiration; he the saviour, deserving the gratitude of all. Newspapers praised him, his "firmness of spirit and gentleness of heart" which had "raised humanity to a new level"; clergymen offered thanks for him, detecting God's hand in efforts which had resulted in the "sudden and unexpected lifting of an oppressive burden." In Heaven, if not in Czechoslovakia, the Agreement he had concluded at Munich might be expected to make a strong prima facie appeal. Chamberlain dolls were offered for sale, and sugar umbrellas; in Scandinavia there was a movement to present him with a trout stream, in Portugal and in France it was proposed to name streets after him. Letters were published suggesting that a fund should be started for some charitable purpose to commemorate his triumph, and commercial firms took the unusual step of buying newspaper space in which to express their gratitude. The *Sunday Dispatch* used for its contents bill, "When the Prime Minister was a fairy prince"; and Mr. Godfrey Winn praised God and Mr. Chamberlain, saying that he saw "no sacrilege, no bathos, in coupling those two names." [1]

---

[1] Quoted in *Britain* by Mass Observation, which contains a selection of the more striking among Press and individual outpourings at this time; notably a leader which appeared in the *Sunday Pictorial*—

"*Let us now praise ourselves. The peoples of Britain.*

For the last few weeks we have walked in the Valley of the Shadow. And we have been unafraid.

We have looked squarely in the face of evil. And we have seen it vanish. . . ."

After such a triumph—at once, Gladstone at his most compelling, fairy prince, and raiser of humanity's level— the way seemed clear for more appeasement. "If you don't succeed at first, try, try again," Mr. Chamberlain had quoted on his departure for Munich, in his excitement eschewing Shakespeare, and falling back on proverbial wisdom. On that occasion, he had tried again, with the fortunate result that German troops marched peacefully into Czechoslovakia, and Londoners went peacefully to bed; and he proposed to go on trying, come what might. Before he could again turn his attention to the larger European field, however, appeasement was required at home. Among junior Ministers some uneasiness was apparent; and Mr. Duff Cooper, First Lord of the Admiralty, had found it necessary to resign on account of his disapproval of the Government's foreign policy. After the exhilaration of being presented with peace with honour when the alternative had appeared to be war and peace with dishonour, came a perceptible hang-over, intensified by the German Government's total disregard of the Munich Agreement, and the savage pogroms which were ordered in Germany as retaliation for the murder by a young Jew of a German Embassy official, vom Rath, in Paris. Ideologues lifted up their heads and their voices; Cliveden Set was rediscovered, and suspended defiance, resumed. Like remembered steamer confidences, the emotion generated by Mr. Chamberlain's flights and dramatic announcement of the Munich Conference soon staled, and in retrospect was distasteful. Had there really been a crisis at all? it began to be wondered. Was the whole thing a cunning stratagem to facilitate concessions to the Nazis? What part had M. Bonnet played, lugubrious, large-nosed French Foreign Minister? How had the French Press come so unanimously to advocate surrender? Why did even the Tabouis cease from troubling? Why was she at rest? Relieved from fear's paralysis, speculation flourished, and to feed it there soon appeared much printed matter—eye-witness accounts, day by day journals, angles innumerable, viewpoints diverse, greatest torrent of recorded words so far released. A thunderclap sounds, and the jungle is still; then, when the silence is found to persist, a chattering begins, a babble of sounds, each creature large and small giving tongue, until another thunderclap, another silence.

A source of uneasiness was the frequently expressed opinion that Mr. Chamberlain had been forced to yield because he knew that England was inadequately defended, and ill-equipped to enter upon a war. Ecstatically waved document of contractual peace notwithstanding, a strong desire manifested itself that now at last strength should be acquired. "We must be strong, we must be strong——" even Mr. Chamberlain said it, despite expectation of peace in our time; "On Britain's strength depends the peace of the world——" even the *Times* said it, despite a Czechoslovakia blessedly relieved of fringe of alien populations. Yet with this almost universal longing for strength, it came tardily. Not the means were lacking, but, it appeared, the will—like a patient determined to recover former vigour, ready to take any medicine, submit to any régime, endure any operation, undertake any expenditure; trying autosuggestion—"I'm as well as ever I was," yet somehow the very inmost fount of vitality refusing to be revived, there the mischief. Rearmament proceeded, Sir Thomas Inskip relinquishing co-ordination of defence, Lord Chatfield his successor; elderly generals compulsorily retired, giving place to less elderly ones; ever larger sums of money voted, and aeroplanes purchased in the United States to make good deficiencies in home production; the Territorial Army's strength doubled, and a National Service Handbook, whose reputed author was Mr. Humbert Wolfe, circulated; after some hesitation, conscription introduced without any appreciable opposition, conscripted troops to be called Militia, and to wear, when not in uniform, grey flannel trousers and blue blazer, supplied free of charge. Rearmament proceeded; "We must be strong!", but were we strong?

Strength is as elusive as happiness; like happiness, sought and not found, prepared for and not attained. Goliath was strong, and David was weak; yet David aimed his pebbles accurately, whereas Goliath's massive sword impotently floundered. Ichthyosaurus, enormously protected and armed, became extinct; yet, according to Mr. Aldous Huxley, gentle, sensitive tarsier survived to become ungentle homo sapiens, Goliath, lying on the ground, impregnable armour still around him, muscles all relaxed, may well have wondered wherein lay the secret of his frail adversary's strength; last ichthyosaurus expiring, may well have been puzzled by gentle tarsier's survival.

Faith is strength, however meagrely equipped; to be faithless is to be weak, however amply furnished with the means of aggression. If life is not worth continuing, it is not worth defending; increase and strength expire together. For bread alone, men will not fight and die; at best, only gratefully seize an opportunity, if one offers, to give up the ghost. The Kingdom of Heaven on Earth cannot be defended, whatever wealth may be expended on its defence; whatever garrison may be recruited, armaments manufactured, deadly weapons devised, allies acquired, provisions accumulated. It is not worth defending.

III

In time, even the Munich Agreement was largely forgotten; the last tear shed, righteous indignation all expended,
flood of books reduced to a small trickle, Czechoslovakia's
Fallen Bastions taken as fallen; mourners, after the requisite
forty days and forty nights of wailing and gnashing of
teeth, departed and gone. After all, nothing had happened;
things were as they had been before, with trams still running, money still circulating, glamour girls still glamorous.
How foolish had been all those woeful predictions and
catastrophic anticipations. Lord Runciman decided that
circumstances warranted his taking a recuperative cruise;
Sir Samuel Hoare wagged an admonitory finger at jitterbugs always expecting trouble which never came; diplomatic correspondents were reassuring, and *Punch* produced
a cartoon of John Bull comfortably stretching himself murmuring, as "War Scare" flew out of the windows: "Thank
God that's gone." Confidence returned—like a bankrupt
who has cashed a check which he knows cannot be met,
lived in hourly expectation of having it returned, awaited
each post with beating heart, and then, when his fears are
unrealized, gradually become confident that they never will
be realized.

Recovered equanimity was rudely shattered when German troops marched into Prague, and took possession of
what remained of Czechoslovakia; promised guarantee of
this remainder, inoperative; placidity of Lord Runciman's
cruise not up to expectations, and Sir Samuel Hoare, rather
than jitterbugs, discomfited. Hitherto, Hitler's efforts had
been directed towards recovering lost German populations;
if his aggressive intentions extended to non-Germans as well,
what limits could be set on them, where might they not

reach? Some kind of sense it had hitherto been possible to make of his fury; now none. Even *Mein Kampf* must be considered obsolete—Plan Number One, with Two, Three and Four to follow in rapid succession. Guarantees were hurriedly given to Poland and Roumania, more specific than Czechoslovakia's, intended to be more durable.

Gloom descended, not again to be lifted. Twilight months followed, in which jitterbugs were unrebuked, and recuperative cruises undertaken, if at all, secretly. Idle now to pretend that statesmen might get together round a table, and talk over their differences. Appeasement had gone the way of Collective Security, though one last journey to Italy was undertaken for its sake, Mr. Chamberlain and Lord Halifax conducting amicable conversations with Mussolini, and an Italian lady remarking of the British Premier that his eyes irresistibly reminded her of a grey mountain stream. Whatever hopes the journey raised, were diminished by demands noisily made in Italy shortly before Mr. Chamberlain and Lord Hailfax arrived there, for the cession of Corsica, Tunisia, Nice and other French possessions, and quite dashed when Italian troops occupied Albania, they, too, in quest of living space—*Passo Romano*, and now *Lebensraumo Romano*. Appeasement, after its short glory, fell into disfavour; sugar umbrellas vanished from shop windows, and when, at a Foreign Press Association dinner, Mr. Chamberlain included the Munich Agreement in a list of his policy's achievements, he was greeted with silence, embarrassed and embarrassing.

In these twilight months, grey-out preceding black-out, events were shadowy; individuals concerned in them, difficult to discern. Was it Mr. Chamberlain speaking, or Mr. Attlee, or Sir Archibald Sinclair, or some composite figure

—Sir Archibald Chamberlee. Right Honourable Stalin, Honourable and Gallant Goering, Learned Friend Goebbels—all was confusion. Gas-masked faces all were alike; trousered women might be men; crooner, face spotlit, voice falsetto, telling of his baby, possibly female.

Mayfair playboys held the stage, until sentences given, they forgotten. *Thetis* disaster wrung all hearts; steel monster plunging, never to emerge, bows clearly seen, and within, men gasping for air, until air all exhausted, no more to gasp. A.R.P. active, posters seen, English type required for poster-face and not at first forthcoming, sallow maiden first chosen, replaced by blonde. Lectures now available, usually a colonel discoursing on poison gases and how to know them; notes taken, decontamination mastered, and general amusement that one gas, possibly to be discharged, should be called B.B.C. Wardens were appointed, sirens established, shelters prepared, and sometimes rehearsals arranged, all forlornly pretending has happened what will not happen, cannot happen, must happen.

Like a deep thunder cloud, bringing stillness and gloom; like the glassy sea when a hurricane comes; like the frigid silence before hate explodes—"There will be no war," Lord Beaverbrook said; spend your money, kiss your sweethearts, happy be. Unity Mitford, often photographed, proclaimed her admiration for the Führer; war of nerves proceeded, important engagements directed by Dr. Goebbels and Commander King-Hall. These two curious antagonists, angry dwarf and Naval Commander who has taken to the mightier pen, exchanged angry words.

Still it might be possible to understand, and understanding, avert disaster so unnecessary. Penguin Specials, only sixpence, were not lacking; all Eastern Europe in that man

—then let that man turn inside out. *Nazi Germany Cannot Win, Why Germany Cannot Win, Hitler's Last Year Of Power*—good titles all. Astrologers predicted peaceful years; "Cabinet Minister Says No War"; Hitler was ill, had made a conciliatory speech, built himself an eyrie high in the mountains, been repeatedly to *The Merry Widow*, seen a throat specialist, used a bomb-proof screen, settled down to architectural plans, conversed amicably with Sir Nevile Henderson, cultivated his garden—Hitler!

After all, we had money, they had none. How easy it would be, if they would but lay down their arms, to make some more equitable arrangement for the distribution of raw materials. More than that, cash itself might in certain circumstances be forthcoming; a thousand millions, no less. A Junior Minister, Mr. Hudson, unofficially and without any specific commitment, like Lord Runciman in Prague, investigating and mediating, threw out a hint to Dr. Wohltat —what about it, just supposing it might be arranged; what about it? Consider the immense financial resources of the British Empire, and Germany's empty till, replenished when Austria was taken, again when Prague was taken, a little trickle from the Bank of International Settlement flowing in on Appeasement's backwash; but their replenishments soon exhausted. Mammon against Mars—"Mr. Mars, I'll make it worth your while. I have a large sum in mind, a really large sum, if only . . . if only you'll lay down your arms, Mr. Mars."

Friends were looked for, helpers, sometimes in unlikely places; Papal blessing not despised, and wistful glances cast in the Kremlin's direction; godly and godless a powerful combination. Peace Front was wanted, powerful enough never to be challenged; and all who would join it, were

welcome indeed. Would Russia join it?—ah! if she would,
all troubles ended, peace at last. Onward Marxist Soldiers,
marching into war. Civilization need no longer be feared
for, Democracy would reach harbour at last, civil liberties,
and Government of the people by the people for the people,
might be taken as secured, if only Russia's help were forthcoming. Having appeased Mussolini and appeased Hitler,
it was now attempted to appease Stalin.

Negotiations directed to this end proved lengthy and
laborious, and while they were proceeding, yet one more
crisis, the last, developed. Where it had been Czechoslovakia, now it was Poland; the guarantee hurriedly given
when German troops entered Prague, might at any moment
be invoked. Like a swimmer tired of battling with a contrary current, abandoning the struggle, and letting himself
be carried along by what he had long tried to resist, this
last crisis was left to take its course. Better, perhaps, if it
was not averted; better, perhaps, black-out than grey out.
Penguin Specials did not on this occasion appear; Eastern
Europe remained in whomever it was in, and even Madame
Tabouis's revelations for the moment lost their bloom.

Hopes entertained that Stalin would come forward as
civilization's resolute defender, take Mr. Speaker, Black
Rod, Provost and Fellows, Dean and Chapter all under his
wing, were sorely disappointed. He proposed, not unreasonably, to let civilization look after itself, preferring to
send the Red Army against Polish troops in flight rather
than against German troops advancing. Two forces, bound
to come together, because the same, came together now,
disconcerting their foreign admirers—even Lord Rothermere wondering if Hitler really was a very great gentleman;
even the Dean of Canterbury wondering if the Sermon on

the Mount really did lead via class war to the Soviet régime.
With the possibility of Russian participation in the Peace
Front removed, there was no need to delay a German attack
on Poland; and, when this took place, a British declaration
of war on Germany was inevitable.

Now old uniforms were brought out, put away long ago;
old songs were remembered, thought to have been forgotten;
old ways were resumed, old emotions experienced, old hopes
revived. No new war was possible, so an old one would
have to suffice. Out of the past, a ghost was summoned up,
intervening years cancelled; out of the past, a corpse was
disinterred, made to stand upright and seem alive, all that
had happened since its interment, abolished—like two lovers
meeting, after many years parted, picking up the thread of
their old intimacy—here we dined, here we sat, here we
embraced, and now again dining, again sitting, again em-
bracing; only faces grown haggard, eyes grown tired, passion all spent.

IV

Many had envisaged the horrors of another war, dwelt on
the destruction and suffering and slaughter it would involve.
What happened, none had envisaged—all the circumstances
of war existing, but no war; a war which would not happen,
and yet which was; a war with manifestations of passion,
but passionless; war was coming, coming, coming; then
came, and lo! there was no war. All the outward and visible
signs of war made their appearance—society ladies photographed making splints; land-girls who broadcast their emotions when they put aside typewriters and began to milk
cows; special correspondents Somewhere in France, describing the spirit of the troops, looking for droll or moving

incidents, humble feet which wore socks knitted by Royal Princesses; shops displaying "Business as Usual" notices, ration-books distributed, recruiting offices opened but few recruits wanted, Saarbrücken about to fall but never taken, leaflets dropped instead of bombs.

> *"Never seek to tell your war,*
> *War that never told should be,*
> *For the gentle wind doth blow,*
> *Silently, invisibly."*

On a clear September morning, a Sunday, with church services proceeding, bells lately still, Mr. Chamberlain's voice was heard proclaiming a state of war—peace in our time, now war in our time. His aged voice proclaimed it, announced the forthcoming combat for freedom and truth, all good things, against oppression and tyranny, all bad things. His aged voice proclaimed it, and before its accents had died away, another sound was heard—the sirens. They blared forth triumphantly, and all scattered, finding dug-outs, hiding-places; donned gas masks, as alike then as Opera House parliamentarians; waited trembling or ecstatic, both perhaps, for the catastrophe which was due. In the slight September haze, Dome of St. Paul's floated; silver balloons rose gently, sweetly, into the sky; all was ready, all was set. Dome should be burst asunder, clustering buildings shake and fall, London Town a heap of ruins, London Town, oh London Town.

> *Jerusalem fell from Lambeth's Vale,*
> *Down thro' Poplar and Old Bow,*
> *Thro' Malden and across the sea,*
> *In war and howling, death and woe.*

It did not happen. Even the sirens mocked; what they promised unfulfilled. Like politicians' promises of peace, was theirs of destruction. Those who had scattered to dugouts and hiding-places, left them; like gas masks were taken off to disclose unlike features. Again, yet again, all was as it had been before. War, it seemed, could not come to pass any more than it could be prevented—contraceptive or strip-tease war, *Menschen in Uniform;* rattle its bones over the stones, old war's funeral and new war's birth.

"Perhaps the most fateful moment in our history," the King said, broadcasting on the afternoon of that same September Sunday. Doubtless the moment was fateful, yet its fatefulness was as elusive as previous moments' unfatefulness had been. Its fatefulness could not be comprehended. "Freedom is in Peril, Defend it with all your Might," posters announced and eyes listlessly read; another advertising campaign—"Eat More Bread," "Breathe More Air," "Defend More Freedom." Buildings sprouted sand-bags, some piled high and some with little heaps at their lower extremities; banks and offices were transferred to rural scenes, Cheapside built in England's green and pleasant land, typewriters sounding and money counted in former ancestral mansions, gilded ceilings and portraits staring down at an unfamiliar scene; children were evacuated, cinemas closed, lights put out, London left dark, childless, cinemaless, at night scarcely existing at all, obliterated.

What had seemed so solid, melted; rows of large houses in Kensington stood silent and deserted, bells when rung echoing through their emptiness, no door opened to reveal lighted opulence within, no respectful domestic advancing to relieve visitors of overcoat and hat; occasional householders who remained, boarded up at night, skeleton garrison left behind when the main army had been withdrawn. Shop-windows were plastered over with strips of paper, even small establishments displaying contraceptive appliances and opened books on nudism and other hygieno-sexual subjects, taking this precaution. Gas masks were carried, sometimes in ornamental cases which also contained make-up apparatus; air wardens and sub-wardens stood by, hospital beds were emptied in preparation for casualties who failed to put in an appearance; A.R.P. personnel took turns at waiting through the night, kept watch o'er man's inanity in expectation of an alarm which did not come.

Most noticeable sign of what had befallen, was the black-out; flood-lighting succeeded by flood darkening. In the darkness, hurrying forms groped their way; buses, faintly illuminated, glided past; neon signs, put out, each particle of light, extinguished. Darkness reigned, darkness descended —Fiat Nox! Soon it seemed as though there never had been any lights; as though always at nightfall buildings had vanished from sight after twilight's short, exquisite frailty; as though darkness had never been vanquished, pierced again and again by murderous shafts, until it was all wounds, like a diabetic unable to find unpierced flesh to insert his needle. War brought darkness, not slaughter; darkness, not passion, took the heaviest toll of life—casualties after two months of war:

Black-out	1,130
Navy	586
Air-Force	79
Army	Nil

To some war brought hope. The functionless saw in it a chance to be released from days which were empty and nights which were long. Bayswater wallpaper might

now be no more seen; streets often trodden, trodden no
more; wives, games of bridge, crossword puzzles, afternoon slumber, all laid aside. War meant being wanted.
They wrote letters; renewed acquaintance with influential
persons once, twice, or even thrice removed; went to recruiting offices. War would renew their youth. They would
be young again, back at the point where the last War ended;
uniformed, riotous, singing "If You Were the Only Girl in
the World" with deep emotion.

Outcasts of all descriptions, monied and penurious, hoped
that at last they might be wanted. In peace they were re-
dundant; in war surely some use would be found for them,
vast human waste-product, somehow fed and clothed, given
the means of living without anything being required of
them in return, inhabiting one or several rooms, moving
about or stationary, drowsing by the blue Mediterranean
or on green recreation-ground seats, functionless.

Saddest of all earthly sights, perhaps, are the functionless
—men who may not work, unfertile women. Miserable is
their plight, whether fed or hungry, housed or houseless.
As their number multiplies, despair increases—each a unit
of despair adding to the sum total which must be breathed
by all. To be alive is a little thing, merely alive, unless in
living passion is expended, fruitfulness achieved. What if
the functionless are endowed or fed, still they are functionless, standing aside. The only brotherhood is of work, the
only sisterhood of procreation—except membership of a
family whose father is in Heaven; and if Heaven has been
abolished, how shall that be attainable?

To the functionless, money was given; doles large and
small, poor and rich relief. It was all there was to give them.
If they had money they might live, and living sufficed—

apply money morning and evening to the affected place; "this is my money, spend this in remembrance of me." The treatment did not work. Money was devoutly taken, but no regeneration resulted. The army of the functionless remained, ever growing, occasionally manifesting their existence by Hunger Marches and other public protests—"Jesu Lover of my Soul" heard above the traffic's noise in busy thoroughfares, and a party of demonstrators entering the Ritz Hotel to demand refreshment, over- and under-fed functionless momentarily confronting one another there, and then separating to pursue their separate ways.

War to these functionless seemed fortunate. If they might not collaborate in carrying on the world's business, at least their services might be useful when destruction was required. In destroying, they would revenge themselves on a world which had excluded them. Others tediously occupied, hoped to be released from a monotonous round, take their leave of ledgers, no more struggle onto crowded suburban trains, discard umbrellas, bowler hats, and live dangerously. Mostly, these hopes were disappointed. Pacifists had insisted that in another war it would be necessary to drive unwilling men into battle at the bayonet's point; when war came, willing men greatly exceeded the demand, and only grieved that no battle was available. Those who hoped through another war to recover their lost youth, found that their youth and war were alike irretrievably lost; that neither could be recovered.

V

Having gone to war, it was necessary to discover why the war was being fought. Many minds, previously preoccupied with peace aims, now turned their attention to war aims. A war must have some purpose; if lives and money were to be expended, something must be achieved. Rather wearily, hopes which had done service before were revived. A better world would come of this struggle, a freer world, a world whence war and poverty, cruelty and arrogance, had been banished. The Good Life would come of this struggle. Mr. Vernon Bartlett found it a privilege to be alive when so promising a future opened before mankind; Mr. Harold Nicolson comforted himself with the prospect of the achievement of "a world which is worth fighting for; a world without conceit or cruelty, without greed and lies." [1] The League of Nations was in too derelict a condition to provide even a war aim, but Federation would do instead. Let men federate or utterly perish.

Some imagined it might be so—politicians seated round a table with maps unrolled, drawing frontiers, debating, bargaining, lunching and dining together, emitting cigar-smoke as they fashioned a European, or perhaps a World, Federation. Mistakes which had been made before must not be made again, Czechoslovakia's borders less precariously arranged, Poland's more ingeniously drawn, Federal Covenant securer than League one had proved. Some imagined it might be so, but they were few. Most knew in their hearts that whatever else the outcome might be, it would not, could not, be Mr. Chamberlain, M. Daladier, Lord Halifax, M. Bonnet, drawing a map, devising a Covenant. Their hands would not shape the future, their lips not decree it, their hearts not wish it. They belonged to the past, and with the past must be obliterated; they were dust which a tumultuous wind would scatter.

Their world was passing away—London, that great city.

[1] See *Why Britain Is at War.*

None could revive it, none stay the process of disintegration. Feet treading, found no foothold; arms reaching, no guiding wall or comforting pillar found; mind thinking, nothing grasped. All was dissolving. Lost! lost! in the darkness of change. Chancellor rising, white, so ghostly, announcing expenditure of £2,400,000,000 a year; rotund First Lord by microphone conveying echo of an echo, fury already spent; Prime Minister, as young as he felt, proclaiming the resolution of all to defend freedom with all their might now it was endangered; mighty Red Army by Finland delayed, mighty no longer; German broadcasts nightly heard, millions eagerly listening, Lord Haw-Haw so far the war's only discovery. These, too, were shadows. Even money had become a dream; even the £2,400,000,000 annually expended was no more than sounds made, marks written, figures idly traced.

Groping along darkened streets, dimly it was felt that a way of life was failing, its comfortable familiarity passing away never to reappear. Would these streets ever be lighted again? Would there be other Parliaments after this one, other Archbishops of Canterbury, other occupants of large mansions, other members of clubs seated, pensive, in leather chairs, other riders in Rotten Row and purchasers of what was so alluringly displayed in Regent Street windows? Difficult to project any existing thing into the future, difficult to imagine its continuance.

In such a situation, effort seemed pointless. To-morrow was mysterious, and each day must be sufficient unto itself. Some spent money lavishly, eager to enjoy its benefits while this yet was possible. Night-clubs flourished; nakedness disported itself; the Café Royal still attracted its own, and at labour exchanges waited the workless, new and old. Men

were fighting for freedom, yet neither fought, nor cared to
be free. It was as though there had been a Freedom Ballot
—millions voting that they were in favour of being free, as
millions had voted that they were in favour of being at
peace.

What freedom was to be fought for? they may have won-
dered. We are all free to sleep under the arches of the
Seine, Anatole France had said; we were all free to read what
Lord Beaverbrook decreed should be printed in the *Daily
Express*, to earn money, to buy and to sell, to vote for
Ramsay MacDonald who had saved the country, for Mr.
Baldwin who would make the League of Nations the keystone of our foreign policy, for Mr. Chamberlain who had
brought us peace with honour from Munich. How varied
was our freedom—stockbrokers freely buying and selling
shares, lawyers freely obtaining briefs and clergymen freely
obtaining benefices, each individual freely struggling to feed
and clothe and house himself as best he might. This so varied
freedom was in peril, and needed to be defended. "Lend to
defend the right to be free," posters pleaded; "Your resolution, your courage, will defend our freedom."

Calamity unspeakable if our freedom were allowed to
perish; calamity unspeakable if dearly prized and hardly
won liberties were lost—no Members of Parliament appealing for votes, no *Daily Express* appealing for readers, no
advertisements appealing for money; no appeals at all, only
orders, to be obeyed under the threat of loss of liberty, and
sometimes of life. In the darkness of change, men tried
to formulate their freedom in order to defend it; in the
darkness of change, they watched their world disintegrating
under their eyes, and knew not whether they were happy

or regretful that it should thus pass away—Oh, let it pass! or, Oh, let it stay!

In so confused a state of mind, the Thirties drew to an end—looking for freedom that it might be defended, looking for a war that it might be fought; Shape of Things to Come, coming, come. Soldiers were ready; aeroplanes flew through the sky, dropped leaflets which might have been bombs; threats were uttered—like Lear's "I will do such things— what they are yet I know not, but they shall be the terrors of the earth"; back to London drifted some of those who had fled, opened cinemas which had been closed, recovered their self-confident voices which had momentarily become plaintive; when no sirens sounded, bravely demanding cessation of bureaucratic control, bravely railing against regulations imposed. After all, though there was a war, still there might be no war; after all, still it was only on other countries that bombs fell—Poland, Finland, Holland perhaps; after all, the Nazi régime might collapse, Hitler die, or, under the stress of a blockade, sue for peace. Fighting a war which might not have to be fought, defending what no more existed to defend, following campaigns which did not take place, mourning for the living and looking for strength to the dead, strangely, sadly and rather foolishly, the Thirties drew to a close.

Index